Modern Syntax

This practical coursebook introduces all the basics of modern syntactic analysis in a simple step-by-step fashion. Each unit is constructed so that the reader discovers new ideas, formulates hypotheses and practices fundamentals. The reader is presented with short sections of explanation with examples, followed by practice exercises. Feedback and comment sections follow to enable students to monitor their progress. No previous background in syntax is assumed. Students move through all the key topics in the field including features, rules of combination and displacement, empty categories, and subcategorization. The theoretical perspective in this work is unique, drawing together the best ideas from three major syntactic frameworks (Minimalism, HPSG and LFG). Students using this book will learn fundamentals in such a way that they can easily go on to pursue further study in any of these frameworks.

ANDREW CARNIE is Professor of Linguistics at the University of Arizona, where he teaches syntactic theory and Celtic linguistics. His previous publications include *Constituent Structure*, second edition (2010), *Irish Nouns* (2008) and *Syntax: A Generative Introduction*, second edition (2006).

Modern Syntax:
A Coursebook

ANDREW CARNIE
University of Arizona

CAMBRIDGE
UNIVERSITY PRESS

CAMBRIDGE UNIVERSITY PRESS
Cambridge, New York, Melbourne, Madrid, Cape Town, Singapore,
São Paulo, Delhi, Dubai, Tokyo, Mexico City

Cambridge University Press
The Edinburgh Building, Cambridge CB2 8RU, UK

Published in the United States of America by Cambridge University Press, New York

www.cambridge.org
Information on this title: www.cambridge.org/9780521682046

First published 2011

Printed in the United Kingdom at the University Press, Cambridge

A catalogue record for this publication is available from the British Library

ISBN 978-0-521-86335-3 Hardback
ISBN 978-0-521-68204-6 Paperback

For my mother, Jean

CONTENTS

ACKNOWLEDGMENTS

I'd like to start these acknowledgments with a big thank you to the staff at Cambridge University Press. They've been unprecedentedly helpful and patient with an author who has taken far too long to produce this book and has been known to occasionally have a bit of authorial pique. In particular, many thanks to both Helen Barton and Andrew Winnard in the commissioning office and to Jodie Barnes in the production staff. Thanks also to Kay McKechnie, Ann Mason and Servis Filmsetting for their help in copy-editing, proof-reading and typesetting this work.

Somewhat unconventionally, I'd also like to thank an editor at a different press, Danielle Descoteaux from Wiley-Blackwell, who was both gracious enough to grant me permission to write a competing book to my other textbook (Carnie 2006) and who was very flexible in our negotiations over the naming of the present work. It should be noted that some of the exercises and definitions used in this work are adapted from Carnie (2006) and used with permission.

Several anonymous reviewers gave me great advice in putting together this book. As did comments from William Alexander, Fiona Carnie, Oded Haber, Heidi Harley and Arthur Torrance. Mistakes and missteps in this book exist despite all their best efforts. Finally, I'd like to thank my supportive colleagues and co-workers (Mike Hammond, Diane Ohala, Diana Archangeli, Adam Ussishkin, Andy Wedel, Heidi Harley (again), Simin Karimi, Amy Fountain, Marian Wiseley, Kimberley Young, Jennifer Columbus and Andy Barss) and my family Jean, Fiona, Morag and Pangur.

AHC, March 21, 2010

HOW TO USE THIS BOOK

This book is different from many other syntax textbooks in that it attempts to teach syntax through discovery rather than through simple presentation. Like other books in the Cambridge Coursebook series, this book is structured as a series of definitions, comments, discussion, and exercises that allow you, the reader, to explore the material on your own. Learning syntactic analysis is best done in consultation with an experienced linguist, so if you are tackling this book on your own, you might contact your local university to see if there is an advanced undergraduate or (post-)graduate student who would be willing to answer those questions that you have.

Unlike other books in the Coursebook series you will need your own notebook to answer many of the questions in this volume. You will be drawing syntactic diagrams, which take up a fair amount of space. In order to reduce production costs, we haven't included that space in this book. All the questions that you should try to answer are marked with a **Q** followed by a number. The questions are divided into three types.

> 1. *Notebook questions:* These questions should be answered in your own notebook or on a sheet of blank paper. They are marked by an open book symbol (📖). The answers to these questions can be found at the end of each chapter.

> 2. *Answer-on-the-page questions:* These questions are usually *yes/no*, multiple choice or short-answer questions. They can either be answered right in this book or recorded in your own notebook. These are marked with a pencil symbol (✏). The answers to these questions can be found at the end of each chapter.

> 3. *Challenge questions:* Throughout the book there are a few questions that are more challenging than the others. These challenge questions are designed to make you critically evaluate the theory being presented to you. I have not provided answers to these questions. You'll have to figure them out for yourself. Some of these questions have clear answers. Others present mysteries that puzzle even experienced syntacticians. Perhaps you'll be the one to figure them out!

I hope that these questions will not only give you plenty of practice in syntactic analysis but will help you to discover the basic methodologies and formalisms that syntacticians use in analyzing sentences.

Inevitably, mistakes, errors and inconsistencies creep into a book like this as it is written, revised, rewritten, edited, and typeset. I've done my best to minimize this, but you should look for the errata sheet on the website: http://dingo.sbs.arizona.edu/~carnie for any corrections.

A NOTE ON THE THEORETICAL PERSPECTIVE OF THE BOOK

Before we set out on our voyage of discovery in syntax, I want to offer a few words about the theoretical perspective of this book. The title of this book, *Modern Syntax: A Coursebook*, is deliberately vague about the particular theory you'll be learning in this book. There are almost as many syntactic theories as there are syntacticians and most syntax textbooks take you down very specific theoretical paths.

One of the things I've tried to do in this book is offer a theoretical perspective that is compatible with several different theories. I've chosen the three most popular modern approaches to syntactic analysis: Chomskyan Minimalism (also known as the Minimalist Program or MP), a relatively simplistic version of Head-Driven Phrase Structure Grammar (HPSG), and Lexical–Functional Grammar (LFG); and I've picked out what I liked best out of each theory. The result is *nothing* that usual practitioners of any of these theories will recognize as uniquely their own. For example, the system of syntactic constituent analysis given here is taken almost exclusively from MP, as is the analysis of DP movement. From HPSG and LFG, I've drawn upon their rich and precise featural notations, but the features I'm using are more like those in MP. From HPSG, I've borrowed the tagging notation (albeit slightly differently construed from the normal view in HPSG) and their system of subcategorization. From LFG, I've borrowed their view of head movement/head mobility (with a twist) and their treatment of long-distance dependencies.

It should be obvious, then, that by the time you finish this book you will not be completely fluent in any of the current major theories. But this isn't a drawback! My goal is to take you to a place where you can successfully pursue *any* of them in depth. I think this is better than making you choose one approach before you have the tools to decide what makes the most sense to you. Unit 26 of this book offers you some guidance on good textbook material that will help you pursue one or more particular frameworks of analysis in more detail.

1 Some basic ideas in syntax

UNIT 1 DEFINING SYNTAX

Objectives:
- Understand the definition of "syntax."
- Understand the scientific method as applied to sentence structure.
- Understand the role of negative evidence.
- Understand the importance of structure in sentence construction.

1.1 Introduction

Definition Syntax is the scientific study of sentence structure.

Comment There are two important parts to this definition: science and sentence structure. Let's look at each of these parts in some detail.

1.2 Science

Discussion When hearing the word *science*, what leaps to mind for most people are the hard sciences like biology, chemistry, physics. But the word *science* actually refers to a methodology for study. The study of syntax uses this methodology, so it is properly considered a science. The scientific method is expressed in the following diagram:

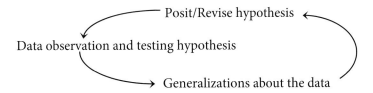

Posit/Revise hypothesis

Data observation and testing hypothesis

Generalizations about the data

The scientific method involves taking a hypothesis about the subject matter, testing it by observing and gathering data, making generalizations about the patterns in that data and then revising the hypothesis to account for the new generalizations.

We are going to apply this definition to an example from syntax, but first we have to start with some definitions.

Definition A **declarative sentence** asserts that an event or state of affairs has occurred (or hasn't occurred): e.g. *Susan ate an apple. Susan didn't eat an apple.*

Definition A *yes/no* **question** is a question that can be answered by *yes, no* or *maybe*: e.g. *Did Susan eat an apple?*

Exercise **Q1** ✍[1] Identify which of the following sentences are *yes/no* questions, which are declarative sentences and which are neither.

(1)	John hasn't eaten anything.	Y/N	Decl.	Neither
(2)	Does Bill really prefer meatballs?	Y/N	Decl.	Neither
(3)	Has Peter eaten his smoked salmon yet?	Y/N	Decl.	Neither
(4)	What has Peter done now?	Y/N	Decl.	Neither
(5)	Heather smokes too much.	Y/N	Decl.	Neither
(6)	John did WHAT?	Y/N	Decl.	Neither

With this background about *yes/no* and declarative questions in mind, consider the following hypothesis:

Hypothesis 1: Yes/no *questions are formed by moving the second word in the equivalent declarative sentence to the front.*

Now look at the following sentences:

(7) Frodo will eat the magic beans. (declarative)

(8) Will Frodo eat the magic beans? (*yes/no* question)

Q2 ✍ Are sentences (7-8) consistent with hypothesis 1? (Pay careful attention to the wording of the hypothesis!)   Y   N

Now consider the next two sentences

(9) The little hobbit will eat the magic beans. (declarative)

(10) Will the little hobbit eat the magic beans? (*yes/no* question)

Q3 ✍ Are these two sentences consistent with hypothesis 1? (Pay careful attention to the wording of the hypothesis!)   Y   N

Q4 ✍ Instead of (10), what sentence does hypothesis 1 actually predict to be the grammatical *yes/no* question equivalent to (9):

(11) ....

In order to explain why the sentence you wrote above on line (11) is ungrammatical, but the one in (10) is OK, we will need to revise the hypothesis.

---

[1] This symbol means that this question can be answered directly in this book.

Q5 📖² Try to come up with a hypothesis that accounts for the grammaticality of (10). (Hint 1: words such as *will* are called **auxiliaries.** Hint 2: use as much of the language in hypothesis 1 as you can, making only minimal changes.)

Hypothesis 2: Yes/no *questions are formed by moving . . . (complete this sentence)*

Comment   Once a hypothesis has been revised, we re-evaluate it and see if it needs further revisions. This involves considering the **predictions** of the hypothesis. There are two kinds of predictions for syntactic theory. A good hypothesis will predict that some sentences are grammatical (more on this notion in unit 2), and others will be ungrammatical. For example, hypothesis 1 (incorrectly) predicted that sentence (11) would be grammatical, and sentence (10) would be ungrammatical. Hypothesis 2, by contrast, correctly predicts that sentence (10) is grammatical and sentence (11) is ungrammatical.

If we consider the case above again, we observe that often it is the *un*grammatical sentences that inform us as to how to revise our hypotheses.

Notation   In syntax, ungrammatical sentences are marked with an asterisk (*).

Exercise   Consider the following set of sentences:

(12) The hobbit who will dance at the party has eaten the magic beans.

(13) *Will the hobbit who dance at the party has eaten the magic beans?

(14) Has the hobbit who will dance at the party eaten the magic beans?

Q6 ✑ Does hypothesis 2 predict that sentence (13) will be grammatical?   Y   N

Q7 ✑ Does hypothesis 2 predict that sentence (14) will be grammatical?   Y   N

Comment   In order to revise our hypothesis we're going to have to make reference to the **structure** of the sentence. The subject in sentence (12) contains a *relative clause*. We'll define relative clauses precisely in a later chapter. In this case, the relative clause is *[who will dance at the party]*. This relative clause is embedded (contained) in the main clause (the entire sentence).

Exercise   **Q8** 📖 Try to come up with a hypothesis that accounts for the grammaticality of (12) and (14). (Hint: you should refer to whether the auxiliary is embedded inside of a relative clause or appears in the main clause.)

---

²   This symbol means that you should answer this question in your notebook or on a separate piece of paper.

Hypothesis 3: Yes/no questions are formed by moving . . . (complete this sentence)

Challenge Can you think of a sentence that hypothesis 3 *fails* to predict correctly? The sentence could be grammatical or ungrammatical. How would you revise the hypothesis to account for this sentence? (There is no feedback for this question.)

1.3 Structure

Comment This leads us to the second part of our definition of syntax: the structure of sentences. The formation of *yes/no* questions makes reference to whether the auxiliary is embedded or not. Sentences are hierarchically structured.

Comment If you add up the values of a series of numbers, it doesn't matter what order they are added in:

$$7 + 8 + 14 + 2 = 2 + 14 + 8 + 7 = 8 + 7 + 2 + 14 \text{ etc.}$$

This is a property of simple addition.

Exercise Take the following words:

yellow, singing, a, the, elephant, mouse, sniffed

Q9 ✐ Using each word only once, and using every word, try to come up with as many grammatical sentences as possible (there are at least eight; more may be possible). One is done for you as an example

(15) A singing elephant sniffed the yellow mouse.

(16) ....

(17) ....

(18) ....

(19) ....

(20) ....

(21) ....

(22) ....

Q10 ✐ Do these sentences mean the same thing?   Y   N

Q11 ✐ Is syntax like addition, in the sense that order is irrelevant?   Y   N

Comment The fact that these sentences do not mean the same thing indicates that the sentence isn't just a linear string of symbols like addition. The position of the words relative to one another makes a difference in meaning. This, taken together with the importance of structure for hypothesis 3 above, is evidence that sentences are structured entities. In particular we're going to claim that certain words are more closely grouped together than others. We can represent this with a tree structure (a), bracketing (b) or boxes (c) (we will return to the notations and the abbreviations you see below in detail in later parts of the book):

(a)

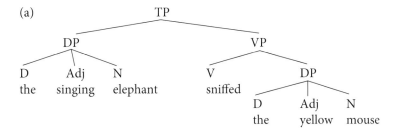

(b) $[_{TP}[_{DP}[_{D}$ the$][_{Adj}$ singing$][_{N}$ elephant$]][_{VP}[_{V}$ sniffed$][_{DP}[_{D}$ the$][_{Adj}$ yellow$]$
$[_{N}$ mouse$]]]]$

(c)

Summary   In this unit, we've defined the study of syntax as the scientific approach to sentence structure. We looked at the scientific method, and how it involves looking for the predictions that a hypothesis makes in terms of the grammaticality and ungrammaticality. In probing this using *yes/no* questions as an example, we also found that sentences aren't merely strings of words, but are objects with structure. This was confirmed by noting that the meaning of a sentence is more than the sum of the meanings of its parts.

In the next unit, we'll look at where syntacticians get their data.

Suggested further reading

(full references are given at the end of the book)
- Carnie (2006), chapter 1
- Larson, (2010), units 1-2
- Sapir (1929)
- Tallerman (2005), chapter 1
- Wikipedia[3] article on syntax: http://en.wikipedia.org/wiki/Syntax

---

[3]   Wikipedia is a mixed bag as far as academic sources go. Sometimes Wikipedia articles are well written and knowledgeable, and sometimes they definitely are not. Sometimes Wikipedia contains some helpful basic information, but you should always use it with caution.

- Wikipedia article on Scientific Method: http://en.wikipedia.org/wiki/Syntax
- Wikipedia article on Hypotheses: http://en.wikipedia.org/wiki/Hypothesis

Answers to questions

Q1 (2) and (3) are Y/N questions, (1) and (5) are declaratives, (4) and (6) are neither (they are questions but they cannot be answered with *yes, no* or *maybe*).

Q2 and Q3 Sentences (7) and (8) are predicted by the hypothesis: the first word in the declarative form is the second word in the Y/N question, and vice versa. Sentences (9) and (10), however, are not predicted. In sentence (10), it is the fourth word of sentence (9) that appears first.

Q4 and Q5 Hypothesis 1 predicts that the *yes/no* question form of sentence (9) would be *Little the hobbit will eat the magic beans*. The second word (*little*) is inverted with the first (*the*). Hypothesis 2 should be something like "*Yes/no* questions are formed by moving the auxiliary of the equivalent declarative sentence to the front."

Q6 and Q7 Hypothesis 2 isn't specific about which auxiliary in a sentence will move to the front. So both sentences are predicted to be grammatical. We need to revise our hypothesis to explain why (13) is ungrammatical.

Q8 Hypothesis 3 needs to make reference to the difference between the embedded auxiliary and the main clause auxiliary. There are several ways to phrase this, but one way would be: Yes/no *questions are formed by moving the main clause auxiliary to the beginning of the sentence.*

Q9, Q10 and Q11 You should have eight sentences, manipulating whether you use *a* or *the* to modify *elephant* or *mouse*, and the same for *yellow* and *singing*. (*A yellow elephant sniffed the singing mouse; A singing elephant sniffed the yellow mouse; A yellow mouse sniffed the singing elephant; A singing mouse sniffed the yellow elephant; The yellow elephant sniffed a singing mouse; The singing elephant sniffed a yellow mouse; The yellow mouse sniffed a singing elephant; The singing mouse sniffed a yellow elephant.*) Either noun phrase can be used in either subject or object position. The answers to the next two questions are both No.

UNIT 2 SYNTACTIC DATA

> **Objectives:**
> - Understand the role of corpora vs. judgment tasks.
> - Learn to read and analyze foreign language examples.
> - Use and apply judgment tasks.
> - Distinguish syntactic from semantic judgment tasks.

Comment   The scientific method requires data, so it's reasonable to ask how we gather that data and what kind of data we use. One obvious source of data is what we hear spoken around us or find written in books and newspapers.

2.1 Corpora

Definition   A collection of written or spoken material representing real-world usage of a language is called a **corpus** (plural: **corpora**).

Discussion   Corpora have a wide variety of uses, but also have a wide variety of limitations. In this unit, we will look at the role of corpora and the role of another data-gathering technique called the "judgment task" in the analysis of sentence structure.

Definition   A corpus with an **interlinear gloss** or word-aligned gloss has three lines: (a) The example in the original language; (b) a word-by-word gloss, where the English for each word (or morpheme[1]) is aligned with the original language; (c) an idiomatic translation into English.

(1) (a)   Níor bhuail mé Seán.   *Actual language data*

     (b)   NEG strike I   John   *Word-by-word gloss*

     (c)   "I didn't strike John."   *Idiomatic translation*

Discussion   For most syntacticians the most important part of this is the *second line*: the word-by-word gloss. The glosses are lined up word for word (and sometimes morpheme for morpheme) with the foreign language on the line above. This line tells you (i) what each word in the foreign language example means, and more importantly, (ii) the order of the words in the foreign language.

---

[1]   A morpheme is a word part such as a suffix or prefix or the root of a word.

9

When trying to determine the phrase structure of a foreign language or the behavior of a word or phrase, this is the line to look at! Remember: do not do an analysis of the idiomatic translation of the sentence, because then you are only doing an analysis of English!

Comment   Sometimes you will also run into example sentences where there is no word-by-word gloss, only an idiomatic gloss. This often happens with "side-by-side" corpora. Often you can deduce the meaning of words that aren't glossed by comparing and contrasting these forms with other sentences that you already know the meaning of. Consider the Irish sentence in (2) and compare it to (1):

(2)   Níor rith mé.

   "I didn't run."

I haven't provided a word-by-word gloss here. However, from sentence (1) we see that *mé* is glossed as "I" and *Níor* is glossed as "Neg" (i.e. "not"). What's left is *rith*. Since the verb *bhuail* "strike" appears between the negation and the word meaning "I," we might conclude that *rith* is also a verb, and means "run" which we take from the idiomatic translation.

Exercise   Consider the following sentences from Japanese.

Q1 ✎ Fill in the blanks for the meanings of the words without word-by-word interlinear glosses. For the moment ignore the *-ga, -o* and *-ni* particles.

(3)   Taroo-ga Mieko-o mita.

   Taro   Mieko   saw

   "Taro saw Mieko."

(4)   Taroo-ga Mieko-o sensei-ni shookaisata.

   Taro   Mieko   teacher   introduced

   "Taro introduced Mieko to the teacher".

(5)   Mieko-ga sensei-o mita.

   Mieko   .... saw

   "Mieko saw the teacher."

(6)   Taroo-ga tuita.

   Taro   ....

   "Taro arrived."

(7)   Taroo-ga isu-ni. suwatta

   Taroo   ....

   "Taro sat on the chair."

Comment   Now let's figure out the meanings of the suffixes *-ga*, *-o* and *-ni*. First some
          definitions to help you; for now we'll assume an intuitive understanding
          of what a "subject" and a "direct object" and "indirect object" are. In the
          English sentence *Calvin gave the peanuts to Scott*, *Calvin* is the subject, *the
          peanuts* is the direct object, and *Scott* is the indirect object.

Definition **Nominative case** is the marking associated with subjects. For example, in
           English the pronouns *I, he, she, we* and *they* are in the nominative case;
           they only ever appear in subject position (in other words, before the
           verb).

Definition **Accusative case** is the marking associated with direct objects. For example,
           in English the pronouns *me, him, her, us* and *them* are in the accusative case.
           They appear in object position (in other words, after the verb).

Definition **Dative case** is the marking (often) associated with indirect objects and nouns
           marking the location of the event. In English we mark the dative case by
           adding prepositions such as *to, in, at* or *on* to the noun.

Exercise   **Q2** ✏ Using the above terms and looking at sentences (3–7), define the
           Japanese suffixes:

           -o   ....

           -ga   ....

           -ni   ....

Exercise   In English, the order of words is

           Subject + Verb + Direct Object + Dative.

           Q3 📖 What is the order of words in Japanese?

Comment   It is possible to extract a lot of information from corpora. For example,
          they often can give us a rough idea how frequent a particular construction
          is and how that construction is used relative to other constructions.
          Corpora are often a good place to look for counterexamples to negative
          predictions, for example, if the theory predicts that a sentence is impossible.
          Checking a corpus allows an efficient method of seeing if there are frequent
          counterexamples.

          However, there are limits to the kinds of generalizations that can be
          found in corpora. The next exercise probes the advantages and limitations of
          corpus data.

Exercise   Consider the following short corpus of Irish sentences taken from the first few pages of a novel;[2] the text has been edited slightly for the purposes of simplifying this exercise.

(8)   Rith Sorcha amach an doras[3]
       Ran Sarah   out   the door

       nuair a   chuala sí Sibéal ag   béiceach.
       when PRT[4] heard she Sybil PROG shout
       "Sarah ran out of the door, when she heard Sybil shouting."

(9)   Cheap sí go raibh an páiste tite   sa   tobar.
       thought she that was   the child fallen in the well
       "She thought that the child had fallen in the well."

(10) Chonaic muid an t-ainmhí, a   mhamaí.
       Saw   we   the animal,   VOC mummy
       "We saw the animal, mummy!

(11) Cén   áit?
       Which place
       "Where?"

(12) Ag Tobar Ghobnait a   bhí sé,
       at Tobargobnata   PRT was he

       ag   ól   uisce as an tobar.
       PROG drink water out the well
       "It was at Tobargobnata where he was, drinking water out of the well."

(13) An raibh adharca air?
       Q was   horns   on.it
       "Did it have horns?"

(14) Ní   raibh, ach bhí clúmh chuile áit   air.
       NEG was,   but was hair   every place on.him
       "No, but he was hairy."

---

[2] Standún (1992). Glossing and translation for this quote by Andrew Carnie.
[3] When a sentence is too long to fit on one line it is split as in this example, with the original language and interlinear gloss lined up and split on two lines, followed by the literal translation in quotation marks.
[4] Grammatical morphemes, words that indicate tense, and other grammatical functions will be indicated in SMALL CAPS in this book. The particular meaning of these morphemes isn't crucial here. We will return to them in later units.

There are many questions that we can answer using this data. Try your hand at these:

Q4 ✏ Do verbs (words like *was, ran, thought, saw*) come before or after their subjects?   Before   After

Q5 📖 How do you form a *yes/no* question in Irish? (See example 13.)

Q6 ✏ Does Irish put prepositions like *to, from* etc. before or after the noun they are attached to?   Before   After

Q7 ✏ Where do objects normally appear: before or after the subject?   Before   After

Q8 📖 How many forms of the verb translated as "was" can you find in the data? Can you guess which form appears where? (advanced)

Q9 ✏ How many sentences in this data are declarative sentences? .... How many are questions? ....

Comment Corpora are useful for many things, including looking for ordering patterns, alternations in forms as well as statistical information.

Exercise **Q10** 📖 Look again at sentences (8)–(14). Can you tell if objects and subjects ever can precede the verb? Can you tell if a preposition ever follows the noun? Is there enough evidence to answer these questions?

2.2 JUDGMENT TASKS

Comment Corpora, even very large ones, contain a limited amount of information about a language. Language is a creative venture. Consider the sentence *Big pink elephants argued whether the naked unicorns danced polkas in the city center.* I'm willing to bet you've never heard nor read that before. If the capacity for language is infinite, how can a finite corpus capture all the facts? The situation is made worse by virtue of the fact that corpora generally only contain acceptable sentences. Recall from the last unit that sometimes to confirm or dismiss a hypothesis we want to know about what sentences are *unacceptable* or *ungrammatical*. This kind of information is almost never contained in corpora. Due to our creative capacity for language, we can't even conclude that the absence of constructions from some corpus means that such forms are unacceptable.

Exercise Consider now the following five sentences of English:

(15) John said <u>that</u> Bill loved peanuts

(16) John said   Bill loved peanuts

13

(17) What did John say <u>that</u> Bill loved?

(18) What did John say   Bill loved?

(19) Who did John say   loved peanuts?

Q11 📖 Given *just* these five sentences, what hypothesis can you make about the word "that"? (i.e. is the word "that" freely optional?)

Consider now (20); compare it to sentence (19).

(20) *Who did John say <u>that</u> loved peanuts?

Q12 📖 Does this sentence cause any problems for the hypothesis you stated in Q11? What is the problem? Does your hypothesis in Q11 predict the unacceptability of (20)?

Comment   The difference between sentences (17) and (18) on one hand and (19) and (20) on the other has to do with whether the *wh*-question word (*what* and *who*) at the beginning of the sentence started out as the object (17 and 18) or as the subject (19 and 20).

Exercise   **Q13** ➥ Were you ever taught by a teacher that you can't say a sentence like (20)?   Y   N

Q14 ➥ Is an unacceptable sentence like (20) likely to appear in a corpus?   Y   N

Comment   You probably weren't taught in grammar classes about this effect, and unacceptable sentences like this aren't part of corpora. But the effect seen is a clear generalization (hypothesis) we can make about English. If we restrict ourselves to corpora we cannot access this kind of information.

Definition   The second kind of data syntacticians use is a **native-speaker judgment task** (NSJT) (or just "judgments"). This is a method of gathering data whereby we ask a native speaker if a carefully constructed sentence is acceptable or not.

Comment   The judgment task is sometimes referred to as native-speaker "intuition." In this book we will avoid this terminology because it suggests something unscientific. Judgment tasks, *when properly applied*, can be quite rigorously scientific and statistically provable.[5]

Definition   Native speakers will judge sentences on a continuum with **acceptability** at one end, and **unacceptability** at the other end, or several degrees of **marginality** in the middle.

---

[5] For more on the role of judgments see Schütze (1992) and Bard, Robertson and Sorace (1996).

Notation Acceptable sentences are not marked. Unacceptable sentences are marked with an asterisk (*) or even two in especially bad cases (**). Marginal sentences are marked with question marks, usually one to three of them (?, ??, ???).

Comment It is important to note that not every native speaker will necessarily agree on all judgments, but this does not invalidate the task. Variation among speakers may reflect dialectal (regional) or idiolectal (personal) differences; it may also reflect the linguistic sophistication of the speaker and the understanding of what is in question. You may come across sentences in this book marked as acceptable vs. unacceptable, and you may not agree with those judgments. If you disagree with the judgments consider how the hypothesis might be modified to take into account your own personal judgments or those of your native speaker consultants.

Definition Let us formally distinguish between acceptable and unacceptable on one hand and grammatical and ungrammatical on the other. **Acceptability** refers to native-speaker judgments. **Grammaticality** refers to what our *hypotheses* predict, and may or may not accurately capture acceptability.

Comment The formal distinction above is one we will try to keep throughout the rest of this book. If we are saying a sentence is acceptable, we mean a native speaker has identified it as such. If we say a sentence is grammatical, we mean that our hypothesis predicts that a native speaker should accept it (whether or not the speaker does so is another question). This distinction is an important one; but students should note that *many* linguists (including this author) sloppily use the terms "grammatical" and "acceptable" interchangeably.

Definition Native speaker judgments come of two kinds: **syntactic judgments**, which are about the form of a sentence and **semantic judgments,** which are about the content or meaning of the sentence.

Comment Consider the following:

(21) *John peanuts the ate.

(22) #The coffee table brushed its teeth.

Sentence (21), for all speakers of English I know, is totally ill-formed syntactically, but most speakers can assign it a meaning ("John ate the peanuts"). Sentence (22), is unacceptable for different reasons. The structure or form of the sentence is fine (as shown by the fact that we can generate sentences like *The coffee drinker brushed his teeth*). Sentence (22) is odd because coffee tables don't have teeth, and they certainly aren't capable of brushing them[6]. The unacceptability of (21) is due to a syntactic problem. The unacceptability of (22) is due to the semantic problem. Chomsky (1957) came up with the famous sentence in (23) to show the independence of meaning and structure:

(23) Colorless green ideas sleep furiously.

The sentence is well-formed syntactically, but semantically meaningless on a literal (non-poetic) level. (One can of course construe such sentences poetically or metaphorically, but that requires an extra level of analysis which we won't concern ourselves with here.) Note also that some syntactically ill-formed sentences may not be semantically interpretable either.

Notation   When a sentence is either uninterpretable or semantically odd, we mark it with the pound sign (also known in the UK as the hash mark) (#).

Exercise   **Q15** ➮ Take the following sentences and mark them with your own judgments of syntactic or semantic unacceptability. Try to rely on your inner "voice" rather than on what you might have been taught in school. Some of these cases may be both syntactically and semantically ill-formed; some of the sentences may be entirely acceptable. When determining acceptability, you may wish to compare the relative acceptability of sentences (e.g. is (k) better or worse than (l)?).

(a)   .... The book was arrived by John.

(b)   .... Susan taught Tom mathematics.

(c)   .... Michael thought that mathematics bored himself.

(d)   .... Susan said that Bill books read.

(e)   .... The stone ate a carrot.

(f)   .... Tom learned Susan chemistry.

(g)   .... I think Louis bought a syntax book.

(h)   .... I wonder who bought what.

(i)   .... Who do you think bought a syntax book?

(j)   .... What do you think Louis bought?

(k)   .... What do you wonder who bought?

(l)   .... Who do you wonder who read a book by?

(m)   .... John's sister is not his sibling.

(n)   .... Who do you think that saw Bill?

---

[6] You might object that (22) is perfectly acceptable as a poetic or metaphorical form. However, that is simply a restatement of the claim that these are semantically odd; the *reason* that this sounds "poetic" or "metaphorical" rather than literal is because it is semantically odd!

(o) .... William gave a book to Marian.

(p) .... William gave Marian a book.

(q) .... William donated a book to the charity.

(r) .... William donated the charity a book.

Summary   In this unit we've looked at two different kinds of data for syntactic study. The first are corpora of naturalistic text. When analyzing these we make use of interlinear word-by-word glosses. We found that while much information could be gathered from such texts (generalizations about word order, frequency, alternations, etc.), one kind of evidence we need to confirm or dismiss our hypotheses (unacceptable sentences) isn't present in the data. We have no way of knowing whether the absence of certain forms from a corpus is an accident or coincidence, or follows from something deeper. In order to get at these kinds of sentences, we considered the NSJT. We saw that judgments come of two types: semantic or syntactic judgments (although the line between these may be obscure). In the next unit we consider the form of syntactic hypotheses.

Suggested further reading

(full references are given at the end of the book)
- Bard, Robertson and Sorace (1996)
- Carnie (2006), chapter 1
- Culicover (2009), chapter 1
- Kim and Sells (2008), chapter 1
- Schütze (1992)
- Wikipedia article on syntactic corpora: http://en.wikipedia.org/wiki/Text_corpus

Answers to questions

Q1 *sensei* "teacher," *tuita* "arrived," *isu* "chair," *suwatta* "sit."

Q2 *-o* "accusative," *-ga* "nominative," *-ni* "dative."

Q3 Subject + Object + Dative + Verb.

Q4 before

Q5 put the particle *an* before the sentence

Q6 before

Q7 after

Q8 *raibh* and *bhí*; *raibh* is found after particles

Q9 Six declaratives, two questions

Q10 There really isn't enough information in this corpus to tell you the answer. While the forms don't occur in the corpus, you don't know if that means they can't occur, or are just not present in this corpus.

Q11 From this data it appears that the word *that* is optional. It can either be present or absent.

Q12 This data seems to show that for this sentence at least the word *that* cannot be optionally present. It must be omitted. This is inconsistent with Q11. The unacceptability of (20) is unexpected.

Q13 and Q14 Unless you had a very sophisticated grammar teacher, you were probably never taught "A *wh*-question word cannot originate in subject position if it is preceded by *that*." Nor, since the sentence is unacceptable, will it ever appear in a naturalistic corpus.

Q15 There are no correct answers to this exercise. Your judgments may well differ from mine. Here are my answers to the question: (a) * or #, (b) OK, (c) *, (d) *, (e) #, (f) # or *, (g) OK, (h) OK, (i) OK, (j) OK, (k) ??, (l) *, (m) #; (n) *, (o) OK, (p) OK, (q) OK, (r) ? or #.

UNIT 3 HYPOTHESES

> **Objectives:**
> - The phrasing of hypotheses as rules, constraints and grammars.
> - Distinguish between descriptive and prescriptive grammatical rules.
> - Learn about the evaluation of grammars in terms of observational, descriptive, explanatory and formal adequacy.

Comment   We've considered the sources of data, now we need to look briefly at the kinds of hypotheses that syntacticians use. In the variety of syntax[1] described in this book, hypotheses are described in terms of **formal rules** and **formal constraints**.

3.1 Rules

Definition   A **rule** is a statement phrased in a positive form that describes possible structures – structures that are claimed to be acceptable to a native speaker.

Discussion   Rules are a useful way to express generalizations about the data; they are always written as directives about what the grammatical form is.

Recall from the last unit our definitions of nominative and accusative case forms in Japanese; now consider the following paradigm of nouns in English.

---

[1]   Since this is an introductory textbook, I am deliberately keeping the text as theory-neutral as possible. However, it goes without saying that no science can progress without taking some theoretical stances and making some assumptions. At its broadest, the approach taken in this book falls under the family of theories known as *Generative Linguistics*, which was founded by Noam Chomsky in the 1950s, and includes such theories as the Extended Standard Theory (EST), Government and Binding Theory (GB) (also known as Principles and Parameters (P&P)), The Minimalist Program (MP), Lexical–Functional Grammar (LFG), Generalized Phrase Structure Grammar (GPSG) and Head-driven Phrase Structure Grammar (HPSG). At its narrowest, the version of the theory presented here is a mix of MP, LFG and HPSG. This should allow students to take the material they learn in this book and apply it at a more advanced level in whichever of these theories they or their instructors choose. I made a choice to pursue a generative approach to the material for two reasons: (i) it is my perception that most research into syntax these days is conducted with some variety of generative assumptions; (ii) this is the approach I am most familiar with personally. However, I hope that scholars from outside this general set of assumptions will find this book equally useful, as a descriptive tool at least.
   See the note at the beginning of this book and unit 26 for some discussion of the differences between these various frameworks of syntactic description and analysis.

Definitions A **paradigm** is a list or table of forms that represents the combination of different grammatical dimensions. For example, the paradigm here compares the dimensions of **person** marking (first person = speaker, second person = listener, third person = some other person), **gender** (masculine = male, feminine = female, neuter = genderless), and **number** (singular vs. plural) with respect to the dimension of case form (nominative vs. accusative).

(1)

	Nominative		Accusative	
	Singular	*Plural*	*Singular*	*Plural*
1st	I	we	me	us
2nd	you			
3masc	he	they	him	them
3fem	she		her	
3neuter	it		it	

Now consider the following sentences:

(2) (a) I kissed him.

     (b) *Me kissed he.

     (c) She loves her.

     (d) *Him ate it.

Exercise **Q1** ✆ On the basis of this limited data, state the restriction on which case form can appear where relative to the tensed verb (*kissed, loves, ate*). In other words, which forms appear before the verb and which appear after it.

Rule 1:   Use the nominative case when the pronoun appears .... the verb.

Rule 2:   Use the accusative case when the pronoun appears .... the verb.

3.2 Constraints

Definition A **constraint** is a formal statement of structures that are impossible – structures that are claimed to be unacceptable to native speakers.

Comment Rules and constraints are two sides of the same coin. Rules state what you must do, constraints tell us what you cannot do. More often than not it is possible to translate a positive rule into a negative constraint. For example, in English declarative clauses, the subject is usually the first noun in the sentence. This can be stated as the rule:

Rule 3:   To form an affirmative statement, put the subject noun before the verb.

But this can be turned on its head and restated as a constraint:

Constraint 3:   In affirmative statements, do not put the subject anywhere except before the verb.

Or alternately:

Constraint 3':   In an affirmative statement, if you put the subject anywhere but before the verb, the sentence will be unacceptable.

Exercise   **Q2** 📖 Translate rules 1 and 2 from Q1 into two constraints.

Challenge   Can you come up with a counterexample to constraint 2 as it is listed in the answer to Q2 at the end of this unit? Try sentences that begin with *I want . . .* and have another verb in them (such as *to leave*). What case does the noun before the second verb take?

Comment   As discussed above, there is a certain interchangeability between positively stated rules and negatively stated constraints. However, if you tried the challenge, you'd see that rules and constraints sometimes make very subtly different predictions. In this book, we will use both rules and constraints. The choice of which to use requires some experience, which will come with time as you become more adept at syntactic analysis.

Definition   A **derivation** is a formal description of how the grammatical structure is formed. It is usually a stepwise description, like a recipe. (First you mix the sugar and the flour, then you add the butter and chocolate chips, next you form the dough into spoon-sized portions, put them on a greased pan, and then bake for ½ an hour at 350°F.)

Definition   A **representation** is the output of the derivation. So, with any luck, the representation of the recipe given above will be well-formed chocolate chip cookies.

Comment   Rules are usually stated over derivations. They tell you how to form the sentence (or cookie). For example, it is a rule in the recipe that at a certain stage you add chocolate chips. By contrast, constraints are usually stated over the representations.[2] For example, a cookie without any chocolate chips in it is not a well-formed chocolate-chip cookie. In our hypotheses, we will have both rules and constraints.

---

[2] This isn't necessarily the case, for example, it is possible to state a constraint over the way a derivation functions. (Indeed, in syntax one occasionally finds such constraints.) So this should be viewed as a bit of an oversimplification.

3.3 Prescriptive vs. descriptive rules and constraints

Comment   Syntacticians – in fact, all linguists – distinguish between two types of "rules" or "constraints." First let's consider the traditional view of grammatical rules (as opposed to the way linguists view rules).

The traditional notion of a grammatical rule or constraint is what one might find in a style book or an English grammar book, or what you learned in school is "proper" or "correct" writing. Some examples of this kind of rule are seen below:

A   Never end a sentence in a preposition:

e.g. avoid sentences such as *Who did Bill give the book to?*

B   Do not split infinitive verbs (i.e. do not put an adverb like *boldly* between the *to* and the verb):

e.g. avoid sentences such as *To boldly go where no man has gone before.*

C   In comparatives, use the nominative form of a pronoun:

e.g. avoid sentences such as *He has eaten more apples than me.*

instead use *He has eaten more apples than I.*

D   Avoid the passive voice:

e.g. do not use sentences such as *Bill was attacked by a sudden bout of coughing.*

E   The adverb *hopefully* can only be used attributively as a manner adverb. It cannot be used to express the notion "it is hoped that."

e.g. do not use sentences such as *Hopefully, Bill will remember to bring the wedding cake today.*

unless you mean that Bill will be bringing the wedding cake in a hopeful manner.

F   Do not use a noun as a verb.

e.g. do not use sentences such as *He input the data* or *He floored the car.*

Exercise   **Q3** 📖 Using your native-speaker judgment (not what you were told was correct in school, but what your "inner voice" tells you), decide which of the "ungrammatical" sentences above (in A-F) truly sound "strange" or unacceptable. Is there any possibility that you yourself might say any of these? Or might you hear one of these sentences said by someone you know? If you are not a native speaker of English, ask a friend who is.

Comment   The kind of sentences that are usually marked as "ungrammatical" by English teachers, and English style books, are often very prevalent in corpora and in everyday speech. Indeed, they even do not strike our native-speaker intuitions as being as unacceptable as a sentence such as:

(3)   *Who did Bill think that ate the apple?

Exercise   **Q4** ✎ Consider now the following five sentences of English. Grade their acceptability using your own native-speaker intuitions. If you are not a native speaker ask a friend who is.

(4)   ....The apple, which we found in the garbage can, was a tasty treat.

(5)   ....The apple, that we found in the garbage can, was a tasty treat.

(6)   ....The theory that Bill proposed was wrong.

(7)   ....The theory which Bill proposed was wrong.

Comment   Sentences (4) and (5) use what is traditionally called a non-restrictive relative clause (a clause modifying a noun that provides additional information, but information that isn't crucial to our understanding of the noun). In traditional grammar books, however, (4) is supposed to be acceptable, and (5) unacceptable. Whereas (6) and (7), which have restrictive relative clauses, are supposed to be equally OK.[3] The intuitions of many (but not all) speakers go against this description. For some speakers of English, in fact, the intuitions are entirely the reverse of what traditional grammars tell us, and (5) is better than (4) and (7) is better than (6).

Exercise   **Q5** 📖   Recall that syntax is supposed to be a science. How should we evaluate these traditional rules (both the one discussed here and in A–F on page 22), given what I've asserted about corpora and native-speaker judgments here?

Comment   What leaps to the mind of the average non-linguist when they hear the expression "grammatical rule" are these rules that you may (or may not!) have been taught in school and admonished to use lest you appear ignorant or uneducated.

Definition   Rules such as the ones in A–F above are called **prescriptive rules**. They prescribe how we should speak.

Definition   Rules that represent actual corpus and judgment data are called **descriptive rules**. They describe how we actually speak.

Comment   Since we are claiming that syntax is a science, our focus from now on will be on descriptive rules. We will, for the most part, ignore prescriptive rules.

Exercise   **Q6** 📖   Prescriptive rules aren't scientific; often they don't even correctly reflect our judgments about our native language. Yet they are an important part of society today. For example, in writing this book, I am expected to follow prescriptive rules, even though I know that they are unscientific.

---

[3]   See for, example, the discussion of the usage of *which* or *that* in non-restrictive and restrictive relative clauses in Kane (1994), p. 702.

Speculate on why prescriptive rules are so important to us, and why they continue to be taught in schools and used in publishing.

Comment Some people argue that prescriptive rules help avoid ambiguity or aid in clarity in language. While this may be the basis for some prescriptive rules (for example, the distinction between *which* and *that* in non-restrictive relative clauses), for others it isn't at all clear they serve that function. Take, for example, the ban on splitting infinitives. Consider the sentences below:

(8)   I asked him to eat the apples quickly.

(9)   I asked him to quickly eat the apples.

Sentence (8) obeys the prescriptive rule of not splitting an infinitive. The adverb *quickly* appears at the end of the sentence. (9), by contrast, is a clear violation of this "rule." But note that while (9) is entirely unambiguous – *quickly* modifies the verb *eat* – the prescriptively correct form is ambiguous: it can either mean that the eating of apples should be done quickly or that the asking was done quickly. The prescriptively grammatical sentence is ambiguous in a way that the prescriptively unacceptable sentence is not. The claim that prescriptive rules aid in "clarity" and "resolving" ambiguity seems to be a towering statue with clay feet.

3.4 Levels of adequacy

Definition A **grammar** is a collection of descriptive rules and constraints.

Comment The hypotheses we build in syntactic theory are stated as grammars. As an essential component of our scientific approach it is important to be able to evaluate the quality of the grammars. In his classic work *Aspects of the Theory of Syntax*, Noam Chomsky delineates three levels of grammatical "adequacy." We will extend this to include a fourth.

Definition An **observationally adequate grammar** accounts for all the data that can be outwardly observed in corpora and other real-world usages. It is characterized by predicting the acceptability of all the sentences in the corpus, and excluding all the sentences not in the corpus. It does not distinguish between those sentences which are accidentally absent and those that are truly not part of the language.

Definition A **descriptively adequate grammar** accounts not only for corporal data, but also for the judgments that a native speaker has about the acceptability of sentences. It captures both whether sentences are acceptable and whether they are unacceptable. Descriptively adequate grammars identify patterns in the data, and account for those patterns in a way that corresponds to the judgments of native speakers.

24

Definition An **explanatorily adequate grammar** offers an explanation for why the grammar is structured the way it is. These explanations might involve information from how children learn language, how people use language, psychological aspects of language, or even from history. In the generative tradition, explanation is often limited to questions of language acquisition, although there is no real reason to exclude other kinds of explanation if they occur.

Comment Thus far, we haven't attempted to offer explanations for any of the rules or constraints we have proposed, so the rules we've provided don't yet meet this level of adequacy. Indeed, we won't really attempt such explanations until much later in the book. However, you should keep this goal in mind as we work along. Chomsky doesn't discuss our fourth level of adequacy, but it follows from the general principles of science.

Definition A **formally adequate grammar** is one that is stated in a formal mathematical manner; one that is precise and simple, and makes its predictions obvious, yet does so in the most perspicuous way.

Comment Again, thus far we haven't attempted anything like formal adequacy. We have stated all our rules in prose, and haven't been very careful in their formalization. As we progress through this book our rules will become more and more formal. You should not let this formalization intimidate you. It is there for precision and accuracy. But as a beginning linguist you should aim for an intuitive understanding of the concepts even if the formalism seems daunting.

Comment In an ideal world, then, our grammar will meet all four of these criteria. We can represent the set of grammars that meet these requirements as the intersection of the four adequacies. Our ideal grammar will lie at the intersection of all of them:

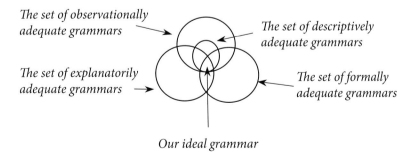

The set of observationally adequate grammars

The set of descriptively adequate grammars

The set of explanatorily adequate grammars

The set of formally adequate grammars

Our ideal grammar

Exercise **Q7**[4] 📖 Below, you'll find the description of several different linguists' work. Determine what levels of adequacy apply to each case. (Note that they may meet more than one level, or partially meet the requirements of that level.)

(a)   Roman Lubwicz has been working on reducing the number of grammatical constraints necessary for accounting for the frequency of passive constructions in a corpus of Polish telephone conversations. His goal is to come up with a single precise constraint to capture these facts.

(b)   Juan Martínez has been working with speakers of Chicano English in the barrios of Los Angeles. He has been both looking at corpora (rap music, recorded snatches of speech) and working with adult native speakers.

(c)   Fredrike Schwarz has been looking at the structure of sentences in eleventh-century Welsh poems. She has been working at the national archives of Wales in Cardiff.

(d)   Boris Dimitrov has been working with adults and corpora on the formation of questions in Rhodopian Bulgarian. He is also conducting a longitudinal study of some two-year-old children learning the language to test his hypotheses.

Comment Attaining all four levels of grammatical adequacy is a high bar to clear, but it is the ideal kind of hypothesis we wish to eventually achieve. At each step in our hypothesis building you should consider which of these evaluation metrics we have achieved, and what is necessary to get us to the point to achieve all four.

Summary In this unit we have concluded our investigation of what it means for syntax to be a science, by looking at the nature of the hypotheses we consider.

- Hypotheses in syntax are usually phrased as rules or constraints.
- Rules and constraints are often interchangeable, but may be subtly different in the predictions they make.
- Rules are usually stated as the directives for derivations; constraints are usually stated as restrictions on representations.
- Collections of rules and constraints are called grammars.
- Grammars can be evaluated on a number of levels including their observational, descriptive, explanatory and formal adequacy.
- They are not, however, evaluated as to how well they meet the expectations of English teachers and style books! We distinguish between

---

[4] This exercise is a modified version of one found in chapter 1 of Carnie (2002).

prescriptive and descriptive rules, with the observation that only the latter are scientific.

Suggested further reading

- Adger (2003), chapter 1
- Carnie (2006), chapter 1
- Chomsky (1965), chapter 1
- Culicover (2009), chapter 1
- Kim and Sells (2008), chapter 1
- Larson (2010), unit 4
- Pinker (1994) and (1995)
- Poole (2002), chapter 1
- Radford (1988), chapter 1
- van Gelderen (2010), chapter 1
- Van Valin and LaPolla (1997), chapter 1
- Wikipedia article on prescriptive grammar: http://en.wikipedia.org/wiki/Prescriptive_grammar
- Wikipedia article on grammar: http://en.wikipedia.org/wiki/Grammar
- Wikipedia article on levels of adequacy: http://en.wikipedia.org/wiki/Levels_of_adequacy

Answers to questions

Q1 Rule 1: before; rule 2: after

Q2 There are many ways this could be phrased, but it should be something like the following: Const. 1: Putting a nominative pronoun anywhere but before the verb will result in unacceptability. Const. 2: Putting an accusative pronoun anywhere but after the verb will result in unacceptability.

Q3 For many native speakers of English, even exceptionally well-educated ones, all of the sentences given above are acceptable. Instead, these sentences act as markers of social, educational or economic class. Speakers may well use them, especially in informal contexts, and they are very likely to have heard them. If you find any of them unacceptable, it's likely that you were drilled in the construction in an English grammar class!

Q4 There are no correct answers here. However, many native speakers of English (especially from North America) will find both (4) and (5) and (6) and (7) equally acceptable. People not trained in grammar classes will often prefer (7) to (6) and (5) to (4). People heavily trained in traditional grammar will prefer (4) to (5) and will treat (6) and (7) equally.

Q5 If syntax is a science then these rules would probably be rejected, because they are not consistent with our data sources.

Q6 Some might attribute the persistence of prescriptive rules to the conservatism of the educational and publishing establishment. However, it may well be the case that prescriptive rules serve some important social function. For example, they may well serve to help choose among dialect forms. Alternatively, they might well serve as a social class marker; if you obey the prescriptive rules, then you have achieved a level of education that marks you as a member of the intellectual elite.

Q7 (a) Formally and observationally adequate. (b) Observationally and descriptively adequate. There is not enough information to tell if it is formally adequate or explanatorily adequate. (c) Observationally adequate, not descriptively adequate. There isn't enough information to tell about explanatory or formal adequacy. (d) Observationally, descriptively and explanatorily adequate. There isn't enough information to make a determination about formal adequacy.

GROUP 1 REVIEW

The following were the major ideas introduced in group 1:

Philosophical/methodological issues
- Syntax is a science and uses the scientific method.
- The scientific method is characterized by data analysis and hypothesis testing.
- Corpora are collections of attested data.
- Corpora don't contain all the information a syntactician needs to do their job.
- Syntactic data is supplemented by native-speaker judgment tasks (marked by * and ?).
- Acceptability refers to whether a native speaker accepts the sentence or not.
- Grammaticality refers to whether a hypothesis predicts a sentence to be OK or not.
- We can distinguish between syntactic and semantic judgments.
- Hypotheses are cast as grammars, which can be collections of rules, constraints or both.
- Grammars can be observationally, descriptively, explanatorily and formally adequate.
- Rules are positive statements that tell you how to identify a grammatical form.
- Constraints are negative statements that tell you how to identify an ungrammatical form.
- Rules and constraints can often be exchanged.
- Rules are stated over derivations (a stepwise description of the formation of a sentence).
- Constraints are stated over representations (the final form of the sentence).
- Rules and constraints in syntax are descriptive, not prescriptive.

Linguistic analysis issues
- The subject is the noun before the verb in English and is often marked with nominative case.

- The object is the noun after the verb in English and is often marked with accusative case.
- Dative case is found on nouns marking the direction or location of an event. In English these are marked with prepositions like *to, for, in, on,* etc.
- A declarative sentence asserts that an event has occurred or will occur.
- Auxiliaries are "helping verbs" like *is, have* and *do.*
- *Yes/no* questions are questions formed by inverting the structurally most prominent auxiliary with the subject. They can be answered with *yes, no* or *maybe.*
- Sentences are structured entities with hierarchical organization.
- Paradigms are lists or tables that represent the forms of nouns that vary along a given dimension.
- Person refers to the participants in the conversation. First person is the speaker, second person is the listener, third persons are other participants or entities outside of the conversation.
- Gender: masculine (male), feminine (female), neuter (neither).
- Number: singular (only one), plural (more than one).

2 Categories and subcategories

UNIT 4 PARTS OF SPEECH AND LEXICAL CATEGORIES

Objectives:
- Understand how words are the basic building blocks of syntax.
- Distinguish between semantically based definitions for word class and those based on distribution.
- Identify Nouns, Verbs, Adjectives and Adverbs using distributional criteria.

4.1 Parts of speech

Definition **Syntactic categories** or **parts of speech** are the groups of words that let us state rules and constraints about the form of sentences. Typical parts of speech are **Nouns** (abbreviated as N), **Verbs** (V), **Adjectives** (Adj) and **Adverbs** (Adv).

Comment Certain words can appear in certain places. This is one of the central insights of syntactic theory. We want to be able to capture where some words appear and others do not in our rules. Parts of speech allow us to make generalizations about which types of elements appear in which positions.

Discussion Almost every student taking an elementary class in grammar will learn something like the following traditional definitions of parts of speech:

Traditional semantic definitions

(i) Noun: word describing a person, place or thing

(ii) Verb: word describing an action, occurrence or state of being

(iii) Adjective: word that expresses quality, quantity or extent

(iv) Adverb: word that expresses manner, quality, place, time, degree, number, cause, opposition, affirmation or denial

These definitions are based in meaning or semantics. To a certain degree, they have some intuitive validity. Nouns do typically refer to things, and verbs typically do refer to actions or states. However, from our linguistic perspective these definitions are inadequate.

Exercise Consider the italicized words in the following examples:

(1) the *assassination* of the president

33

(2)   The *sincerity* of the student was unquestioned.

Look carefully at the traditional definitions of parts of speech.

Q1 📖 Does *assassination* refer to a thing (i.e. a noun) or an action (i.e. a verb)? Can you tell?

Q2 📖 Does *sincerity* describe a thing (i.e. a noun) or a quality (i.e. an adjective)? Explain your answer.

Exercise **Q3** ✍ The following sentence has a number of nonsense words in it. Can you tell what part of speech they are? Do not try to use the definitions above or a dictionary – that won't work because these words are meaningless!

(3)   The yinkish dripner blorked quastofically into the nindin with the pidibs.

yinkish	N	V	Adj	Adv
dripner	N	V	Adj	Adv
blorked	N	V	Adj	Adv
quastofically	N	V	Adj	Adv
nindin	N	V	Adj	Adv
pidibs	N	V	Adj	Adv

Discussion   Many people can identify the part of speech of a word without knowing what it means; if the definition of a part of speech is based in its meaning, then this should not be possible. It appears as if we can identify an item's part of speech without knowing anything about its meaning.

4.2 Distributional definitions

Definition   Parts of speech are determined by looking at their distribution, not their meaning. **Distribution** refers to the places the word appears, both with respect to other words and with respect to the prefixes and suffixes the word has on it.

Discussion   Look again at sentence (3). We can determine the part of speech of these nonsense words by looking at where each word appears and which suffixes and prefixes it takes.

(4) (a)   yinkish   Adj   between *the* and a noun

takes *-ish* adjective ending

(b)   dripner   N   after an adjective (and *the*)

takes *-er* noun ending

subject of the sentence

(c)	blorked	V	after subject noun
			takes *-ed* verb ending
(d)	quastofically	Adv	after a verb
			takes *-ly* adverb ending
(e)	nindin	N	after *the* and after a preposition
(f)	pidibs	N	after *the* and after a preposition
			takes *-s* noun plural ending

Definitions   What follows is a list of distributional criteria for identifying **nouns**. This list works for English.

> **Derivational suffixes:** In English, nouns often end in derivational endings such as *-ment (basement), -ness (friendliness), -ity (sincerity), -ty (certainty), -(t)ion (devotion), -ation (expectation), -ist (specialist), -ant (attendant), -ery (shrubbery), -ee (employee), -ship (hardship), -aire (billionaire), -acy (advocacy), -let (piglet), -ling (underling), -hood (neighborhood), -ism (socialism), -ing (fencing).*

> **Inflectional suffixes:** Nouns in English dont show much inflection, but when pluralized can take suffixes such as *-s (cats), -es (glasses), -en (oxen), -ren (children), -i (cacti), -a (addenda)*. Note that the following endings have homophonous usage with other parts of speech: *-ing, -s, 's, -er, -en.*

> **Syntactic distribution:** Nouns often appear after determiners such as *the, those, these* (e.g. *these peanuts*) and can appear after adjectives (*the big peanut*). Nouns can also follow prepositions (*in school*). All of these conditions can happen together: *in the big gymnasium*. Nouns can appear as the subject of the sentence (we will define subject rigorously in a later unit): <u>*The syntax paper*</u> *was incomprehensible*; or as the direct object: *I read* <u>*the syntax paper*</u>. Nouns can be negated by *no* (as opposed to *not* or *un-*): *No apples were eaten.*

One easy way to see if something is a noun is to see if you can replace it with another word that is clearly a noun. So if we want to see if the word *people* is a noun or not, we can substitute another word we know for sure to be a noun, e.g. *John (I saw people running all over the place* vs. *I saw John running all over the place).*

Exercise   **Q4** ✏ Underline all the nouns in the following passage:[1]

> "If you'll watch my feet, you'll see how I do it," said she; and lifting her skirt above her dainty ankles, glided across the floor on tiptoe, as lightly

---

[1]   From Bacheller (1903).

as a fawn at play. But Sidney Trove was not a graceful creature. The muscles on his lithe form, developed in the school of work or in feats of strength at which he had met no equal, were untrained in all graceful trickery. He loved dancing and music and everything that increased the beauty and delight of life, but they filled him with a deep regret of his ignorance.

Definition What follows is a list of distributional criteria for identifying **verbs**. This list works for English.

Derivational suffixes: Verbs often end in derivational endings such as *-ate (dissipate)* and *-ize/-ise (regularize)*.

Inflectional suffixes: In the past tense, verbs usually take an *-ed* or *-t* ending. In the present tense, third person singular (*he, she, it*), they take the *-s* ending. Verbs can also take an *-ing* ending in some aspectual constructions (*she was walking*) and take either an *-en* or an *-ed* suffix when they are passivized (more on passivization in later units): *the ice cream was eaten*. Note that the following endings have homophonous usage with other parts of speech: *-ate, -ing, -s, -er, -en, -ed*. So these aren't entirely reliable guides. For example, *-ing* and *-s* often also occur on nouns; *-en* and *-ed* can appear on adjectives.

Syntactic distribution: Verbs can follow auxiliaries and modals such as *will, have, having, had, has, am, be, been, being, is, are, were, was, would, can, could, shall, should* and the special infinitive marker *to*. Verbs follow subjects, and can follow adverbs such as *often* and *frequently*. Verbs can be negated with *not* (as opposed to *no* and *un-*[2]).

Exercise **Q5** ✎ Go back to the passage in Q4 above and circle all the verbs.

Definition What follows is a list of distributional criteria for identifying **adjectives**. This list works for English.

Derivational suffixes: Adjectives often end in derivational endings such as *-ing (the dancing cat), -ive (indicative), -able (readable), -al (traditional), -ate (intimate), -ish (childish), -some (tiresome), -(i)an (reptilian), -ful (wishful), -less (selfless), -ly (friendly)*.

Inflectional suffixes: Adjectives can be inflected into a comparative form using *-er* (alternately they follow the word *more*). They can also be inflected into their superlative form using *-est* (alternately they follow the word *most*). Adjectives are typically negated using the prefix *un-* (in its sense meaning "not," not in its sense meaning "undo"). Note that the

---

[2] There are verbs that begin with *un-*, but in these circumstances, *un-* usually means "reverse" not negation.

following affixes have homophonous usage with other parts of speech:
-ate, -ing, -er, -en, -ed, un-, -ly.

Syntactic distribution: Adjectives can appear between determiners
such as *the, a, these* etc. and nouns (*the <u>big</u> peanut*). They also can
follow the auxiliary *am/is/are/was/were/be/been/being* (warning: this
distribution overlaps with verbs). Frequently, adjectives can be modified
by the adverb *very.* They can also appear in *as . . . as . . .* constructions
(*as <u>big</u> as Bill*). Note that the last two criteria also can identify adverbs.

Definition What follows is a list of distributional criteria for identifying **adverbs.** This
list works for English.

Derivational suffixes: Many adverbs end in *-ly: quickly, frequently,* etc.

Inflectional suffixes: Adverbs generally don't take any inflectional suffixes.
However, on rare occasions they can be used comparatively and follow
the word *more: She went <u>more quickly</u> than he did.* Adverbs typically
don't take the prefix *un-* unless the adjective they are derived from does
first (e.g. *unhelpfully* from *unhelpful,* but **unquickly, *unquick*).

Syntactic distribution: The syntactic distribution of adverbs is most easily
described by stating where they can't appear. Adverbs can't appear
between a determiner and a noun (**the quickly fox*) or after the verb
is and its variants.[3] They can really appear pretty much anywhere
else in the sentence, although typically they either appear at the
beginning or end of the clause/sentence. Frequently, like adjectives,
they can be modified by the adverb *very* or appear in *as . . . as*
constructions.

Comment In unit 13, we'll actually claim that adverbs and adjectives are part of one
larger class that we call "A." But for now, it's helpful just to assume that they
are different. Don't be surprised later on when we come up with the slightly
more sophisticated analysis!

Exercise **Q6** ✎ Go back to the passage in Q4 above and put a box around all the
adjectives and a dotted underline under any adverbs.

Comment As you can see from trying to identify the parts of speech in this passage,
parts of speech are not always obvious or straightforward. It requires some
practice and some experience. Next, we have several other exercises to help
you practice identifying parts of speech.

---

[3] In some prescriptive variants of English, there are a limited set of adverbs that can appear
after *is.* For example, *well* is prescriptively preferred over *good,* in such constructions as *I
am well* vs. *I am good* (referring to your state of being rather than the acceptability of your
behavior). Most speakers of American English don't allow any adverbs after *is.*

Exercise **Q7** 📖 Identify the main parts of speech (i.e. <u>N</u>ouns, <u>V</u>erbs, <u>Adj</u>ectives/<u>Adv</u>erb) in the following sentences.

(a)   The old rusty stove exploded in the house quickly yesterday.

(b)   The brainy assistant often put vital files through the new efficient shredder.

(c)   The large evil leathery tiger complained to his aging keeper about his unappetizing snacks.

(d)   I've just eaten the last piece of cake.

Exercise **Q8** ✏ Consider the following data from Lummi (Straits Salish),[4] assume that (a) *t'iləm=lə=sxʷ* is a verb. What part of speech are the (b) and (c) forms?

(a)   t'iləm=lə=sxʷ

sing=past=2SG.NOM

"You sang."   *verb*

(b)   si'em=lə=sxʷ

chief=past=2SG.NOM

"You were a chief."   ....

(c)   sey'si=lə=sxʷ

afraid=past=2SG.NOM

"You were afraid."   ....

Q9 📖 What does the data from Lummi tell us about the value of semantic definitions of parts of speech?

Exercise **Q10** ✏ Consider the following selection from *Jabberwocky*, a poem by Lewis Carroll (from *Through the Looking-Glass and What Alice Found There*, 1872). Identify the parts of speech of the underlined words. Indicate what criteria you used for determining their part of speech. Note that since these words are nonsense words you cannot use semantic criteria like "it's a thing" to determine what part of speech they are!

Twas brillig and the <u>slithy</u> toves   ....

Did <u>gyre</u> and <u>gimble</u> in the <u>wabe</u>;   ....

All mimsy were the borogoves,

And the mome raths <u>outgrabe</u>.   ....

---

[4]   Data from Jelinek and Demers (1994).

"Beware the Jabberwock, my son!

The jaws that bite, the claws that catch!

Beware the Jubjub bird, and shun

The <u>frumious</u> <u>bandersnatch</u>!"   ....

He took his <u>vorpal</u> sword in hand: ....

Long time the <u>manxome</u> foe he sought –   ....

So rested he by the <u>tumtum</u> tree   ....

And stood a while in thought.

And as in <u>uffish</u> thought he stood   ....

The <u>Jabberwock</u> with eyes of flame, ...

Came whiffling through the <u>tulgey</u> wood, ...

and burbled as it came.

Summary   In this unit we have covered the following major concepts:
- We use syntactic categories to make generalizations about what words can appear in which positions.
- Traditional semantic criteria are too vague to be effective; they also don't work in the light of nonsense words.
- Syntacticians use distributional criteria based on suffixes, prefixes and the relation of the word to other words.

Suggested further reading

- Aarts (1997), chapter 3
- Baker (2003)
- Carnie (2006), chapter 2
- Culicover (2009), chapter 2
- Huddleston and Pullum (2005), chapters 2, 3, 5, 6
- Larson (2010), unit 9
- Radford (2004), chapter 2
- Tallerman (2005), chapter 2
- van Gelderen (2010), chapter 2
- Williams (1983)
- The following is a website that teaches the traditional semantic definitions of parts of speech: www.funbrain.com/grammar/
- Wikipedia article on nouns: http://en.wikipedia.org/wiki/Noun
- Wikipedia article on verbs: http://en.wikipedia.org/wiki/Verb
- Wikipedia article on adjectives: http://en.wikipedia.org/wiki/Adjective
- Wikipedia article on adverbs: http://en.wikipedia.org/wiki/Adverb

Answers to questions

Q1 and Q2 The semantic definitions are pretty vague and don't always give us a clear answer. To me, *assassination* is at the very least an action, similarly *sincerity* is a quality, but once we investigate these cases syntactically we will find that they are both nouns.

Q3 *yinkish* Adj; *dripner* N; *blorked* V; *quastofically* Adv, *nindin* N, *pidibs* N.

Q4 The following are pronouns, which are a special type of noun: *you('ll)*, *my, I, she, her, his, he, him, they.* The following are clear nouns: *feet, skirt, ankles, floor, tiptoe, fawn, Sidney Trove, creature, muscles, form, school, work, feats, strength, equal, trickery, music, everything, beauty, delight, life, regret, ignorance. Play* and *dancing* are also nouns in this sentence even though they express actions.

Q5 For the moment I'll leave auxiliary verbs like *will* or *had* out of the list; we'll return to these in unit 5. The following are clear verbs: *watch, see, do, said, lifting, glided, was, developed, met, were loved, increased, filled.*

Q6 Adjectives: *dainty, graceful, lithe, deep;* Adverbs: *lightly. How* is also an adverb, but may not be obvious from the criteria listed above.

Q7 (a) N: *stove, house;* Adj: *old, rusty;* Adv: *quickly, yesterday;* V: *exploded*

(b) N: *assistant, files, shredder;* Adj: *brainy, vital, new, efficient;* Adv: *often;* V: *put.*

(c) N: *tiger, keeper, (his), snacks;* Adj: *large, evil, leathery, aging, unappetizing;* V: *complained*

(d) N: *I, piece, cake;* Adj: *last;* Adv: *just;* V: *eaten*

Q8 and Q9 Both (b) and (c) are also verbs; we can tell this by virtue of the fact that they bear the same basic inflection as the verb. This tells us that semantic definitions aren't valid, because presumably the words that mean the same thing in English are nouns and adjectives respectively.

Q10

gimble: V	this one is tricky. I think it's a verb based on the parallel between it and "did shimmer," but other analyses are possible.
wabe: N	after *the*
outgrabe: V	*out-* prefix
frumious: Adj	after *the*, *-ious* ending
bandersnatch: N	after *frumious*
vorpal: Adj	after *his*, before *sword*, possibly *-al* ending

manxome: Adj	after *the*, before *foe*
tumtum: Adj	after *the*, before *tree*
uffish: Adj	after *in*, before *thought*, *-ish* ending
Jabberwock: N	after *the*
tulgey: Adj	between *the* and *wood*, *-y* ending

UNIT 5 FUNCTIONAL CATEGORIES

> Objectives:
> - Learn the difference between open and closed-class parts of speech.
> - Learn the difference between functional and lexical parts of speech.
> - Be able to identify the major functional parts of speech, such as prepositions, determiners, conjunctions and complementizers.
> - Learn about parts of speech that are open but functional (such as interjections).
> - Learn about parts of speech that are closed but lexical (such as intensifiers).

5.1 Open vs. closed classes

Comment   When a new concept comes into our worldview, we almost immediately label it with a new word, a borrowing from another language or reassigning an old word a new meaning. When we borrow a word or make up a new word, we have what is called a **neologism**.

Definition   Parts of speech that allow neologisms are known as **open classes**. Examples of open classes include Nouns, Verbs, Adjectives and Adverbs.

Comment   By contrast, some parts of speech resist new words. For example, it would be a rare event when a language invents a new preposition (words like *in, on, under,* etc.).

Definition   Parts of speech that generally do not allow neologisms are known as **closed classes**. Examples of closed classes include prepositions, auxiliaries, conjunctions, articles, etc.

Exercise   Most standard varieties of English don't have a gender-neutral singular pronoun that can refer to humans (other than the very awkward *one*). There have been numerous attempts to introduce gender-neutral singular human pronouns into English. The following list is a subset of the ones found on John Chao's gender-neutral pronoun FAQ:[1]

---

[1] http://www.aetherlumina.com/gnp/index.html

42

ae, ar, co, e, em, ems, en, es, et, ey, fm, ha, hann, he'er, heesh, heir, hem,
her'n, herim, herm, hes, hesh, heshe, hey, hez, hi, himer, hir, hirem, hires,
hirm, his'er, his'n, hisher, hizer, ho, hom, hse, hymer, im, ip, ir, iro, jhe,
le, lem, na, ne, ner, nim, on, per, po, rim, s/he, sap, se, sem, ser, sheehy,
shem, shey, shim, sie, sim, ta, tem, term, tey, thim, thon, uh, ve, vim, vir,
vis, xe, z, ze, zie, zim, zir

None of these has caught on. Instead, the otherwise plural *they/them/their/*
themselves is usually felt to be more natural by native speakers, even though
it is the bane of prescriptive editors.

Q1 📖 Why have the above forms not caught on, but instead we have co-
opted a plural pronoun (*they, their*) for this usage?

5.2 Lexical vs. functional categories

Definition Categories that express content are called **lexical categories**. In English the
lexical categories are the ones we looked at in the previous unit (N, V, Adj,
Adv). Categories that express grammatical notions are known as **functional
categories**. Functional categories are the glue that holds sentences together.
Some typical examples are articles (*the, a*), prepositions (*on, under*), modal
verbs (*can, will*) and auxiliary verbs (*have, be, do*). Functional categories are
typically closed (although, as we will see in the next unit, there isn't a one-to-
one correspondence).

Exercise **Q2** ✏ In the last unit you saw the following passage and identified some
words as nouns, others as verbs, adjectives and adverbs. Go through the
passage and see if you can tell what words are functional words. Underline
them (Hint: they're all the words you didn't previously identify as N, V, Adj
or Adv!)

> "If you'll watch my feet, you'll see how I do it," said she; and lifting her
> skirt above her dainty ankles, glided across the floor on tiptoe, as lightly
> as a fawn at play. But Sidney Trove was not a graceful creature. The
> muscles on his lithe form, developed in the school of work or in feats
> of strength at which he had met no equal, were untrained in all graceful
> trickery. He loved dancing and music and everything that increased the
> beauty and delight of life, but they filled him with a deep regret of his
> ignorance.

Comment You'll notice that all the words in Q2 marked as functional categories are
quite hard to define. Take the word *of* as an example; its meaning lies in how
it acts to link other material together in the sentence. In the last line, *of* tells
us that his *regret* is about *his ignorance*. *Of* is the grammatical item that ties
these words together.

5.3 Functional categories

Definition Let's start with a simple example of a functional category. These are **prepositions**. These usually express the relationship between a noun and a verb. For example, if I say *Alex went to the computer lab*, the preposition *to* indicates the goal/end point of Alex's going. Distributionally, prepositions always come before the articles/determiners – if there are any – that come before the noun (i.e. *to* comes before *the* in the above sentence). Here are some typical prepositions of English:

(1)   *Some prepositions of English* (P):

      (a)   Dave ran <u>to</u> the cave.

      (b)   Sumayya hid her taxes <u>from</u> the federal government.

      (c)   Jeff put his paper <u>under</u> my coffee cup.

      (d)   Dan saw the tallships <u>over</u> the horizon.

      (e)   Art cleaned the pipe <u>without</u> an air compressor.

      (f)   Jennifer likes to sit <u>by</u> the seashore.

      (g)   Heidi bobbed <u>above</u> the waterline.

      (h)   Leila presented her paper <u>before</u> the princess.

      (i)   Jerid smoked everyday <u>after</u> work.

      (j)   Sylvia trudged <u>through</u> the bog.

      (k)   Jorge was seen <u>near</u> the student union building,

      (l)   Calvin knocked the clock <u>off</u> the bedside table.

      (m)   Shannon bought a piano <u>for</u> his son.

      (n)   Dainon jumped head first <u>into</u> the hot tub.

      (o)   Alex gasped <u>during</u> the shocking concert.

      (p)   Jenny jumped <u>across</u> the lobby.

      (q)   Kimberley hasn't eaten <u>since</u> Friday.

      (r)   Alina didn't wait <u>until</u> 5pm.

      (s)   Marian got sick <u>at</u> the hot dog stand.

Exercise **Q3** ✏ In the passage given above in Q2, we can find examples of the prepositions *across, above* and *at* but there are also four other prepositions not listed in (1). Identify what they are and give the sentence that contains them below:

      (t)   ....

      (u)   ....

      (v)   ....

      (w)   ....

Comment Prepositions are part of a larger class known as **adpositions**. **Prepositions** come before the noun. **Postpositions** come after the noun. English doesn't have postpositions, but many languages such as Japanese and Mandarin Chinese do. Note that many linguists use the term "preposition" even when referring to words that are more correctly postpositions.

Definition **Determiners** are a class of items that appear before nouns, but typically after prepositions. There are a number of different subtypes of determiners. Here are some of them:

    (2)   *Determiners of English* (D)

        (a)   *Articles:* the, a, an

        (b)   *Deictic articles:* this, that, these, those, yon

        (c)   *Quantifiers:* every, some, many, most, few, all, each, any, less, fewer, no

Exercise **Q4** ✏ Go back to the passage given above in Q2. How many articles, quantifiers, deictic markers can you find? Be very careful: the *that* on the second last line is *not* a deictic marker (it is a complementizer – which we return to below)

    Articles ....   Deictics ....   Quantifiers ....

Comment Many linguists treat possessive pronouns like *my, your, his, her, our, their* as determiners too. We can see several examples of this kind of determiner in the paragraph too.

Definition Next we consider two kinds of function words that link various categories together. First we have **conjunctions** (Conj), also known as **coordinators**. These words tie together two words or phrases (groups of words) on an equal level. For example, the conjunction *and* ties together two determiner–noun sequences in (3a), two verb phrases in (3b) and two sentences in (3c).

    (3)   (a)   I ate [the pizza] *and* [the eggroll]

        (b)   I [ate the pizza] *and* [drank the soda]

        (c)   [I ate the pizza] *and* [Dave drank the soda]

In each case the conjunction links the two coordinated elements on an equal level. Here is a list of some English conjunctions:

    (4)   *Conjunctions of English* (Conj): and, or, nor, neither . . . nor, either . . . or, if . . . then . . . , both . . . and . . ., however, nevertheless

Some of these are composed of two words, we will ignore this complication for the moment.

Comment If you have taken any formal logic, you probably would not describe *or* as a "conjunction" (as in formal logic *or* (∨) is known as a "disjunction").

45

Linguists use the term "conjunction" differently: we use it the same way that a logician uses the term "connective." For linguists the term "conjunction" includes all the forms listed above in (4) and is not limited to *and* or &/∧.

The second kind of connecting word we will look at is known as a **complementizer**. In traditional grammar, complementizers are sometimes known as **subordinators** or **subordinating conjunctions**. They differ from conjunctions in that they link two items in an asymmetric unbalanced fashion. They also generally link clauses (roughly speaking, a clause is a sentence – we'll return to this in a later unit). Take, for example, the sentence *Amy thinks that Dave forgot to pay his bar tab*. This sentence includes a smaller sentence: *Dave forgot to pay his bar tab*. This smaller sentence is a part of the larger sentence that includes *Amy* and *thinks* as well. The complementizer *that* signals that the second sentence is subordinate to (i.e. included in) the larger sentence. Below are some complementizers of English.

(5)   *Complementizers of English* (C): that, for, if, whether, because, after, although, while, since, until, before, provided, unless, though

Comment   There are some other words that might be analyzed as complementizers, such as *which* and *when*. For reasons that will become clear later we're actually going to give those a different analysis, but you might see other words listed as complementizers in some syntax books.

Exercise   **Q5** ✏ In each of the following sentences there is a blank. Fill in the appropriate conjunction or complementizer. More than one form is possible for many of the sentences. Indicate whether the form you used is a conjunction (Conj) or complementizer (C).

(a)   Mark .... Susan cut down the tree.   Conj   C

(b)   I wonder .... Mark cut down the tree.   Conj   C

(c)   I'm sure .... Mark cut down the tree.   Conj   C

(d)   .... Mark cut down the tree .... Susan did.   Conj   C

(e)   Bill asked .... Mark cut down the tree.   Conj   C

(f)   .... Mark cut down the tree .... I'll be really angry.   Conj   C

(g)   Mark cut down the tree .... Susan didn't.   Conj   C

Definitions   There are a few other functional categories that we have not included here: for example, words like *not* may be a special category that is used to indicate **negation**. We also have the class of elements that we can loosely group together as **interjections**. Interjections can be combined with sentences, but are more often uttered in isolation. These include such words as *oh, darn* (and the ruder variants of *darn!*), *yes, no, maybe, hot diggity*, etc.

Comment While it is the case that many functional categories are closed (i.e. it is very hard to add new words to these classes), it is not the case that all closed classes are functional categories. For example, non-possessive pronouns are closed class, but they are distributed at least partly like nouns, which are lexical.

Exercise **Q6** 📖 Interjections are functional items, in that they express a grammatical notion (such as the speaker's agreement or attitude with respect to the thing being said), but are they closed class? Is it possible to make up new interjections? Think about swear words.

Q7 📖 There is a class of adverb that includes *very, rather, too*. We call these **intensifiers**. They typically serve to modify adjectives and other adverbs as in *very big* or *too rude* or *rather quickly*. Is the group of intensifiers open class or closed class? How do you know?

Comment In this unit, we've distinguished between those words whose function is fully grammatical (functional categories) and those that express the content in a sentence (lexical categories). In the next unit we will look at one case (pronouns) that isn't so clear cut, in that these words have properties of both functional and lexical categories. In later units we'll look at two other types of words (modals and auxiliaries) that also have both functional and lexical properties.

Suggested further reading

- Aarts (1997), chapter 3
- Bresnan (1972)
- Carnie (2006), chapter 2
- Culicover (2009), chapter 2
- Huddleston and Pullum (2005), chapters 2, 7, 8 and 10
- Radford (2004), chapter 2
- van Gelderen (2010), chapter 2.
- http://en.wikipedia.org/wiki/Open_class_word
- http://en.wikipedia.org/wiki/Closed-class_word
- http://en.wikipedia.org/wiki/Preposition
- http://en.wikipedia.org/wiki/Grammatical_conjunction
- http://en.wikipedia.org/wiki/Determiner_%28class%29
- http://en.wikipedia.org/wiki/Interjection

Answers to questions

Q1 If pronouns are closed-class parts of speech, then the fact that new pronouns aren't easily introduced follows directly.

Q2 if, ('ll for will), do, above, across, and, on, as, a, was, not, the, in, the, of, or, at, which, had, no, were, all, that, but, with

Q3 ... glided across the floor *on* tiptoe ... developed *in* the school of work ... delight *of* life ... they filled him *with* a deep regret *of* his ignorance. . .

Q4 articles: *the* 4, *a* 3; deictic articles 0; quantifiers: *all* 1, *every*(thing) 1

Q5 (a) *and* or *or*; Conj; (b) *if* or *whether*; C; (c) *that*; C; (d) *either* ... *or* or *neither* ... *nor* ; Conj; (e) *if* or *whether*; C; (f) *if* ... *then* or *either* ... *or* or *neither* ... *nor* ; Conj; (g) *but*; Conj

Q6 Interjections seem to be an open-class part of speech. You can make up new ones to disguise taboo forms (such as *foop* for the f-word), and new words regularly come into the grammar, such as Homer Simspon's *doh!* or *oof!*, which have recently been added to English.

Q7 Adverbs are typically open-class, but intensifiers seem to be an exception. They are mostly closed class. It is very hard to add new ones. However, recently in the American English of younger speakers, we have acquired a new intensifier: *hella* as in *These cookies are hella good.* One can also find the swear word *fuckin'* used this way. The British can use *bloody* as an intensifier too. The open/closed isn't a firm and clear distinction in every situation.

Comment While lexical categories are typically open and functional categories are typically closed. There is no one-to-one correspondence between the two notions. There are functional categories that are open (such as interjections) and lexical categories that are closed (such as intensifiers and pronouns).

UNIT 6 SUBCATEGORIES 1: PRONOUNS

> Objectives:
> - Understand the basic concept of subcategories.
> - Learn about the use of features to distinguish among subcategories.
> - Learn about pronouns which have some of the properties of functional categories and some of the properties of nouns.

6.1 Pronouns vs. other nouns

Comment In unit 4, we learned about the lexical categories of N, V, Adj and Adv; in unit 5, we examined the behavior of functional categories. In this unit we're going to look at a group of words that has properties of both lexical categories and functional categories.

Exercise In (1)–(4) below, compare the behavior of the underlined words in each (a)/(b) pair.

(1) (a) John ate the beef waffles.

    (b) He ate the beef waffles.

(2) (a) The kitten snuggled into Susan.

    (b) The kitten snuggled into her.

(3) (a) The TV was annoying Susan and Frank.

    (b) The TV was annoying them.

(4) (a) George's coat was shredded at the cleaners.

    (b) His coat was shredded at the cleaners.

Q1 📖 *John, Susan, Susan, Frank, George* are all nouns. What does the data in (1)–(4) tell us about the part of speech of *he, her, them* and *his*?

Exercise Other distributional tests for being a noun include being able to take a determiner (*the* man), being able to be modified by an adjective (*the big* man), and being able to take plural morphology (*the dogs*).

Q2 ✏ Are any of the following examples acceptable? Mark the unacceptable forms with *.

(5)   (a)   the him

      (b)   big him

      (c)   hims

Exercise   Look at the data in (6). Notice the alternation in forms between the (a) and (b) example. Compare this to the examples in (7).

(6)   (a)   <u>He</u> left.

      (b)   Peter kissed <u>him</u>.

(7)   (a)   <u>Peter</u> left.

      (b)   Erin kissed <u>Peter</u>.

In unit 3, we saw that the difference between *he* and *him* was one of case. (See question 1 of unit 3.)

Q3 ✏ Do nouns that aren't pronouns show overt signs of case in English?   Y   N

Discussion   In some ways pronouns are like other nouns. They can appear in subject and object position just like nouns (see 1–4), but in other situations they are different. For example, English pronouns inflect for case, but other English nouns do not. Similarly, most English nouns can follow a determiner, can be modified by an adjective, or take plural morphology, but pronouns cannot.

Definition   **Subcategories** are subtypes of larger categories. So nouns are a category, and pronouns are a subcategory of nouns.

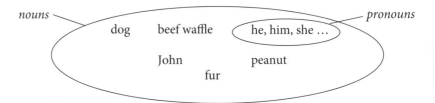

6.2 Feature notation

Notation   One way we can indicate a subcategory is with a feature structure. Feature structures are notations associated with a word, which indicate some particular (or several particular) properties of a word. In this book, we'll indicate features between square brackets, where the attribute being associated with a word is on the left followed by its value.[1] For example, let's

---

[1] The basic form of the feature structures given here is borrowed from the theories of HPSG and LFG. However, the particular arrangement of features and the feature values themselves are different from what you'll find in the HPSG/LFG literature. Nothing much hangs on the arrangement given here, except to make it relatively consistent with Chomskyan Minimalist theory. The geometry of the features and their relationships is ultimately an empirical question, and the organization I've given here could well be wrong.

consider a partial feature structure that might be associated with the word dog:

(8) *dog*

[CATEGORY   N]

The word *dog* has an attribute (or features) of having a CATEGORY. The value of that CATEGORY feature is N. More complicated feature structures are required to reflect the category status of pronouns. We want to mark that pronouns are nouns too, so we'll leave in the value N. This tells us that pronouns can appear in subject and object position (and other such positions). But then we want to mark it for the fact that they don't take plural marking, can't appear after determiners, etc. For the moment, we'll mark this with a feature SUBCAT with the value +D (the reason for the choice of +D will be made clear in a minute). Because being a pronominal is a subproperty of being a noun, we embed this feature inside of a pair of brackets associated with the value N. So a partial feature structure for a pronoun like *he* will look like (9):

(9) *he*

$$
\left[
\text{CATEGORY}
\left[
\begin{array}{l}
\text{N} \\
\\
\text{SUBCAT } +D
\end{array}
\right]
\right]
$$

We can read this as "*he* is of the category N, with a subcategory of D" (making it a pronoun). We can enrich this even further. The pronoun *he* is the special form used in nominative case. Further, it is singular, third person and masculine. It is not a big jump to add the features CASE, GEND (gender), PERS (person) and NUM (number). While these are properties associated with being pronouns, they don't mark subcategories, so we're going to mark these properties as being something different. We're going to let CASE stand on its own, and we're going to group GEND, PERS and NUM together into a group we're going to call AGR-φ features. This stands for "agreement" features. The symbol φ is the Greek letter *phi*, which is the standard marker for this kind of inflectional feature in Chomskyan grammar. Here is a fuller feature structure for *he*:

(10) *he*

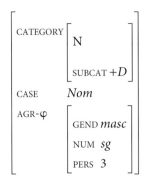

This reads that *he* is a pronoun (N with subcategory +D), in the nominative (*nom*) case, that expresses masculine (*masc*) gender, singular (*sg*) number and third (3) person agreement features.

If a particular form is used for more than one possible usage (this is known as a **suppletion**) – for example, the pronoun *you* can be both singular or plural and can be used to address both masculine and feminine entities – then we don't specify a value for the number or gender features. *You* is also used in both nominative and accusative environments, but is never found in possessive (*you book, cf. *your book*). To indicate this we put a ¬ sign before a feature value that this word cannot bear. So the feature structure for *you* looks a little different than the feature structure for *he*.

(11) *you*

$$
\begin{bmatrix}
\text{CATEGORY} & \begin{bmatrix} \text{N} \\ \text{SUBCAT } +D \end{bmatrix} \\
\text{CASE} & \neg Poss \\
\text{AGR-}\varphi & \begin{bmatrix} \text{GEND } masc \\ \text{PERS } 2 \end{bmatrix}
\end{bmatrix}
$$

Exercise **Q4** ✏ Using (8), (10) and (11) as models, and using the following features with the listed values, fill in the blank feature values for each of the following pronouns. The case for pronouns like *his*, *our*, etc. is called the **possessive** or **genitive** case.

Feature	Possible values (so far!)
CATEGORY	N
	SUBCAT
SUBCAT	+D
CASE	*nom* (nominative)
	acc (accusative)
	poss (possessive)
AGR-φ	GEND (gender)
	NUM (number)
	PERS (person
GEN	*masc* (masculine)
	fem (feminine)
	neut (neuter)
NUM	*sg* (singular)
	pl (plural)
PERS	1 (first person, speaker)
	2 (second person, addressee)
	3 (third person, non-participant)

(a)   *him*

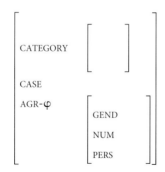

(b) *she*

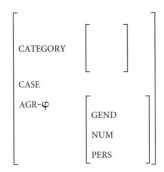

(c) *I*

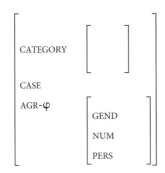

(d) *our*

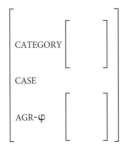

(e) *her (warning!* her *is tricky. Note that* her *can be used two ways:* her book *and I saw* her. *Use a ¬ feature to capture this!)*

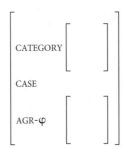

(f)   *girl*

$$\left[\right]$$

6.3 Possessive pronouns

Exercise   Confine yourself to the following data.

(12) (a)   the suitcase

(b)   the big suitcase

(c)   every suitcase

(d)   every big suitcase

(e)   my suitcase

(f)   my big suitcase

(g)   *the every suitcase

(h)   *every the suitcase

(i)   *the my suitcase

(j)   *my the suitcase

(k)   *every my suitcase

(l)   *my every suitcase

Look carefully at what other words can appear with the word *suitcase*.

Q5 ✏ Can both a determiner (like *the* or *every*) and an adjective
(*big*) occur together before *suitcase*?   Y   N

Q6 ✏ Can a possessive pronoun (like *my*) and an adjective occur
together before *suitcase*?   Y   N

Q7 ✏ Can two determiners (like *the* or *every*) occur together before
suitcase?   Y   N

Q8 ✏ Can a determiner and a possessive pronoun occur together
before *suitcase*?   Y   N

Q9 📖 What does the distribution described by questions 5–8 tell us about
the distribution of possessive pronouns? Are they in any way like Adjectives
or Determiners?

Exercise Now consider the following data:

(13) (a) We linguists love a good fight.

(b) How do you like them apples? (*OK in non-standard speech*)

(c) You clowns never know when to stop.

(d) *The we linguists love a good fight.

(e) *How do you like those them apples?

(f) *The you clowns never know when to stop.

Q10 📖 Although this is a fairly rare phenomenon in English, what does the data in (13) tell us about the part of speech of pronouns?

Discussion The reason that we mark the pronominal subcategory with the feature value of +D is to evoke the fact that there is some overlap between the distribution of pronouns and determiners.

6.4 Reflexive pronouns

Exercise Consider the following underlined words.

(14) (a) I saw myself.

(b) He saw himself.

(c) You saw yourself.

(d) She saw herself.

(e) We saw ourselves.

(f) You saw yourselves.

(g) They saw themselves.

(h) *I saw herself.

(i) *You saw myself.

(j) *He saw themselves.

The underlined pronouns are called **anaphors** or **reflexive pronouns**. In English these all end in -*self* or -*selves*.

Q11 📖 Describe in your own words the pattern that explains why (a)–(g) are acceptable, but (h)–(j) are not. You should make reference to the first noun (i.e. the subject) in your answer.

Definition Anaphors (also known as reflexive pronouns) are a subcategory of nouns that behave in most ways like pronouns (i.e. anywhere they appear a noun can appear instead, they cannot co-occur with determiners or adjectives), but they are more restricted, in that they can only appear in object position and they have to have the same AGR-φ features as the subject.[2]

Notation Anaphors are indicated by the +R (mnemonic for "reflexive") value to the SUBCAT feature. Here's the feature structure for the anaphor *himself*:

(15) *himself*

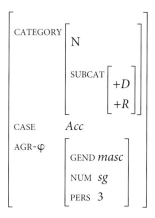

Exercise **Q12** ✍ Fill in the feature structure for *yourself*. Important hint: note that anaphors never appear in the nominative or possessive case, so be careful about the value of the CASE feature.

yourself

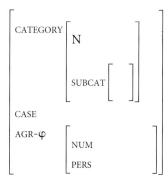

---

[2] Actually, their distribution is a little more complex than this; we'll return to this in later units.

Summary In this unit, we've looked at one particular subcategory of nouns: pronouns. We've observed how their distribution overlaps somewhat with determiners. We also looked at how to capture the properties of pronouns using feature structures. This included a subcategory of the pronoun subcategory: anaphors.

Suggested further reading

- Adger (2003), chapter 2
- Falk (2001), chapter 3
- Huddleston and Pullum (2005), chapter 5
- Larson (2010), unit 14
- Sag, Wasow and Bender (2003), chapters 3 and 4
- van Gelderen (2010), chapter 2
- Wikipedia article on pronouns: http://en.wikipedia.org/wiki/Pronoun
- Wikipedia article on anaphors: http://en.wikipedia.org/wiki/Reflexive_pronoun
- Wikipedia article on feature structures: http://en.wikipedia.org/wiki/Feature_structure

Answers to questions

Q1 Pronouns like *he, her, them* and *his* all appear in positions where nouns appear. Since part of speech is based on distribution, this means that pronouns have something noun-like in their category.

Q2 Pronouns may not be modified by determiners, adjectives or take plural marking. As we will see later, pronouns have some of the properties of determiners as well as nouns.

Q3 Non-pronominal nouns do not showcase morphology in English (although they frequently do in other languages).

Q4 (a) *him*

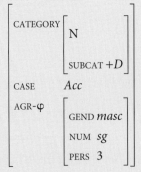

(b) *she*

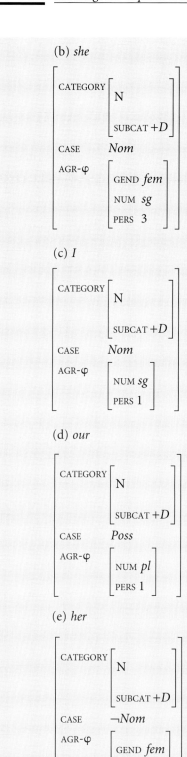

$$\begin{bmatrix} \text{CATEGORY} & \begin{bmatrix} \text{N} \\ \\ \text{SUBCAT} +D \end{bmatrix} \\ \text{CASE} & Nom \\ \text{AGR-}\varphi & \begin{bmatrix} \text{GEND } fem \\ \text{NUM } sg \\ \text{PERS } 3 \end{bmatrix} \end{bmatrix}$$

(c) *I*

$$\begin{bmatrix} \text{CATEGORY} & \begin{bmatrix} \text{N} \\ \\ \text{SUBCAT} +D \end{bmatrix} \\ \text{CASE} & Nom \\ \text{AGR-}\varphi & \begin{bmatrix} \text{NUM } sg \\ \text{PERS } 1 \end{bmatrix} \end{bmatrix}$$

(d) *our*

$$\begin{bmatrix} \text{CATEGORY} & \begin{bmatrix} \text{N} \\ \\ \text{SUBCAT} +D \end{bmatrix} \\ \text{CASE} & Poss \\ \text{AGR-}\varphi & \begin{bmatrix} \text{NUM } pl \\ \text{PERS } 1 \end{bmatrix} \end{bmatrix}$$

(e) *her*

$$\begin{bmatrix} \text{CATEGORY} & \begin{bmatrix} \text{N} \\ \\ \text{SUBCAT} +D \end{bmatrix} \\ \text{CASE} & \neg Nom \\ \text{AGR-}\varphi & \begin{bmatrix} \text{GEND } fem \\ \text{NUM } sg \\ \text{PERS } 3 \end{bmatrix} \end{bmatrix}$$

(f) *girl*

$$\begin{bmatrix} \text{CATEGORY} & N \\ \text{AGR-}\varphi & \begin{bmatrix} \text{NUM } sg \end{bmatrix} \end{bmatrix}$$

Comment (f) was a bit of a trick. Although it is obvious that *girl* is talking about a female, in English we don't express gender marking on nouns. We also don't express any special marking for case or person (although *girl* is also obviously third person). In other languages (such as Spanish or French) these relations might be expressed on regular nouns, and in such cases they would be expressed in the feature structure. We do indicate that *girl* is singular, however, since we can distinguish it from *girls*.

Q5 Y

Q6 Y

Q7 N

Q8 N

Q9 Possessive pronouns are appearing the same positions as determiners, and like determiners they cannot co-occur with other determiners (at least in the data given).

Q10 In these limited cases, it looks as if other pronouns are also appearing in the same positions as determiners, and like determiners they cannot co-occur with other determiners (at least in the data given).

Q11 The anaphor must bear the same AGR-φ features as the subject noun in the sentence. So if you have a masculine, singular third person anaphor, then the subject must match up in number, gender and person.

Q12 The value of the SUBCAT feature is +D, +R. The CASE feature must be *acc* (contrast that with *you* – see above). The value of the NUM feature is *sg* (again unlike *you* which is ambiguous in its number value). The plural anaphor is *yourselves*, which will have a *pl* NUM feature. The PERS is 2.

UNIT 7 SUBCATEGORIES 2: OTHER SUBCATEGORIES OF NOUNS

Objectives:

- Learn about the subcategories of proper nouns, animate nouns, mass nouns and count nouns.

Comment In the last unit we learned about two subcategories of nouns: pronouns and anaphors. In this unit, we look at some other subcategories of nouns.

7.1 Proper nouns

Exercise Compare the behavior of the underlined words in (1a–c)

(1) (a)   Andrew loves bagpipes.

    (b)   *The Andrew loves bagpipes.

    (c)   Big Andrew loves bagpipes.

Q1 📖 Names, such as *Andrew*, are called **proper nouns**. What is the distribution of proper nouns relative to determiners and adjectives? How is the distribution of proper names different from that of pronouns?

Exercise Consider the following data from Italian:

(2)   Il   Gianni mi ha   telefonato.

    the Gianni me has telephoned

    "Gianni called me up."

Q2 📖 What does the evidence from Italian tell us about whether the distribution of proper nouns overlaps with that of determiners?

Notation In order to mark the limited distribution of the subcategory of proper nouns we will use the feature value +*prop*, illustrated in the following partial feature structure.

(3)   *Andrew*

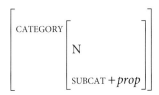

Challenge What are we to make of data like that in (4)? Is this evidence for our claim that unlike pronouns, proper names are not +D? Is this data counterevidence to our claim that proper names can't appear with determiners? Is the phenomenon in (4) available to any proper name or is it possible with just a subcategory of the subcategory?

(4) (a) We Harleys love a good family challenge.

(b) Those Rosenbaums are famous for their chili.

(c) The Carnies are coming over tonight for dinner.

7.2 Animate nouns

Definition Next we consider another subcategory: that of **animate** nouns. Animate nouns refer to living things. This class is a little trickier to identify, since there is no obvious morphological mark of it in English, but we can find syntactic evidence for this group.

Exercise **Q3** ✍ Start by evaluating the acceptability of the following sentences. Assume that nothing poetic or metaphorical is being asserted in the following forms. Give each sentence a "*" if it is bad, a "?" if it is OK but a bit weird, and leave it blank if it is OK.

(5) (a) .... Peter sent an email to Dave.

(b) .... Peter sent Dave an email.

(c) .... Peter sent a letter to Detroit.

(d) .... Peter sent Detroit a letter. (Where *Detroit* is the city, and does not mean something like "the Detroit office.")

(e) .... Susan bought some flowers for her mother.

(f) .... Susan bought her mother some flowers.

(g) .... Susan bought some flowers for her birthday.

(h) .... Susan bought her birthday some flowers.

Discussion The (a), (c), (e), (g) examples are known as **prepositional ditransitives**. These are cases where there is both an indirect object (e.g. *to Dave*) and a direct object (e.g. *an email*), where the indirect object is marked with a preposition. The (b), (d), (f) and (h) examples are known as **dative constructions**. In the dative, the indirect object comes first and is not marked with a preposition. Notice that in the dative construction, the sentence is better when an indirect object (the first noun after the verb) refers to a person or an animate group.

Comment Observe the following data from Spanish (taken from Legate 2005). In (6) we see that an animate object in Spanish like *Juan* is marked with a special marker *a*, by contrast the inanimate *Juan's house* is not marked with *a*.

(6) (a) Vimos a   Juan.

saw.1PL DAT Juan

"We saw Juan."

(b) Vimos la   casa   de Juan.

saw.1PL the house of Juan

"We saw Juan's house."

Notation We will represent animate nouns with the SUBCAT value of *+Animate* (highlighted for you in the diagrams below). In many cases this will overlap with pronouns and proper names, but not necessarily:

(7)   *Andrew*

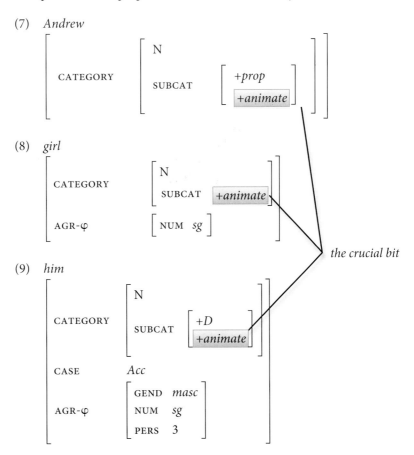

(8)   *girl*

(9)   *him*

63

7.3 Common nouns: mass vs. count

Definition   Nouns that are not pronouns or proper names are known as **common nouns**.

Exercise   Common nouns fall into two main subcategories. We'll examine these two subcategories in the exercises.

> **Q4** ✆ For each of the words below indicate whether it can occur with the quantifier *much* or the quantifier *many*.
>
> | | | | |
> |---|---|---|---|
> | (a) | apples | Much | Many |
> | (b) | sincerity | Much | Many |
> | (c) | air | Much | Many |
> | (d) | cats | Much | Many |
> | (e) | water | Much | Many |
> | (f) | sugar | Much | Many |

Definition   There is a clear-cut distinction between nouns that can appear with *much* and those that can appear with *many*. We call nouns that appear with *much* **mass nouns**. We call nouns that appear with *many* **count nouns**.

Discussion   At first pass it may look as if the difference between mass and count nouns is one of plurality (e.g. *apples* is plural but *air* is not), but further data will show us that plurality isn't the main determinant for distinguishing count from mass nouns. We look at this in the next exercise.

Exercise   Consider the following data:

> (10) (a)   *I ate apple.
>
> (b)   I ate the apple.
>
> (c)   I ate sugar.
>
> (d)   I ate the sugar.
>
> (e)   He is filled with sincerity.
>
> (f)   I doubt his sincerity.
>
> (g)   The sincerity of the President's claims is in dispute.

We know from Q4 that *apple* is a count noun but *sugar* and *sincerity* are mass nouns.

> **Q5** 📖 What is the rule or pattern that determines the co-occurrence of count nouns with determiners? What about mass nouns?

Comment   In some ways, mass nouns are like plural count nouns. Plural count nouns in English can appear with or without a determiner (11c and d). This is like the

64

pattern of mass nouns (see (10c–g) above). By contrast, singular count nouns always require a determiner (11a and b).

(11) (a) *Cat ate the spider.

    (b) The cat ate the spider.

    (c) Cats ate the spider.

    (d) The cats ate the spider.

There are, however, restrictions on which determiners can appear with mass nouns. For example, *several* and *every* cannot appear with mass nouns:

(12) (a) Every cat ate the tuna.

    (b) *Every water drowned the man.

    (c) Several cats ate the tuna.

    (d) *Several waters drowned the man.[1]

The overall pattern appears to be the following:

(13)	Count nouns		Mass nouns
	Singular	*Plural*	
Determiner	Required	Optional	Optional
Much/Many	–	Many	Much
Every	OK	*	*
Several	–	OK	*

Comment Humans are very good at imagining situations different from the usual situation. As such, it isn't difficult to construct situations where we find count nouns functioning like mass nouns. For example, we know that *cat* is a count noun from the tests given above, but imagine a sci-fi movie where there were giant lizard people who liked snacking on cats. We can imagine these Felinivorous Lizards announcing at dinner "Tonight we have a fine dinner of cat served with peas." As disgusting as this may appear to many of us, we understand immediately that the lizards are using *cat* as a mass noun.

But one doesn't have to go to science fiction to find cases were we have nouns that can be used as both as mass and count nouns. In fact, such situations are the norm.

(14) (a) That soda is filled with *sugar*. (mass)

    (b) I'd like two *sugars* in my coffee please. (count)

    (c) *Fire* is a dangerous thing. (mass)

    (d) He had a *fire* in his fireplace. (count)

---

[1] This is of course OK if we are talking about cups of water; we return to this point below.

Usually the mass and count versions have subtly different meanings. For example, (14a) is about the ingredient of sugar with no amount specified, whereas (14b) is about two teaspoons or two packets of sugar. Frequently count nouns or count noun usages of mass nouns are identified as having a boundary that allows them to be counted. If I'm looking at a warehouse filled with coffee, I refer to the mass unbounded notion of coffee. If I'm at my favorite café and I ask for a coffee, I'm looking for the bounded notion of a cup of coffee, which I can count.

This flexibility in subcategory muddies the water in trying to determine if a noun is count or mass when looking at the word in isolation. However, we have already learned that parts of speech, including subcategories, can only be determined by looking at their distribution. This is no less true here. We can tell if a noun is count or mass only in the context in which it appears, even though semantically there are some concepts that seem to be more "massy" (e.g. water) and some that appear to be more "county" (e.g. a person).

Exercise **Q6** ✏ Using the chart in (13) as a guide and keeping in mind the proviso given immediately above this exercise, determine whether the following nouns are mass nouns, plural count nouns or singular count nouns. (Circle the relevant answer.) Some of these may fall into more than one category, but don't change the endings of the words (i.e. do not turn *cow* into *cows*).

(a)	cow	Singular count	Plural count	Mass
(b)	people	Singular count	Plural count	Mass
(c)	corn	Singular count	Plural count	Mass
(d)	dogs	Singular count	Plural count	Mass
(e)	cattle	Singular count	Plural count	Mass

Notation We will mark count nouns with the feature +*Count*. Mass nouns are −*Count*. +*Count* nouns can bear the additional feature of ±*Plural*.[2] −*Count* nouns don't bear this feature. This restriction can be stated as the constraint in (15):

(15) *Mass/Pl Feature Co-occurrence Restriction:*

$$* \begin{bmatrix} -count \\ \pm pl \end{bmatrix}$$

---

[2] Note that sometimes I use *sg* (i.e. singular) as an abbreviation for −plural.

±*Count* is a value for the SUBCAT, just like +*animate* and +*proper*. So the representation for *girl* (in its normal count usage) would be:

(16) *girl*

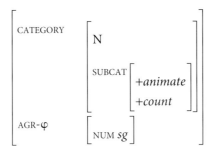

Exercise **Q7** 📖 Draw two feature structures for the word *water*. One is for its normal mass noun usage (*The lake didn't have much water in it*); the other will be for its count usage (e.g. *I drank the water*).

Summary In this unit we've identified the following different subcategories of nouns:
- Proper nouns (+*proper*)
- Animate nouns (±*animate*)
- Count nouns (+*count*), which can be ±*plural*
- Mass nouns (−*count*)

We also saw that these features don't draw out discrete classes of nouns; there is overlap among them. For example, a noun could be both a proper name and animate. Similarly, we saw that depending upon context nouns may shift in their subcategory, particularly between mass and count usages.

Here are the additional features we have added:

Feature	Possible values (so far!)
CATEGORY	N
	SUBCAT
SUBCAT	+D
	+*prop*
	±*animate*
	±*count*

Suggested further reading

- Huddleston and Pullum (2005), chapter 5
- Kim and Sells (2008), chapter 6
- Lobeck (2000), chapter 4
- Wikipedia article on count nouns:
  http://en.wikipedia.org/wiki/Count_noun
- Wikipedia article on mass nouns:
  http://en.wikipedia.org/wiki/Mass_noun
- Wikipedia article on proper nouns:
  http://en.wikipedia.org/wiki/Noun#Proper_nouns_and_common_nouns
- Wikipedia article on animacy: http://en.wikipedia.org/wiki/Animacy

Answers to questions

Q1 Like pronouns, proper names in English cannot appear with a determiner, but they can appear with an adjective

Q2 In Italian, and other languages, proper names can co-occur with determiners. This suggests that proper names should not be identified with the +D feature.

Q3 a, b, c, e, f, g, should all be acceptable; d is decidedly strange unless "Detroit" refers to some group of people in Detroit; h is just awful.

Q4 *Much* can appear with *sincerity, air, sugar* and *water. Many* can appear with *apples* and *cats.*

Q5 (Singular) count nouns like apple must co-occur with a determiner, there is no such restriction on mass nouns.

Q6 (a) *Cow* is a singular count noun in its usual usage. It might be used in a mass context with enough imagination (e.g. there is a horrible highway accident and the mangled remains of several cows are scattered everywhere, and the police say "We really have to clean all this cow off the road").

(b) *People* is a plural count noun. It cannot be a mass noun (*much people).

(c) *Corn* can be both a count noun (*Pass me a corn* (on the cob)) and a mass noun (*Corn is used to make corn syrup; Is there much corn in that soup?*).

(d) *Dogs* is a plural count noun.

(e) *Cattle* is a mass noun. In standard usage it cannot be used as a count noun although for many Americans a count noun usage (synonymous with singular cow or "head of cattle") is coming into use.

Q7   *Mass noun usage:*

$$\begin{bmatrix} \text{CATEGORY} & \begin{bmatrix} \text{N} \\ \\ \text{SUBCAT } -count \end{bmatrix} \end{bmatrix}$$

Count noun usage:

$$\begin{bmatrix} \text{CATEGORY} & \begin{bmatrix} \text{N} \\ \\ \text{SUBCAT } +count \end{bmatrix} \\ \\ \text{AGR-}\varphi & \begin{bmatrix} \text{NUM } sg \end{bmatrix} \end{bmatrix}$$

69

UNIT 8 SUBCATEGORIES 3: TRANSITIVITY

Objectives:
- Understand the notions of argument structure, predicates and arguments.
- Be able to identify subcategories of verbs based on the number and type of arguments they take (i.e. valency or transitivity).
- Represent these subcategories with features.

Comment In the last unit, we looked at the various ways we can subcategorize nouns capturing the restrictions they place on what other words they can appear with. For example, we saw that mass nouns can appear with *much* and count nouns with *many*. In this unit, we take a similar approach to the subcategorization of verbs based on the number of nouns they take as obligatory companions.

8.1 Arguments vs. adjuncts

Definition A **predicate** expresses a relation between individuals in the world (which can be abstract). The entities involved in the predicate are known as the **arguments**. Take for example the following sentence:

(1)   Calvin ate the stinky tuna.

The verb *ate* is the predicate. The arguments are *Calvin* and *the stinky tuna*. Predicates are typically verbs, but they can also involve other parts of speech. We will focus on verbal predicates here. Arguments can be nouns like *Calvin*, or determiners with nouns (and possibly modifiers) like *the stinky tuna*. We'll call all of these structures **Determiner Phrases** or DPs. Arguments can also be nouns and related structures marked with a preposition, which we'll call **Prepositional Phrases** or PPs. In the following sentence, *sent* is the predicate; the DP arguments are *Andrew* and *a package*; the prepositional phrase *to Dan* is the third argument.

(2)   Andrew sent a package to Dan.

We can also find cases where embedded clauses (sentences inside of sentences), which we'll call **Complementizer Phrases** or CPs, serve as arguments:

(3)   I thought [$_{CP}$ that Calvin ate the stinky tuna].

In (3), the CP *that Calvin ate the stinky tuna* (marked in [ ] brackets) is an argument of the verb *thought*. In the next unit, we'll see cases where verb phrases (VPs) and other structures can also serve as arguments, but for our purposes in this unit DPs, PPs and CPs will suffice. If these notions seem a bit obtuse right now, don't panic, we'll give them more precise definitions in later units. For the moment, just try to remember that DPs are essentially the group of words associated with nouns, PPs are the same but with a preposition at the front, and that CPs are clauses (essentially embedded sentences).

Comment In school you may have learned a definition of the notion "predicate" where sentences are divided into subjects and predicates and the predicate includes everything after the verb. In this book we use the definition used by logicians and linguists, where the predicate does not include the object.

Discussion Arguments only include the elements that are necessary for completing the meaning of the verb. Any additional DPs or PPs are called **adjuncts**. Figuring out what is an argument and what is an adjunct requires some practice and skill, but roughly speaking, arguments typically are the doer of the verb, any element that is having the verb done to it, and in the case of verbs of motion the end point of the event described by the verb. Any other DP or PP is an adjunct. This is pretty fuzzy for now. Here are some examples:

(4) (a) Calvin   ate   the tuna   with a fork

          argument   *predicate*   *argument*   *adjunct*

     (b) Art   built   the sun room   on Friday

          argument   *predicate*   *argument*   *adjunct*

     (c) Heidi   put   the avocado   in the fridge

          argument   *predicate*   *argument*   *argument(!)*

In general, being obligatory is a good guide to whether an element is an argument or an adjunct. For example, you can leave the PPs in (4a) and (4b) off without making the sentence unacceptable, but you can't leave off the PP in (4c), making it an argument:

(5) (a) Calvin ate the tuna.

     (b) Art built the sun room.

     (c) *Heidi put the avocado.

But the test of obligation can throw you off too. For example, the verb *eat* takes two arguments, but one can easily be left off:

(6) (a) Calvin ate the tuna.

     (b) Calvin ate.

But note that the meaning of the verb *eat* in (6a) is different from the verb *eat* in (6b). One means "consumed" and the other means "consumed something." The difference between the optionality of *the tuna* (in 6b) vs. *with a fork* (in 4a) is very subtle and hard for students to identify. Try the next exercise to see how you do, but don't be frustrated if you have trouble with this! The definitions here are sufficiently hazy that this isn't easy even for experienced syntacticians.

Exercise **Q1** 📖 Identify the predicates, the arguments and the adjuncts in the following sentences.

(a) I smiled.

(b) Susan kissed Calvin with too much lipstick.

(c) Pangur hit Art with the cat toy.

(d) I passed Dave the beef waffles last week.

8.2 Argument structure

Definition One traditional way to subcategorize verbs is to make reference to the number of arguments that they take (this is known as the verb's valency). A verb that takes one argument is said to be **intransitive**; those that take two are **transitive** and those that take three are **ditransitive**:

(7)

Transitivity	Valency	Example
Intransitive	1 argument	arrive
Transitive	2 arguments	love
Ditransitive	3 arguments	give, put

Exercise **Q2** ✏ Go back to Q1 and identify if the following verbs are intransitive, transitive or ditransitive based on the sentences given there. Note that adjuncts do not count in determining transitivity!

(a) *smile* ....

(b) *kiss* ....

(c) *hit* ....

(d) *pass* ....

Comment While the notions of transitivity are useful descriptive abbreviations, in most cases syntacticians need a more fine-grained notation. For example, we want to be able to distinguish between verbs like *ask*, which allow either a DP (determiner phrase) or a CP (a clause) as one of its arguments (8), from a verb like *hit*, which requires that the argument that follows be a DP and never a CP (9).

(8) (a) I asked [$_{DP}$ the question].

      (b) I asked [$_{CP}$ if you knew the answer].

(9) (a) I hit [$_{DP}$ the ball].

      (b) *I hit [$_{CP}$ that you knew the answer].

Notation We will distinguish external arguments (typically the subject, or the noun that comes before the verb) from those that come after the verb (called the direct and indirect objects). Restrictions on external arguments/subjects will be marked in a special EXTERNAL feature. Those on the arguments that come after the verb will be marked on the INTERNAL feature. Both of these features are values of the SUBCAT feature.

Take, for example, the fact that the verb *laugh* requires that its subject be capable of laughing. Leaving aside poetic usages, this is only possible when the subject is +*animate*. Furthermore, the subject argument of *laugh* must be a DP. A partial feature structure looks like (10):

(10) *laugh*

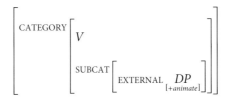

This says that *laugh* is a verb, with the subcategorical properties such that its external argument (i.e. its subject) must be an animate DP.

Other verbs have other external properties. For example, the verb *bother* can take either a DP (11a) or a CP (sentential) subject (11b), but does not allow a PP (prepositional phrase) subject (11c).

(11) (a) [$_{DP}$ Undercooked beef waffles] bother John.

      (b) [$_{CP}$ That Susan baked her beef waffles] bothers John.

      (c) [$_{PP}$ With butter and jam] bothers John.

When there is a choice between two categories, we use the notation of a pair of curly brackets around the choices. So the value of the EXTERNAL feature is {DP/CP} for *bother*. This means that the external argument can be either a DP or a CP.

INTERNAL arguments (roughly objects and indirect objects) can be treated the same way. Take the verb *bother* again. The object of this verb must be animate and must be a DP:

(12) (a)   #/*Undercooked beef waffles bother the stone.

(b)   *Undercooked beef waffles bother [$_{CP}$ that the man left.]

(13) *bother*

$$
\begin{bmatrix}
\text{CATEGORY} & \begin{bmatrix} V \\ \\ \text{SUBCAT} & \begin{bmatrix} \text{EXTERNAL } \{DP \, / \, CP\} \\ \\ \text{INTERNAL } \underset{[+animate]}{DP} \end{bmatrix} \end{bmatrix}
\end{bmatrix}
$$

Next consider (14): here are two more examples, this time with ditransitive verbs. Ditransitives take two internal arguments. We will list the arguments in the order they have to appear in the sentence, placing them between < > brackets which indicate an ordering. A verb like *put* requires that the first argument be an DP and the second a PP:

(14) (a)   I put [$_{DP}$ the book][on the table]

(b)   *I put [$_{DP}$ the book][$_{DP}$ the table]

(15) *put*

$$
\begin{bmatrix}
\text{CATEGORY} & \begin{bmatrix} V \\ \\ \text{SUBCAT} & \begin{bmatrix} \text{EXTERNAL } \underset{[+animate]}{DP} \\ \\ \text{INTERNAL } < DP, PP > \end{bmatrix} \end{bmatrix}
\end{bmatrix}
$$

Contrast this with a verb like *give*, which allows more than one possible order. One order allows a DP and a PP; the other allows two DPs:

(16) (a)   I gave the book to Chris.

(b)   I gave Chris the book.

(17) *give*

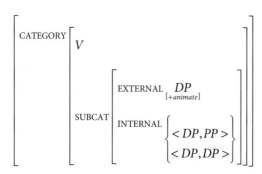

In (17) you'll notice that the INTERNAL feature has a choice (indicated by the {} brackets) of two orderings, each indicated by the < > brackets. The top line in the choice (<DP, PP>) corresponds to (16a), the second line (<DP, DP>) corresponds to (16b).

Exercise For each of the verbs that follow, I've given you a paradigm of sentence that should allow you to figure out the values of the INTERNAL and EXTERNAL features. You may need to reference the categories DP, PP and CP, and in some circumstances the feature ±*animate*. Model your answers on the examples in (10, 11, 13, 15, 17). PPs are tricky – don't include them in the feature structures unless they are obligatory; optional PPs are adjuncts. Assume the judgments given even if you don't agree with them. Assume literal meanings are all we're looking for here. Poetic meanings may be possible but we aren't going to attempt to account for them. Be sure to read the points after each set of sentences for additional instructions and hints.

Q3 📖 *arrive*

(a) I arrived.

(d) *[_pp_To the store] arrived.

(e) *[_CP_ That Calvin sang] arrived.

(f) *I arrived [_DP_ the package].

(g) *I arrived [_CP_ that Calvin sang].

   • Ignore the PPs in sentences like *I arrived at the station*, because they are adjuncts. You do **not** need to refer to ±*animate*.

Q4 📖 *rub*

(a) *I rub.

(b) I rubbed [_DP_ the genie's lamp].

(c) *I rubbed [_pp_ to the genie].

(d) *I rubbed [_CP_ that Calvin sang].

Q5 📖 *kiss*

(a) *I kissed.

(b) I kissed [_DP_ the policeman].

(c) *I kissed [_pp_ to the policeman].

(d) *I kissed [_CP_ that Calvin sang].

(e) *The store kissed the policeman.

(f) I kissed the stone.

(g) I kissed water.

(h) *[$_{PP}$ To me] kissed the policeman.

(i) *[$_{CP}$ That Calvin sang] kissed the policeman.

- Ignore the sentence *We kissed*. You will have to make reference to ±animate for the external argument. Do you have to refer to it for the internal argument?

Q6 📖 *kill (transitive usage)*

(a) *I kill.

(b) I killed [$_{DP}$ the policeman].

(c) *I killed [$_{PP}$ to the policeman].

(d) *I killed [$_{CP}$ that Calvin sang].

(e) The stone killed the policeman.

(f) *I killed the stone.

(g) *I killed water.

(h) *[$_{PP}$ To me] killed the policeman.

(i) *[$_{CP}$ That Calvin sang] killed the policeman.

- For the purposes of this question ignore the sentence *I killed*. You will have to make reference to ±animate for the external argument. Do you have to refer to the ±animate for the internal argument?

Q7 📖 *ask (transitive usage only)*

(a) I asked [$_{DP}$ the question].

(b) I asked [$_{CP}$ if you knew the answer].

(c) *The stone asked the question.

(d) *[$_{PP}$ To me] asked the question.

(e) *[$_{CP}$ That Calvin sang] asked the question.

- For the purposes of this question, ignore the sentences like *I asked* or *I asked for the bacon* or *I asked John the question*. You will have to make reference to ±animate for the external argument. Do you have to refer to the ±animate feature for the internal argument?

Q8 📖 *think*

(a) I thought [$_{DP}$ the answer].

(b) I thought [$_{CP}$ that you knew the answer].

(c) *The stone thought the answer.

(d) *[$_{PP}$ From me] thought the answer.

(e) *[$_{CP}$ That Calvin sang] thought the answer.

- For the purposes of this question ignore the sentences like *I thought*. You will have to make reference to ±*animate* for the external argument. Do you have to refer to the ±*animate* for the internal argument?

Q9 📖 *send (ditransitive usage)*

(a) I sent [DP Daniel] [DP the story].

(b) *I sent [DP Daniel] [CP that the exam was cancelled].

(c) I sent [DP the story] [PP to Daniel].

(d) *I sent [PP to Daniel] [DP the story].

(e) *I sent [CP that the exam was cancelled] [DP Daniel].

(f) *I sent [DP the story] [DP Daniel].

- Assume the subject is a DP. Ignore intransitive and transitive usages of this verb. Don't worry about ±*animate*.

Q10 📖 *spray (ditransitive usage only)*

(a) *I sprayed [DP the paint] [DP the wall].

(b) *I sprayed [DP the paint] [CP that the exam was cancelled].

(c) I sprayed [DP the paint] [PP on the wall].

(d) *I sprayed [PP on the wall] [DP the paint].

(e) *I sprayed [CP that the exam was cancelled] [DP Daniel].

(f) *I sprayed [DP the wall] [DP the paint].

- Assume the subject is a DP. Ignore intransitive and transitive usages (such as *I sprayed*, or *I sprayed the wall*). Don't worry about ±*animate*.

Q11 📖 *tell (ditransitive usage only)*

(a) I told [DP Daniel] [DP the story].

(b) I told [DP Daniel] [CP that the exam was cancelled].

(c) I told [DP the story] [PP to Daniel].

(d) *I told [PP to Daniel] [DP the story].

(e) *I told [CP that the exam was cancelled] [DP Daniel].

(f) *I told [DP the story] [DP Daniel].

- Assume the subject is a DP. Ignore intransitive and transitive usages (such as *I told* or *I told the teacher*). Don't worry about ±*animate*.

Summary In this unit, we've subcategorized verbs by their argument structure and the requirements placed on their arguments.

We have only scratched the surface of subcategorization in this book. We have not extensively looked at the subcategorization of adjectives or of adverbs or of functional categories, although we will touch on these in future units. These categories have subcategories as well. The methodology for discovering these will now be obvious (I hope!)

Suggested further reading

- Aarts (1997), chapter 6
- Carnie (2006), chapters 2 and 8
- Grimshaw (1990)
- Huddleston and Pullum (2005), chapter 4
- Levin (1993)
- Larson (2010), unit 13
- http://en.wikipedia.org/wiki/Transitive_verb
- http://en.wikipedia.org/wiki/Intransitive
- http://en.wikipedia.org/wiki/Ditransitive_verb

Answers to questions

Q1 (a) *predicate:* smile; *argument:* I

   (b) *predicate:* kissed; *arguments:* Susan, Calvin; *adjunct:* with too much lipstick

   (c) *predicate:* hit; *arguments:* Pangur, Art; *adjunct:* with the cat toy.

   (d) *predicate:* passed; *arguments:* I, Dave, the beef waffles; *adjunct:* last week.

Q2 *smile:* intransitive; *kiss:* transitive; *hit:* transitive; *pass:* ditransitive.

Q3 *arrive*

$$\begin{bmatrix} \text{CATEGORY} \begin{bmatrix} V \\ \text{SUBCAT} \begin{bmatrix} \text{EXTERNAL } DP \end{bmatrix} \end{bmatrix} \end{bmatrix}$$

Q4 *rub*

$$\begin{bmatrix} \text{CATEGORY} \begin{bmatrix} V \\ \text{SUBCAT} \begin{bmatrix} \text{EXTERNAL } DP_{[+animate]} \\ \text{INTERNAL } DP \end{bmatrix} \end{bmatrix} \end{bmatrix}$$

78

Q5   *kiss*

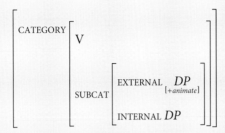

Q6   *kill*

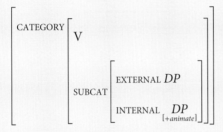

Q7   *ask (transitive usage only)*

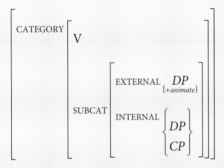

Q8   *think*

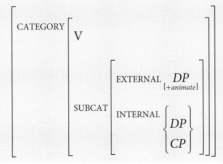

Q9 *send*

$$
\left[\text{CATEGORY} \left[V \atop \text{SUBCAT} \left[\text{EXTERNAL } DP \atop \text{INTERNAL} \left\{ {<DP,PP> \atop <DP,DP>} \right\} \right] \right] \right]
$$

(It would also be reasonable to assume that the EXTERNAL DP must be +animate.)

Q10 *spray*

$$
\left[\text{CATEGORY} \left[V \atop \text{SUBCAT} \left[\text{EXTERNAL } DP \atop \text{INTERNAL} <DP,PP> \right] \right] \right]
$$

Q11 *tell (ditransitive usage only)*

$$
\left[\text{CATEGORY} \left[V \atop \text{SUBCAT} \left[\text{EXTERNAL } DP \atop \text{INTERNAL} \left\{ {<DP,PP> \atop {<DP,DP> \atop <DP,CP>}} \right\} \right] \right] \right]
$$

UNIT 9 TANGENT: TENSE, ASPECT, VOICE AND MOOD

Objectives:

- Learn to distinguish the various tense, aspect, voice and mood properties of English.
- Learn to identify the modals and auxiliaries that represent these distinctions.

Comment In unit 6, we looked at pronouns, which had properties of both lexical and functional categories. Coming up in unit 10, we look at two other categories that seem to be both lexical and functional. These are verbal subcategories of modals and auxiliaries. But understanding what these categories do requires a quick side trip into their meanings. In this unit, we'll do a brief survey of the semantic notions underlying auxiliaries and modals and the features we'll use to represent these ideas.

9.1 Tense

Definition **Tense** refers to the time of an event relative to the time at which the sentence is either spoken or written. If I write or say *John left*, that entails that the act of John's leaving happened before I wrote or said the sentence. Let us use the symbol E to stand for the time at which the event occurred, and U for the time of the utterance or writing. We distinguish three tenses in English:

(1) (a) *past tense*: the event being described (E) happened before the time of speech or writing (U): $E < U$, e.g. *John danced.*

(b) *present tense*: E is at the same time as U: $E = U$, e.g. *He likes Ice cream.*

(c) *future tense*: E is going to happen after U: $U < E$, e.g. *He will eat dinner.*

In English, the past tense is typically marked with an *-ed* suffix (e.g. the past tense of *dance* is *danced*) or the verb comes with a special past tense form (e.g. the past tense of *leave* is *left*). The present tense is either unmarked (for first or second person or plural subjects), e.g. *I hate beef waffles* or marked with an *-s* suffix (in the third person) e.g. *He hates beef waffles.* In formal speech, the future is marked with the modal auxiliary *will* (*He will eat his* *beef waffles*). In less formal speech, the auxiliary *gonna* (or *going to*) is used (*I'm gonna eat my beef waffles*).

Exercise **Q1** 📖 Identify whether the following sentences are in the past, present or future tense by circling the correct answer.

(a)	The parakeet flew home.	Past	Present	Future
(b)	Calvin loves snow cones.	Past	Present	Future
(c)	Otto drank the tuna juice.	Past	Present	Future
(d)	Reggie will wake everyone up.	Past	Present	Future
(e)	Andrew brushed the cat.	Past	Present	Future
(f)	I drink too much.	Past	Present	Future

Notation   We notate tense with a feature TENSE, which takes *past*, *present* and *future* as values. TENSE itself is a value of the feature SEM (for semantics). So the feature we use to represent past tense is [SEM [TENSE *past*]], the features we use for present and future are [SEM [TENSE *present*]] and [SEM [TENSE *future*]] respectively.

9.2 Perfect aspect

Definition   While tense is defined by looking at the relationship between the time of the event and the time of the utterance or writing, **aspect** is a very different notion. Aspect is defined by making reference to some other point, typically other than the speech time, then looking at when the event happens relative to that reference point. Take, for example, sentence (2):

(2)   John had eaten his sandwich before I could get him his pickle.

The event of John eating his sandwich happened before a time distinct from when I wrote the sentence, that is, it happened before I got him his pickle. The time of pickle-getting is a reference point, and John's eating happened before that.

The particular aspect found in (2) is called the **perfect**. The perfect happens when the time of the event (which we might represent abstractly as E) occurs before some reference point (R). So the perfect is E < R.

Definition   The perfect is always indicated in English by using the auxiliary or helping verb *have* (or one of its variant forms: *has* or *had*) combined with a special form of the main verb known as the **participle**. This is sometimes inaccurately called the "past participle"; we will avoid this term because there is nothing particularly "past" about participles as we will see – they can occur in the future!

The participle in English can be formed four ways:

(3) (i)   by attaching an *-en* or *-n* suffix: *eat* → *eaten, fall* → *fallen*

  (ii) by attaching an *-ed* suffix: *dance* → *danced, love* → *loved*

  (iii) by using a special participial form: *drink* → *drunk, sing* → *sung, fly* → *flown*

  (iv) by making no change at all: *hit* → *hit*

The method found in (ii) is especially confusing since the *-ed* suffix is often used to form the past tense. You can tell the difference between a participle and a past tense by the fact that the participle always appears with an auxiliary verb like *be, have* or their variants.

(4) (a)   He danced.   *past tense*

  (b)   He has danced.   *participle form of dance, found in the perfect aspect. (Cf.* He has fallen.)

Learning to identify the perfect requires looking for two things. First you have to look to see if there is a *have/had/has* auxiliary. Second you have to see if there is a participle. Abstractly, then, we can identify the formula HAVE + PARTICIPLE as the defining characteristic of the perfect.

Exercise **Q2** ✏ The following paragraph contains three sentences in the perfect aspect. What are they? Underline or circle the verb and auxiliary marking the perfect. Remember the formula discussed immediately above.

I was driving into Tucson to buy some tortillas, when I noticed that my car was nearly out of gas. I was surprised because I had filled the tank yesterday. I had driven all over town. However, I hadn't gone that far.

Discussion The perfect aspect can be combined with each of the tenses. The aspect is marked by virtue of the fact that we have both a form of the verb *have* and a participle. The tense is indicated by the particular form of the verb *have*: in the past this verb shows up as *had*, in the present as *have* or *has*, and in the future as *will have*. In each of the following examples, we are using the participle of the verb *eat: eaten.*

(5)   *past*
          |

  (a)   I had eaten the beef waffles.   *past perfect (pluperfect)*
             ⌄ $E < R < U$
          perfect

          present
          |

  (b)   I have eaten the beef waffles.   *present perfect*
             ⌄ $E < (R = U)$
          perfect

future
|
(c)   I will <u>have eaten</u> the beef waffles.   *future perfect*
                    ⌄ $U < E < R$
        perfect

Definition   The opposite of perfect is the **imperfect**.[1] The imperfect is not indicated by affixes or auxiliaries; it is marked by the absence of perfect marking.

Exercise   **Q3** ✏ Identify the aspect and tense of each of the following sentences. Be especially careful about the present perfect, which sometimes feels a bit like a past tense (because the event time is before the utterance time). You can identify the present perfect by virtue of the fact that the verb *have* is either in its *have* form (with no *will* before it!) or in its *has* form.

(a)   Susan has danced already.

Tense:	Past	Present	Future
Aspect:	Perfect	Imperfect	

(b)   Calvin will have slept all day.

Tense:	Past	Present	Future
Aspect:	Perfect	Imperfect	

(c)   Heidi danced yesterday.

Tense:	Past	Present	Future
Aspect:	Perfect	Imperfect	

(d)   Art had danced already.

Tense:	Past	Present	Future
Aspect:	Perfect	Imperfect	

(e)   Calvin will sleep all day.

Tense:	Past	Present	Future
Aspect:	Perfect	Imperfect	

(f)   Art drinks whisky sours.

Tense:	Past	Present	Future
Aspect:	Perfect	Imperfect	

(g)   Dave will drink a whisky sour.

Tense:	Past	Present	Future
Aspect:	Perfect	Imperfect	

---

[1]   We will not distinguish between imperfect and imperfective in this book.

(h) Dan had drunk a whisky sour.

    Tense: Past   Present   Future

    Aspect: Perfect   Imperfect

(i) I have never eaten beef waffles.

    Tense: Past   Present   Future

    Aspect: Perfect   Imperfect

9.3 Progressive aspect

Definition The second aspect we will look at is the **progressive**. The progressive aspect indicates an on-going event relative to the reference time. For example, imagine I say (6):

(6) Jeff was dancing with Sylvia, while Amy sat angrily at their table.

This means that there is some reference time that I have in mind (probably the time Amy was sitting at the table) and there was a co-occurrence between the reference time and the time of the dancing.

In English, the progressive aspect is always indicated by combining what is traditionally called the **present participle** form of the verb with some version of the auxiliary verb *be*. Present participles in English are always marked with *-ing*. In this book we're going to refer to present participles as **gerunds**, While this isn't exactly correct (the term "gerund" is more typically used to describe nouns that are homophonous with present participles), it allows us to avoid the confusing "present"/"past" participle terminology. We want to avoid these terms since both kinds of participle can appear with any tense. In English the form of the present participle is always identical to that of the gerund, so there is no harm in conflating the terms.

(7)

form	*traditional name*	*name used in this book*
ends in *-ing*	present participle	gerund
ends in *-en* (etc.)	past participle	participle

To indicate the progressive, the gerund is always combined with the auxiliary verb *be*. The verb *be* in English has quite a complex paradigm. The chart below is provided for your reference:

(8)

	Past		*Present*		*Future*
	Singular	*Plural*	*Singular*	*Plural*	
1st	was	were	am	are	will be
2nd	were		are		
3rd	was		is		

Participle: been

Gerund: being

Like the perfect, the tense marking in progressives is typically indicated on the auxiliary. The progressive aspect is always presented in English by the pairing of the gerund with *be* (i.e. the progressive's formula is BE + GERUND).

(9)

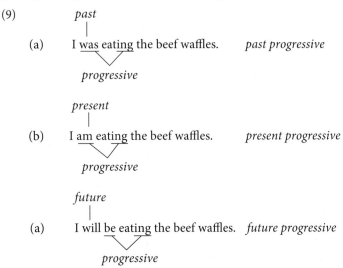

(a) I was eating the beef waffles. *past progressive*

(b) I am eating the beef waffles. *present progressive*

(a) I will be eating the beef waffles. *future progressive*

Exercise **Q4** ✏ Identify the tense and aspect of each of the following sentences. Impf/non-prog stands for any sentence that doesn't have either perfect or progressive aspect morphology (i.e. for an item that is either imperfect or non-progressive):

(a) Calvin is sleeping on top of the fridge.

Tense:	Past	Present	Future
Aspect:	Perfect	Progressive	Impf/non-prog

(b) Otto grabbed at the passing stick.

Tense:	Past	Present	Future
Aspect:	Perfect	Progressive	Impf/non-prog

(c) Heidi will be grading her papers.

Tense:	Past	Present	Future
Aspect:	Perfect	Progressive	Impf/non-prog

(d) Art has pulled down the outer wall.

Tense:	Past	Present	Future
Aspect:	Perfect	Progressive	Impf/non-prog

(e)   Andrew will eat the beef waffles.

Tense:	Past	Present	Future
Aspect:	Perfect	Progressive	Impf/non-prog

(f)   Jean was driving to her daughter's house.

Tense:	Past	Present	Future
Aspect:	Perfect	Progressive	Impf/non-prog

(g)   Jean had driven to her daughter's house.

Tense:	Past	Present	Future
Aspect:	Perfect	Progressive	Impf/non-prog

9.4 Voice

Definition   **Voice** refers to a phenomenon that changes the number of participants that are described in an event. Consider a typical verb like *eat*. In an **active** sentence like *Calvin ate the beef waffles*, we can identify an eater (*Calvin*) – the subject of the sentence – and the eatee (the thing eaten: *beef waffles*). In unit 8, you learned that *Calvin* is a DP that satisfies the EXTERNAL feature of the verb, and *the beef waffles* is a DP that satisfies the INTERNAL feature. The eater is in the subject position (before the verb) and the eatee is in the object position (after the verb). In a **passive**, such as *The beef waffles were eaten,* the eatee appears in subject position. The eater is either mentioned after a preposition (like *by Calvin*) or omitted entirely.

In English, the passive voice is marked with a *be* auxiliary and the participial form of the verb: *The beef waffles <u>were</u> eat<u>en</u>*. The formula for a passive is BE + PARTICIPLE (contrast this with the perfect, where the participle is combined with the verb *have*). Active sentences bear no special marking.

Exercise   **Q5** ✎ Identify the active and passive sentences below:

(a)	Calvin caught the mouse.	Active	Passive
(b)	The retaining wall was torn down.	Active	Passive
(c)	Otto drank the tuna juice.	Active	Passive
(d)	Dave played the game.	Active	Passive
(e)	Art tore down the retaining wall.	Active	Passive
(f)	The game will be played.	Active	Passive

9.5 Combined tense, aspect and voice

Discussion Let's briefly summarize the patterns we've seen so far. We've distinguished three tenses (past, present, future), two aspects (perfect and progressive) and the passive voice. (We also saw imperfects, non-progressives and actives that show no special marking.) The marking of aspect and voice requires both an auxiliary and a special form of the following verb:

(10)	Auxiliary verb	Following verb form
Perfect aspect	have	participle (-en)
Progressive	be	gerund (-ing)
Passive voice	be	participle (-en)

It's possible to combine the three rows in (10) to form complex verb forms:

(11) The soup had been being eaten.   *past perfect progressive passive*

Let's break that down into the relevant bits. Tense is indicated on the first auxiliary (*has* vs. *had*). The fact that the sentence is in the perfect aspect is indicated by a combination of the verb *have* (*had*) and the fact that the following verb is in its participle form (ends in *-en*). The fact that the sentence also bears the progressive is indicated by the next *be* auxiliary (*been*) and the fact that the following verb form is a gerund (*being*). Finally, the fact that the sentence is a passive is indicated by the last *be* auxiliary and the fact that the verb appears in a participle form.

(12)

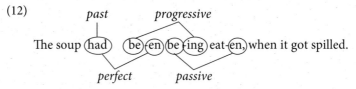

The pattern here is complex, but surprisingly regular. There is an interleaving of tense, aspect markers and voice markers.

Exercise Consider the future perfect progressive passive:

(13)

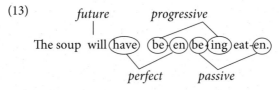

Q6 📖 Look only at the auxiliary forms (*will, have, be, be*). What order do tense, perfect, progressive and passive appear in?

Q7 📖 Keeping all tense, aspect and passive markers in the sentence, is any other order of these elements possible?

Comment: One interesting part of the English auxiliary system is that it requires a combination of items to determine what aspect/voice is being represented. For example, the use of the participle does not by itself tell us if a particular aspect/voice is being used. The participle is used both in the perfect and in the passive. To distinguish between the two, you have to see whether it is being used with the auxiliary *be* or the auxiliary *have*. Similarly, the auxiliary *be* by itself tells us nothing: when it is used with a gerund it is part of the marking of a progressive; when it is used with a participle it marks the passive.

Exercise **Q8** ✎ For each of the following sentences identify its tense, if it is perfect or imperfect, if it is progressive or non-progressive and whether it is active or passive voice:

(a) Pangur was being massaged.

tense:	present	past	future
aspect 1:	perfect	imperfect	
aspect 2:	progressive	non-progressive	
voice:	active	passive	

(b) Surrey will have been adopted.

tense:	present	past	future
aspect 1:	perfect	imperfect	
aspect 2:	progressive	non-progressive	
voice:	active	passive	

(c) Calvin is eating the tuna.

tense:	present	past	future
aspect 1:	perfect	imperfect	
aspect 2:	progressive	non-progressive	
voice:	active	passive	

(d) The tuna has been eaten.

tense:	present	past	future
aspect 1:	perfect	imperfect	
aspect 2:	progressive	non-progressive	
voice:	active	passive	

(e) Calvin has been eating the tuna.

tense:	present	past	future
aspect 1:	perfect	imperfect	
aspect 2:	progressive	non-progressive	
voice:	active	passive	

(f) The wall had been torn down.

tense:	present	past	future
aspect 1:	perfect	imperfect	
aspect 2:	progressive	non-progressive	
voice:	active	passive	

Notation The features we use to represent these are:

Feature	Possible values (so far!)
SEM	TENSE
	ASPECT
	VOICE
TENSE	*past*
	present
	future
ASPECT	*perfect*
	progressive
VOICE	*±passive*

The active, imperfect and non-progressive variants are not indicated with features (the assumption being that these are marked by the absence of a feature – as evidenced by the fact that these variants aren't indicated in the morphology). SEM stands for "semantics."

9.6 Mood

Definition We have only one more inflectional category to deal with. This is the category of **mood**. Mood refers to the speaker's perspective on the event. In particular, whether the event described is a possibility, a probability, a necessity or an obligation. Typically speaking, mood is expressed through modal auxiliary verbs although it can also be expressed through other means including adjectives (*it is possible that. . .*), other auxiliaries or verbs (*Calvin has to eat his tuna*) or adverbs (*Possibly John will leave*). The modals of English that express mood are:

(14) *Modals of English:* can, could, may, might, would, shall, should, must

90

Comment Traditional grammarians use the term "mood" two ways. One is the way we've just defined it. The other is to express particular functions of the sentence such as questions (interrogative mood), statements (declarative mood), orders or commands (imperative mood), expressions of conditions (conditional mood) or expressions of uncertainty (subjunctive mood). These so-called moods aren't expressed using modals.

Notation We use one more SEM feature to indicate mood, unsurprisingly called MOOD. This can have the values of *possibility, probability, necessity* or *obligation.* Sometimes these can be combined.

Exercise **Q9** 📖 Construct sentences combining various modals with the various aspects and voices. Where does the modal verb always appear?

Summary This unit has been a slight detour into the semantics of Tense, Aspect, Mood and Voice, which are the categories typically represented by various combinations of Auxiliaries and Modals. In the next unit, we turn to the syntax of these elements and look at the restrictions on their combination and ordering. We'll see that modals and the future tense auxiliary *will* constitute one closed class category and the auxiliary verbs form another.

Suggested further reading

- Aarts (1997), chapter 3
- Carnie (2006), chapter 9
- Huddleston and Pullum (2005), chapter 3
- Lobeck (2000), chapter 5
- Sag, Wasow and Bender (2003), chapter 8
- http://en.wikipedia.org/wiki/Grammatical_aspect
- http://en.wikipedia.org/wiki/Perfect_aspect
- http://en.wikipedia.org/wiki/Progressive_aspect
- http://en.wikipedia.org/wiki/Grammatical_tense
- http://en.wikipedia.org/wiki/Grammatical_mood
- http://en.wikipedia.org/wiki/Grammatical_voice
- http://en.wikipedia.org/wiki/Auxiliary_verb
- http://en.wikipedia.org/wiki/Modal_auxiliary_verb

Answers to questions

Q1 (a) past, (b) present, (c) past, (d) future, (e) past, (f) present

Q2 I had filled the tank; I had driven all over town; I hadn't gone that far

Q3 (a) present perfect; (b) future perfect; (c) past imperfect; (d) past perfect; (e) future imperfect; (f) present imperfect; (g) future imperfect; (h) past perfect; (i) present perfect

Q4 (a) present progressive; (b) past impf/non-prog; (c) future progressive; (d) present perfect; (e) future impf/non-prog; (f) past progressive; (g) past perfect

Q5 (a) active; (b) passive; (c) active; (d) active; (e) active; (f) passive

Q6 tense (*will*) before perfect (*have*) before progressive (*be*) before passive (*be*) (The same order can be seen in the suffixes on the various verbs.)

Q7 No other order is possible.

Q8 (a) past imperfect progressive passive; (b) future perfect non-progressive passive; (c) present imperfect progressive active; (d) present perfect non-progressive passive; (e) present perfect progressive active; (f) past perfect non progressive passive

Q9 Some examples (many more are possible):

    (a)   Calvin could be eating the beef waffles. (modal + progressive)

    (b)   The beef waffles might have been eaten. (modal + perfect + passive)

    (c)   The beef waffles might have been being eaten.

        (modal + perfect + progressive + passive)

        etc.

The modal always precedes all the other auxiliaries and verbs.

UNIT 10 SUBCATEGORIES OF AUXILIARIES

Objectives:

- Investigate the similarities and differences between main verbs, auxiliaries and modals.
- Discover the differences between auxiliary verbs *be* and *have* and main verbs *be* and *have*.

Comment In the last unit, we investigated the basic semantic relations represented in the English auxiliary system: tense, aspect, voice and mood. In this unit, we're going to look in more detail at the behavior of modals and auxiliaries. We'll see that modal verbs and auxiliaries have certain properties in common, and that auxiliary verbs like *be* and *have* also have properties in common with main verbs. We'll also distinguish between two uses of *be/have*, which can function both as main verbs and as auxiliaries.

10.1 Main verb vs. auxiliary verb uses of *be, have* and *do*

Exercise Consider the following sentences of English:

(1) (a) Calvin has a peanut.

    (b) Susan has a cold.

    (c) Bill had an accident.

(2) (a) Calvin has eaten a peanut.

    (b) Frank has drunk too much.

    (c) Bill has been dancing.

Q1 ▭ In terms of the meaning of the word *have/has/had*, what do the sentences in (1) have in common? In (1) is the verb have followed by another verb? Compare the sentences in (1) to the sentences in (2). Does the verb *have* have the same meaning in (2) as it does in the sentences in (1)?

Exercise Next consider the following sentences:

(3) (a) John is a doctor.

    (b) Bill was the one.

(4) (a) John was eating the popsicle.

    (b) Calvin was sat on by his brother.

Q2 📖 Sentence (4a) is the use of *be* (*was/is*) as part of a progressive sentence. Sentence (4b) is the use of *be* as part of a passive. Do either of the sentences in (3) describe a passive or progressive action? In terms of syntactic categories, what is the difference between the sentences in (3) and (4) with respect to the elements that follow *be*?

Exercise Next consider the following sentences, using the verb *do* (*did*). We're not really going to look carefully at this verb until units later in the book, but since it patterns with *be* and *have* with respect to differences we're discussing here, we're including it here for completeness.

(5) (a) John did his homework.

(b) Calvin did a back flip.

(6) (a) John did not eat.

(b) Calvin did not do a back flip.

Q3 📖 The distinction between (5) and (6) is a little more delicate and harder to describe, so don't panic if you have trouble explaining it; you can look at the answer to this question for more details. Describe at least the difference in category of the elements that follow *do* in each group of sentences. Can you also see a difference in meaning? Note that in sentence (6b) there are two *do* verbs. What does this tell us about *do* in English?

Discussion English appears to have multiple verbs *be*, at least two verbs *have* and two verbs *do*. We're going to hypothesize that the major difference between the first group of sentences in each of Q1, Q2 and Q3 and the second is that the verbs in (1), (3) and (5) are main verbs, and the verbs in (2), (4) and (6) are auxiliary verbs. To distinguish between each usage, from this point forward we'll annotate *be*, *have* and *do* with subscript notations, such as be_{prog} (for progressive), be_{perf} (for perfect), etc.

(7)

Form	Name	Meaning	Subcategory
Calvin is the cutest cat.	be_{cop}	Copula (identity/ property)	Main verb
Calvin is eating.	be_{prog}	Progressive	Auxiliary
Calvin was sat on.	be_{pass}	Passive	Auxiliary
Calvin has a luxurious coat.	$have_{poss}$	Possession	Main verb
Calvin has eaten.	$have_{perf}$	Perfect	Auxiliary
Calvin did his homework.	do_{main}	Accomplishment/ performance	Main verb
Calvin did not eat.	do_{aux}	Present to support tense before negation	Auxiliary

Notation   In terms of features, we will notate the auxiliary usages of these verbs with the feature [SUBCAT +*aux*].

Comment   Next we have to find evidence to support our hypothesis. The next set of questions is meant to help you find supporting evidence for the distinction between main verb usages and auxiliary uses.

Exercise   Recall the rule of Subject/Auxiliary Inversion that we discussed in unit 1. This rule is used to indicate the presence of a yes/no question. Now consider the following data:

(8) (a)   Has Pangur eaten his tuna?

(b)   Is Pangur eating his tuna?

(c)   Did Pangur eat his dinner?

(d)   *Ate Pangur his dinner?

Contrast (8a) with (8d).

Q4 ✏ Can main verbs in English undergo Subject/Aux Inversion?   Y   N

Q5 ✏ Can auxiliary verbs undergo Subject/Aux Inversion?   Y   N

Q6 📖 What generalization can we make about the behavior of main and auxiliary verbs and Subject/Aux Inversion?

Exercise   With your answers to Q4–6 above in mind, consider now the following examples with what we've identified as "main verb" uses of *have* and *do*. This data represents the judgments of most North American speakers. Speakers of British English and many other dialects may disagree with the judgments given. For the purposes of this exercise restrict yourself to the facts of American English, as given in (9). (We leave aside *be* here, as it behaves differently.)

(9) (a)   *Has Calvin a bowl?

(b)   *Did Calvin his homework?

Q7 📖 How does this data support the idea that there are two verbs *do*, and two verbs *have*?

Challenge   The copular main-verb versions of *be* behave differently from *have* and *do*. Copular *be*$_{cop}$ can undergo Subject/Aux Inversion just like auxiliary *be*. So we can have grammatical forms like *Is Calvin the cutest cat?* in all dialects of English. Does this invalidate using Subject/Aux Inversion as a test for the main verb/auxiliary verb distinction we proposed in Q6? Can you think of a way that we might explain the unusual behavior of *be*$_{cop}$ and retain the test? Most speakers of British English will also have found sentence (9a) grammatical. How can we account for this fact if auxiliary *have* and main verb *have* are distinct?

Exercise   Now contrast the behavior of auxiliary verbs with main verbs with respect to the negative word *not*.

(10) (a)   John is not leaving.

    (b)   Calvin has not eaten his dinner.

    (c)   Pangur did not play with his mouse.

    (d)   *Calvin ate not his dinner.

    (e)   *Pangur plays not with his mouse.[1]

Q8 ✐ Can main verbs come before *not*?[2]   Y   N

Q9 ✐ Can auxiliary verbs come before *not*?   Y   N

Q10 📖 Making reference to the feature [SUBCAT +*aux*], make a generalization about the sentences in (10).

Exercise   With your answers to Q8–10 above in mind, consider now the following examples with what we've identified as "main verb" uses of *have*$_{poss}$ and *do*$_{main}$.

(11) (a)   *Calvin has not any catnip.

    (b)   *John did not his homework.

Q11 📖 How does the data in (11) support the hypothesis that there are different auxiliary and main verb uses of *have* and *do*.

Challenge   Again, the copular main verb *be*$_{cop}$ behaves differently from *have* and *do*. Copular *be*$_{cop}$ can precede negation just like auxiliary *be*. So we can have grammatical forms like *Calvin is not the cutest cat* in all dialects of English. Does this invalidate using negation as a test for the main verb/auxiliary verb distinction we proposed in Q10? Can you think of a way that we might explain the unusual behavior of *be*$_{cop}$ and retain the test?

Comment   Parallel to the data in (8)–(11) discussed above, it's also possible to construct an argument distinguishing main verb and auxiliary uses of the verb *have* using temporal adverbs like *often*. So we find that auxiliary uses of *have* can precede *often* (*Calvin has often eaten tuna*), but main verb uses cannot (*Calvin has often his bowl*). The data here are a little more subtle, since there are situations where adverbs like *often* can follow main verbs (*Calvin sleeps often*). For this reason we won't go through this argument in detail.

---

[1]   Assume here that there is no continuation of this sentence with something like . . . *but with his ball*. This sentence is ungrammatical without such a completion.

[2]   We leave aside here the fad that was popular in the late 1990s where people would sarcastically end sentences in *NOT!* (*I love Michael Jackson's music, NOT!*). This slang usage had a different meaning than the *not* we're looking at here. Also note that in that sarcastic usage, the *NOT!* was always preceded by a distinct pause.

For a textbook rendition, see Carnie (2006), chapter 8. For a very technical discussion with a comparison of the English data to French, see Pollock (1989).

10.2 Modals vs. auxiliaries

Comment Modal verbs have a slightly different distribution than other auxiliaries like *have* or *be*. The discussion and exercises in this section are intended to help you figure out what that distribution is.

Exercise **Q12** 📖 Are auxiliaries like *be* and *have* verbs? Go back to unit 4 and look at the distributional definition of verbs. In what ways are they like verbs? In what ways are they not like verbs?

Exercise **Q13** 📖 Are modals like *can* and *should* verbs? Go back to unit 4 and look at the distributional definition of verbs. In what ways are they like verbs? In what ways are they not like verbs?

Exercise **Q14** ✏ Can you construct a sentence with more than one modal?   Y   N

Q15 📖 Can you construct a sentence with more than one auxiliary? If so provide an example.

Exercise Consider the following data. We use *should* to represent the behavior of all modals and *be* (and its variants) to represent the behavior of all other auxiliaries.

(12) (a)   I am not eating the plums.

    (b)   I should not eat plums.

    (e)   I have not been eating plums.

    (f)   *I have not should eat plums.

Q16 ✏ Can modal verbs appear before *not*?   Y   N

Q17 ✏ Can auxiliary verbs appear before *not*?   Y   N

Q18 ✏ Can modal verbs appear after *not*?   Y   N

Q19 ✏ Can auxiliary verbs appear after *not*?   Y   N

Discussion Modals must be in the first position in the string of verbs in an English sentence, and must precede negation. Other auxiliaries can appear in later positions. We have now seen two ways in which modals pattern differently from auxiliaries like *be* and *have*: (i) we're only allowed one modal, but we can have multiple *be/have* auxiliaries; (ii) modals must appear before negation and can never follow it.

We have to conclude, then, that modals are a different type of animal than auxiliaries. What exactly that difference is, we'll discuss in section 10.3. But first let's look at one way that modals are like auxiliaries.

Exercise **Q20** 📖 Turning back to Subject/Auxiliary Inversion, do modals like *should* behave like auxiliaries or like main verbs?

(13) (a)   Pangur has eaten the beef waffles.

(b)   Has Pangur eaten the beef waffles?

(c)   Pangur may eat the beef waffles.

(d)   May Pangur eat the beef waffles?

(e)   Pangur ate the beef waffles.

(f)   *Ate Pangur the beef waffles?

How does the data in (13) argue for the idea that modals and auxiliaries overlap in part of speech/subcategory?

Exercise **Q21** 📖 Turning back to the data about the position of *not* given above in (12), can you make a generalization about which items can appear before *not*, and which items may never appear before *not*?

Discussion While there is categorical evidence to suggest that auxiliaries and modals are different categories (Q12–19), there is also evidence from Subject/Auxiliary Inversion and the position of negation to suggest that they overlap in some ways. How can we account for this contradictory evidence? We are going to capture this by proposing that the similarities among modals and auxiliaries are captured by the feature [SUBCAT +*aux*]. Only words with this feature can undergo Subject/Aux Inversion and appear before negation. Main verbs lack this feature so they don't invert. How then do we explain the differences? We're going to claim that despite the fact they share the [SUBCAT +*aux*] feature, they actually belong to completely different categories. Abstractly, we have the pattern expressed in the diagram in (14), where category T is the main category of modals:

(14) CATEGORY T   CATEGORY V

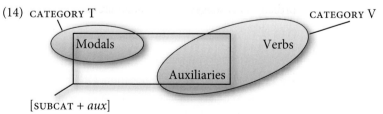

[SUBCAT + *aux*]

The similarities among modals and auxiliaries (and the differences between these and main verbs) are captured by the feature [SUBCAT +*aux*]. The similarities between auxiliaries and main verbs (and the differences between them and modals) are captured by [CATEGORY V]. Finally, the differences between modals and both auxiliaries and main verbs are captured by [CATEGORY T].

10.3 Modals and tense

Comment The T category stands for tense. No doubt you are having a "huh?-What-are-you-talking-about?" moment now. After all, with the exception of the future tense particle *will*, tense actually almost always seems to show up on auxiliaries and verbs (He *is* leaving, He *danced*, etc.) and not on modals. So at first glance the claim that modals are of category T, and not, say, of some category M for modals, seems a bit strange. But there is significant evidence to suggest that English modals are of category T. In this section you'll investigate the interaction of modals and tense and look at the position of tense markers relative to the rest of the system.

Exercise **Q22** ✏ Consider the future tense marker *will*:

(15) (a) Calvin will not eat the beef waffles.

    (b) *Calvin not will eat the beef waffles.

In the data above, does *will* pattern with modals or with *be* and *have* with respect to its positioning relative to the word *not*? (Refer back to the data in (12) if necessary.)   Modals   Auxiliaries

Exercise **Q23** 📖 Can you construct a sentence in English that uses both a modal and the future tense marker *will*? What might this tell us about the category of the future tense marker?

Exercise **Q24** ✏ If there is a modal present do any of the other auxiliaries or verbs in a sentence bear tense affixes (e.g. *-s* or past tense *-ed*)? (Be careful not to confuse tense affixes with the affixes that mark gerunds or participles.)   Y   N

Discussion The exercises above show us two things: (i) the tense particle *will* patterns just like a modal; and (ii) when a modal is present, no tense morphology is present. This suggests that modals are indeed, against first appearances, of the category Tense.

Notation Partial feature structures for *have*$_{perf}$, *be*$_{pass}$, *will* and *should* are given below:

(16) (a)   *be*$_{pass}$

$$\left[\begin{array}{l} \text{CATEGORY} \left[\begin{array}{l} \text{V} \\ \text{SUBCAT} + aux \end{array} \right] \\ \text{SEM} \quad \left[\text{VOICE } passive \right] \end{array} \right]$$

(b) *have*_{perf}

$$
\begin{bmatrix}
\text{CATEGORY} & \begin{bmatrix} \text{V} \\ \text{SUBCAT} + aux \end{bmatrix} \\
\text{SEM} & \begin{bmatrix} \text{ASPECT } perfective \end{bmatrix}
\end{bmatrix}
$$

(c) *will*

$$
\begin{bmatrix}
\text{CATEGORY} & \begin{bmatrix} \text{T} \\ \text{SUBCAT} + aux \end{bmatrix} \\
\text{SEM} & \begin{bmatrix} \text{TENSE } future \end{bmatrix}
\end{bmatrix}
$$

(d) *should*

$$
\begin{bmatrix}
\text{CATEGORY} & \begin{bmatrix} \text{T} \\ \text{SUBCAT} + aux \end{bmatrix} \\
\text{SEM} & \begin{bmatrix} \text{MOOD } obligation \end{bmatrix}
\end{bmatrix}
$$

Notice that *will* and *should* are of syntactic category T, but express different semantic notions (*will* expresses a future tense semantics but *should* expresses an obligation mood semantics). *Be*_{pass} and *have*_{perf} differ from *will* and *should* in that they are of category V. All the forms have [SUBCAT +Aux].

Exercise **Q25** 📖 Assume the modal *can* represents the semantic notion of *ability*. Draw the feature structure for *can*; use (16) as a model.

Q26 📖 Draw the feature structure for *be*_{prog}; use (16) as a model.

Comment There is some important information missing from the feature structures given in (16) and in your answers to Q25 and Q26. These are the facts we discovered in the last unit, where we saw that, for example, *be*_{prog} requires that the form of the following verb be a gerund and other such requirements. We will deal with these questions in detail in unit 13, but we will hint at an explanation below in section 10.4 of where we're going.

10.4 Past and present tense marking in English

Discussion Above, we've claimed that *will* and all modals are instances of the category T. One argument for this is that the future tense marker *will* and modals behave alike; another is that if a modal is present then no other tense marking can be found on English verbs. Of course, this is missing the point that present and past tense marking in English appears on *verbs*, not in a particle like *will*! In this section we'll explore this problem.

Exercise Consider where tense marking appears when there is a negation in a sentence:

(17) (a) Calvin ate the beef waffles.

       (b) Calvin did not eat the beef waffles.

       (c) Calvin likes beef waffles.

       (d) Calvin did not like the beef waffles.

Q27 📖 When there is no negation, present and past tense is marked on the verb. When negation is present where does it appear?

Q28 📖 Now think carefully about the relative position of tense and negation and compare it to the relative position of modals with respect to negation (if necessary refer to the data in (13) a few pages back).

Discussion Somewhat counterintuitively, tense behaves similarly to modals and *will* when it comes to its position relative to negation. Tense (on the auxiliary) precedes the negation. Thus it might be that tense is behaving exactly like *will* and modals in other respects.

Notation Let us propose that there is a category T present in every sentence, even when we don't have a modal or *will*. This will require you to take a leap of faith, but consider for the moment the possibility that there are present tense and past tense equivalents to *will*, but that they have no phonological content, that is, they are totally silent. Let's call these $\emptyset_{pres}$ and $\emptyset_{past}$, where $\emptyset$ is meant to invoke the idea of a silent word. It's OK to be suspicious of the idea of silent words, but note that English, like many languages, makes significant use of the absence of morphology to express content. So, for example, the plural of the nouns *deer* and *sheep* are *deer* and *sheep*. Similarly, the first- and second-person endings on verbs in English are typically silent too: *I walk_, you walk_* (cf. *she walks*), so perhaps silent words aren't quite such a stretch after all.

The consequence of this is that the tense in a sentence like *Calvin ate the beef waffles* isn't in *ate*, but in the silent $\emptyset_{past}$ that precedes it. In essence we're claiming that the structure of such a sentence parallels that of its negative counterpart, or the counterpart with a modal, the minor difference being that the T word is silent in (18a) but pronounced in (18b and c).

(18) (a) Calvin $\emptyset_{past}$ ate   the beef waffles

     (b) Calvin   did   not   eat   the beef waffles

     (c) Calvin   can   eat   the beef waffles

        Subject   *T*   *(neg)*   *V*   *Object*

Exercise **Q29** 📖 Using (18a) as a model, what's the abstract structure of the sentence *Calvin eats the beef waffles?*

Exercise **Q30** ✏ Is there anything in our system so far that predicts the ungrammaticality of the following abstract forms (where we have a mismatch between the abstract T particle and the form of the verb)?   Y   N

(19) (a) Calvin $\emptyset_{past}$ eats   the beef waffles.

     (b) Calvin $\emptyset_{pres}$ ate   the beef waffles.

Discussion We need to find some mechanism for both explaining why tense morphology appears to be on the verb (and not on the T morpheme) and explaining why the correct form of the verb appears with the relevant tense morpheme. To do this we're going to make use of the INTERNAL feature you learned about in unit 8. Internal arguments, you'll remember, are the required elements that come after the verb. In unit 8, these were all DPs and PPs. But here, we're going to claim that verbs can also satisfy internal features of certain elements.

Let's start with the past: we're going to claim that $\emptyset_{past}$ requires that its internal argument be of a special form called the preterite.[3]

Definition The **preterite** is the form a verb takes when it shows up in past tense sentences. Typically this is the form ending in *-ed*, but it can also be an irregular form like *ate, rang, shook, stood, went,* etc.

Notation The feature structure for preterites uses a new feature: FORM, which refers to the morphological shape of the word. The value for preterites is [FORM *preterite*]. For example, a partial feature structure for the preterite of the verb *leave* is seen in (20). (I've left off the SUBCAT features here for simplicity, but they'd be part of the structure too.)

---

[3] The American spelling for this word is "preterit." I'm using the British/Canadian spelling here.

(20) *left*

$$\begin{bmatrix} \text{CATEGORY V} \\[4pt] \text{FORM} \qquad \textit{preterite} \end{bmatrix}$$

The way we ensure that $\emptyset_{past}$ is always followed by a preterite is by specifying that $\emptyset_{past}$ has an internal feature that looks for precisely (and only) following preterite verbs:

(21) $\emptyset_{past}$

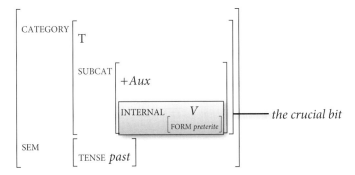

This is a pretty complicated structure so just focus on the bit that is circled. This feature requires that the form of the verb that follows our abstract $\emptyset_{past}$ will be in the preterite form.

Notation Let us claim that corresponding to the preterite, there is a form of the verb found only in the present tense. This form is a little more complicated, as it varies depending upon the person of the subject. With third-person subjects it has an *-s* suffix (for most regular verbs), with first- and second-person subjects it has no marking. Some verbs, *be* and *have* for example, have a variety of forms dependent upon person (e.g. *am, are, is,* etc.). For the purposes of this unit we're going to ignore the differences in person and lump all present tense forms together, describing them with the feature [FORM *present*].

Exercise **Q31** 📖 Using (21) as a model, what's the feature structure for $\emptyset_{pres}$?

Comment By making use of the internal feature of the T, we can ensure that the correct form of the verb follows it. We're going to make extensive use of this device in unit 13, when we return to the English auxiliary system. Before doing that, however, we finally have to address the question of the structure formed out of the feature structures we've been proposing throughout this group of units.

103

Suggested further reading

- Aarts (1997), chapter 3
- Adger (2003), chapter 5
- Carnie (2006), chapter 9
- Huddleston and Pullum (2005), chapter 3
- Kim and Sells (2008), chapter 8
- Lobeck (2000), chapter 5
- Pollock (1989)
- Sag, Wasow and Bender (2003), chapters 5, 13 and 15
- http://en.wikipedia.org/wiki/Auxiliary_verb
- http://en.wikipedia.org/wiki/Modal_auxiliary_verb

Answers to questions

Q1 In (1), the verb *have* indicates possession. The possession can be concrete or it can be a bit more abstract (as in (1c)). In each of these cases the verb *have* is followed by a noun. The sentences in (2) lack this notion of possession; the syntactic structure is also different. In these forms *have* is followed either by a verb (or at least a participle).

Q2 In (3) the verb be *is* used to indicate that the subject has a certain property or is identified with a particular role. It indicates membership in classes or expresses identity. These uses are known as **copular** *be*. By contrast the uses in (4) don't have these functions. Leaving aside the traditional description of gerunds as nouns (we will treat them mostly as verbs), the difference between (3) and (4) in terms of category is that the copular verb is followed by a noun and the progressive and passive usages are followed by verbal forms.

Q3 The answer to this question is much harder to pin down. The *do* in (5) seems to mean something like "accomplish" or "perform." Some speakers might think the same thing is true of the *do* in (6). But here things are more subtle. No *do* is necessary in a simple declarative like *John ate*. But the *do* is required with a negation: *John did not eat*. The *do*s in (5) are followed by nouns, the *do*s in (6) are followed by (negated) verbs. In later units, we'll claim that the *do* in (6) is "meaningless" – in the sense that it is present to support the tense morphology in the environment of negation. The fact that we can have two verbs *do* in a single sentence (6b) suggests that we have two verbs *do*: one to support tense and one to provide the meaning "accomplish/perform."

Q4 N

Q5 Y

Q6 For American English, we can state the generalization thus:

Only verbs with the [SUBCAT +*aux*] *feature can undergo the Subject/Aux Inversion rule.*

Q7 The "main" verb uses of *do* and *have* pattern as if they lack the [SUBCAT +*aux*] feature, as they do not invert. Note, however, that this rule cannot be the end of the story, because main verb *be* also undergoes Subject/Aux Inversion. The challenge question which follows asks you to speculate on why that might be and how we might incorporate such a fact into our generalization.

Q8 N

Q9 Y

Q10 Only verbs with [SUBCAT +*aux*] can appear before the word *not*.

Q11 Main verbs *have*$_{poss}$ and *do*$_{main}$ cannot appear before negation. This is a position associated with auxiliaries, so that suggests that these verbs are not auxiliaries.

Q12 *Be* and *have* take inflectional suffixes just like verbs including tense morphology and the suffixes that turn them into participles and gerunds. They also appear after subjects and before objects. They can be negated with *not*. They follow modals, the infinitive marker *to* (and to a greater or lesser degree other auxiliaries). They can follow adverbs like *often*. All of this suggests that they have some verbal properties, making them a special subcategory of verbs.

Q13 Unlike auxiliaries, modals do not take verbal inflectional endings; they also cannot follow *not*, nor follow other modals or auxiliaries or the infinitive marker *to*. They do however follow subjects and precede objects, and can follow the adverb *often*.

Q14 Most speakers of English only allow one modal in a sentence. There is one exception to this speakers from the South Eastern United States often allow a combination of *might* and *could*: %*He might could leave*.[4] However, there is some evidence to suggest that this is actually a compound. (Only these two modals can combine; they must be in this order, and for many speakers no adverb can appear between them.)

Q15 All speakers of English allow multiple *be/have* combinations such as *I have been dancing* or *I am being taught syntax*. This suggests that modals are different from *be/have* auxiliaries.

---

[4] The % symbol marks that a form is acceptable in a particular dialect.

Q16-19 Modals can only appear before *not*; other auxiliaries can appear before or after *not*.

Q20 Auxiliaries and modals can both undergo Subject/Aux Inversion. Main verbs cannot. This suggests that there is some overlap in category between auxiliaries and modals.

Q21 Auxiliaries and modals can both appear before negation. Main verbs cannot. This again suggests that there is some overlap in category between auxiliaries and modals.

Q22 With respect to *not, will* patterns just like a modal; it cannot follow negation. Even though it does not directly express modality, *will* patterns syntactically like a modal.

Q23 For all speakers of English, the future tense marker *will* is in complementary distribution with the modal verbs. It is impossible to have a single clause that has both a modal and a future tense marker in it: **Calvin could will eat the beef waffles. *Calvin will could eat the beef waffles.* etc. This suggests that maybe *will* is a modal verb in English, because like other modals it typically cannot combine with other modals.

Q24 No, the first verb after a modal is always in its "bare" form with no tense morphology expressed. If you have a modal you cannot have a tense marker.

Q25 *can*

$$
\begin{bmatrix}
\text{CATEGORY} & \begin{bmatrix} \text{T} \\ \text{SUBCAT} + aux \end{bmatrix} \\
\text{SEM} & \begin{bmatrix} \text{MOOD } ability \end{bmatrix}
\end{bmatrix}
$$

Q26 *be*$_{prog}$

$$
\begin{bmatrix}
\text{CATEGORY} & \begin{bmatrix} \text{V} \\ \text{SUBCAT} + aux \end{bmatrix} \\
\text{SEM} & \begin{bmatrix} \text{ASPECT } progressive \end{bmatrix}
\end{bmatrix}
$$

Q27 Tense appears on the *do* auxiliary (in particular, *did* is the past tense and *does* is the present), not on the verb.

Q28 Just as negation always follows modals and *will* (both of category T), negation when it is present must follow the auxiliary expressing tense. As an aside, this is true not only of *do,* but also other auxiliaries.

Q29 Calvin Ø$_{pres}$ eats the beef waffles.

Q30 No, nothing (so far) explains why we couldn't have an abstract present tense T combined with a past tense verb.

Q31 Ø$_{pres}$

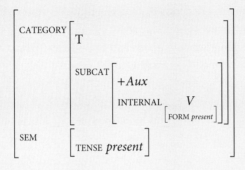

GROUP 2 REVIEW

The following were the major ideas introduced in group 2:
- Parts of speech are determined distributionally rather than semantically.
- The major lexical categories are N, V, Adj and Adv.
- The distinction between open- and closed-class parts of speech is based on whether we can add new words to the class.
- Lexical categories provide the content of the sentence; functional categories provide the grammatical glue that holds the sentences together.
- While functional categories tend to be closed-class parts of speech and lexical categories tend to be open, there are cases where this correlation does not hold.
- There are two cases where the functional/lexical distinction does not work well: pronouns and auxiliaries.
- Subcategories are specific restricted forms of categories. The representation of these with features and feature structures.
- With nouns, the distinction between pronouns, proper nouns, mass nouns and count nouns, and animates.
- With verbs, the distinction between auxiliary and main verbs. Among the main verbs, the distinctions based on argument structure.
- The English tense, mood, aspect and voice system, and these categories are represented by auxiliaries and modals.

3 Constituents, MERGE and trees

UNIT 11 CONSTITUENCY

Objectives:
- Understand the definition of constituent.
- Explore constituency tests including: standing alone, replacement and displacement.
- Start looking at representing these structures in tree format.

11.1 Constituents

Definition   A **constituent** is an identifiable subpart of a sentence. It can either be a single word or a group of words that functions as a unit. Most constituents are called **phrases**. (We'll develop a better definition of "phrase" later.)

Comment   In unit 3, looking at evidence from the formation of yes/no questions, we saw that rules like Subject/Auxiliary Inversion make reference to the internal structure of sentences. Constituents are these internal structures. In this unit, we look at how we identify these structures.

Discussion   As a first step, we can observe that constituents typically correspond to strings of words that are bound together in terms of semantics. The relevant notion here is vague but hopefully intuitive: modification. If one word modifies the meaning of another, they will be linked together in a constituent. Consider the string *the very big can of tuna*. Look at the words *very* and *big*; notice how there is a close relationship between these. *Very* modifies *big*; it tells you how big the can is. Compare this to the relationship between *very* and *can*: *very* does not tell you how can something is! This means that there is a constituent consisting of *very* and *big*, but excluding *can*.

Constituents are usually parts of other constituents. So the constituent *very big* is part of a larger structure *the very big can of tuna*. One important thing you should note from this larger constituent is that words that modify one another need not be adjacent to each other. So, for example, the determiner *the* is not adjacent to the noun *can*, but it tells you that there is some specific can we're talking about. Also, note that phrases can modify words. So the phrase *very big* modifies *can*, as does the phrase *of tuna*.

111

11.2 Tests for constituency

Definition **Semantic modification test for constituency**: if one word modifies another, then they are part of the same constituent.

Exercise **Q1** ✎ Look at the following sentence. Then answer the following questions:

(1) A black cat quickly scratched the rather large couch.

(a)	Does *a* modify *black*?	Y	N
(b)	Does *a* modify *cat*?	Y	N
(c)	Does *black* modify *cat*?	Y	N
(d)	Does *the* modify *rather*?	Y	N
(e)	Does *the* modify *large*?	Y	N
(f)	Does *the* modify *couch*?	Y	N
(g)	Does *rather* modify *couch*?	Y	N
(h)	Does *rather* modify *large*?	Y	N
(i)	Does *rather large* modify *couch*?	Y	N
(j)	Does *quickly* modify *scratched*?	Y	N

Discussion On the basis of the results discussed above we can identify at least the following constituents of sentence (1) (since each word is a constituent by itself, these are also listed):

> *a*
>
> *black*
>
> *cat*
>
> *a black cat*
>
> *the*
>
> *rather*
>
> *large*
>
> *couch*
>
> *rather large*
>
> *the rather large couch*

There are other constituents that aren't obviously revealed by this test. For example, while we know that *quickly* modifies *scratched*, the constituent that contains them is actually *quickly scratched the rather large couch*, not *often scratched*. This can be seen by looking at other tests, which we'll present below.

Notation There are a number of ways to represent constituents. One way is to put brackets around the constituent with a subscript label on the first bracket. Let's go back to our first example: *a very big can of tuna*. *Big* is an adjective, and it is modified by the intensifier adverb *very*. Since *big*, by itself, can modify *can* (as in *the big can*), the whole phrase *very big* is functioning like a big adjective. We call this an **adjective phrase** (abbreviated AdjP). The bracketed notation will also include brackets around each word indicating their category:

(2)   *These brackets indicate the category of the larger constituent.*

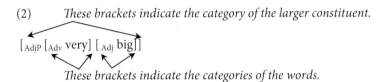

These brackets indicate the categories of the words.

The bracketed notation is very close to another notation – box notation:

(3)

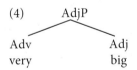

The box notation is difficult to draw, so most linguists use either the bracket notation or a third system: the tree notation. This last notation is the most commonly used in the syntax literature. In the tree notation, the name of the whole constituent is written on top; each subconstituent is connected to this label with a line.

(4)   AdjP

Adv   Adj
very   big

Here are the trees and bracket structures for the entire phrase:

(5)   (a)

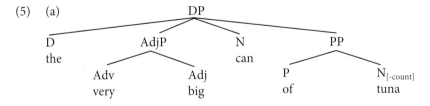

(b) [$_{DP}$ [$_D$ the] [$_{AdjP}$ [$_{Adv}$ very][$_{Adj}$ big]][$_N$ can][$_{PP}$ [$_P$ of] [$_N$ tuna]]]

(Caveat: in later units we'll have a slightly more articulated structure for this kind of DP, so don't get too attached to trees like this!)

Exercise **Q2** 📖 Using (5) as a model, draw the tree structure for the phrase *the rather large couch.*

Comment In the next unit, we'll look at some rules that govern what goes into each constituent. Before that, however, we look at some other tests for constituency.

Definition **Stand-alone test:** if a string of words can stand alone in answer to a question, then it is a constituent.

Discussion Recall that the definition of constituent requires that when a string of words is a constituent it functions as a unit. One such unit would be a sentence fragment answer to a question. We've already established that the sequence *the very big can of tuna* is a constituent, since we have a string of modifiers for the word *can*. Let's see if we can replicate this result with the stand-alone test:

Q: What did you find in the cupboard?

A: The very large can of tuna.

This test will also reveal that the string *very large* is a subconstituent of this:

Q: How big was that can of tuna?

A: very large

Exercise **Q3** 🖝 Going back to sentence (1), use the stand-alone test to see if any of the following strings are constituents or not.

(a)	a black	Y	N
(b)	a black cat	Y	N
(c)	the rather	Y	N
(d)	rather large	Y	N
(e)	the rather large couch	Y	N
(f)	quickly scratched	Y	N
(g)	quickly scratched the rather large couch (Try the question "What did the cat do?")	Y	N

Comment Notice that although *quickly* modifies *scratched*, *quickly scratched* is not a constituent. Instead, what we have is the **verb phrase (VP)** *quickly scratched the rather large couch*:

(6)

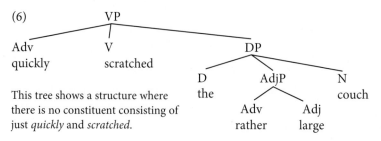

This tree shows a structure where there is no constituent consisting of just *quickly* and *scratched*.

114

Exercise **Q4** 📖 Using (6) and (5) as models, draw the VP tree for *ate the can of tuna*.

Definition **Replacement test for constituency:** if you can replace a string of words with a single word, without changing the meaning of the rest of the sentence, then that string is a constituent.

Discussion Single words are constituents. It follows that if you can use a single word in place of a string of words, then that string is also a constituent. For example, start with the sentence *The fat cat with black and white fur demanded attention*. We can replace *The fat cat with black and white fur* with *Calvin* to give us *Calvin demanded attention*. This shows us that *the fat cat with black and white fur* is a constituent.

Exercise **Q5** 📖 For each of the following sentences, provide another sentence that replaces the underlined string with a single word. All the underlined strings are constituents.

(a)   I took the garbage to the dump.

(b)   The guy with the felt hat fell on the floor.

(c)   Susan arrived from Chicago.

Comment Here is the tree for sentence (a) above (TP is the abbreviation for the sentence; I'll explain this in a later unit):

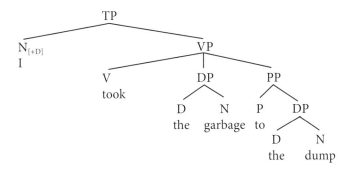

Exercise **Q6** 📖 Using the tree above as a model, draw the tree for sentence (c) (hint: omit the DP inside the VP):

Definition **The displacement (or movement) test:** if a string of words can be displaced (i.e. moved) as a unit, then it is a constituent.

Definition A **cleft** is a displacement, where a string of words is placed at the beginning of the sentence after the words *it is/was/will be* but before a word like *that, who, what, where, how* or *whose* and the rest of the sentence.

115

Discussion If we start with the sentence *I saw the cat with the black and white fur,* one possible cleft structure of this is *It was <u>the cat with the black and white fur</u> that I saw.* The underlined string is a constituent because it can be clefted.

Exercise **Q7** ✎ Try clefting the underlined string in each of the following sentences, and see if they are constituents.

(a) Calvin bought <u>a really expensive ring</u>.

Cleft: ....

Constituent?   Y   N

(b) I was going to <u>the store</u>.

Cleft: ....

Constituent?   Y   N

(c) Pangur ate his tuna <u>very quickly</u>.

Cleft: ....

Constituent?   Y   N

(d) Pangur ate <u>his tuna very</u> quickly.

Cleft: ....

Constituent?   Y   N

Comment If you have trouble with the acceptability of the cleft versions of (a–b), try putting extra stress or emphasis on the clefted string. This should improve the acceptability. This is because cleft constructions typically involve a focus or topicality of the clefted element.

Comment There are two things to note about constituency tests. There are times when two constituency tests give conflicting results. For this reason, it's important to try a couple of different tests when determining constituency of a string of words. Second, there are a wide number of constituency tests that I haven't listed here. For a fairly comprehensive list, see chapters 10 and 11 of Aarts (1997).

Challenge There are verbs that take a preposition after them. This preposition often doesn't take an object: *He passed out.* These special prepositions are often called **particles**. Now, consider the following sentences:

(a) He blew out the candle.

(b) He turned off the light.

(c) He blew up the building.

(d) He rode out the storm.

116

In each of these, we have a preposition followed by a DP. Can you figure out if the constituency of these sentences has the prepositions forming constituents with the DP that follows them ($[_{VP}$ V $[_{PP}$ P DP]]) or are acting as particles and are forming constituents with the verbs that precede them ($[_{VP}$ [V P] DP])? Use the tests you have learned to test this.

Summary   Constituency was the focus of this unit. Constituents are the units of substructure. DP, PP, AdjPs and VPs are all typical constituents. The tests for constituency include semantic modification, stand alone, replacement and movement. In the next unit, we'll look at the rules for building constituent structures and the constraints on those rules.

Suggested further reading

- Aarts (1997), chapters 10 and 11
- Adger (2003), chapter 3
- Carnie (2006), chapter 3
- Falk (2001), chapter 2
- Haegeman (2006), chapter 2
- Kroeger (2004), chapter 2
- Larson (2010), chapter 7
- Lobeck (2000), chapter 3
- Radford (1988), chapter 2
- Tallerman (2005), chapter 5
- http://en.wikipedia.org/wiki/Constituent_%28linguistics%29

Answers to questions

Q1 (a) N, (b) Y, (c) Y, (d) N, (e) N, (f) Y, (g) N, (h) Y, (i) Y, (j) Y

Q2

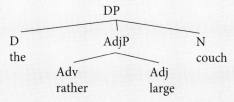

Q3 (a) N, (b) Y, (c) N, (d) Y, (e) Y, (f) N, (g) Y

Q4

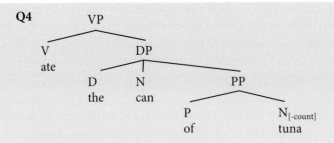

Q5 Your answers will not necessarily be the same as mine, but here is a possible set of sentences: (a) *I took the garbage <u>out</u>*; (b) *<u>Bob</u> fell on the floor*; (c) *Susan came*.

Q6

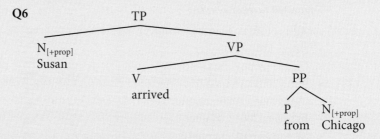

Q7 (a) It was a really expensive ring that Calvin bought.   Y

(b) It was the store that I was going to.   Y

(c) It was very quickly that Calvin ate his tuna.   Y

(d) *It was his tuna very that Calvin ate quickly.   N

UNIT 12 C-merge: COMPLEMENTS

Objectives:

- Correctly apply the rule COMPLEMENT-MERGE, which is used for constructing constituents.
- See how MERGE is constrained by the feature structures of the participating words and the Principle of Full Interpretation.
- Learn about phonologically null categories.

Comment   A formal, explanatory and descriptive grammar must provide a hypothesis for describing the observed phenomenon of constituency. There are a number of such proposals including rule systems called Phrase Structure rules and a widely known approach known as X-bar theory (see Carnie 2006 for detailed versions of these rule systems). In this book, we will pursue a different system that is both simpler and more modern. This system is based on the interaction of feature structures, a constraint that ensures that only appropriate material is joined together in constituents, and a rule called COMPLEMENT-MERGE or C-MERGE.

12.1 COMPLEMENT-MERGE and Full Interpretation

Definition   The **head** of a constituent is the element that subcategorizes for the other elements in a constituent.

Definition   **COMPLEMENT-MERGE** (C-MERGE): combine two (or more) items together into a constituent as required by the INTERNAL features of one of the items. The constituent is given the label of the head (typically followed by a "P" to indicate that the final constituent is a phrase), e.g.

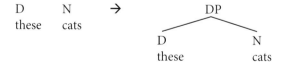

119

Definition   ***Principle of Full Interpretation (FI)*** *(preliminary version): if two items are merged together their feature structures must be compatible.* [1] (A constraint)

Discussion   Assume that the feature structure for a determiner like *these* looks like that in (1):

(1)   *these*

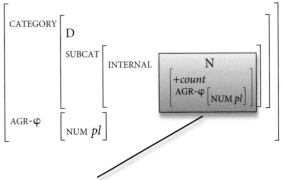

This bit is the important part. It shows that the element satisfying the internal feature of the word these *must meet these various requirements.*

This quite complicated structure says that *these* is a determiner (D); it is plural; and it requires that the word be followed by a count noun, which is also plural (as indicated by the INTERNAL feature).

Imagine the word we want to follow this is *cats*. A partial feature structure for this word is given in (2):

(2)   *cats*

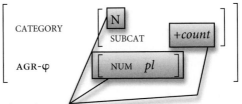

These features are a match for the INTERNAL specification in (1)

---

[1] Professors and students with a little more experience will know I'm playing fast and loose here with this constraint. The name of the constraint here is often used in the Chomskyan tradition to refer to a constraint that requires the resulting structure to have a semantic representation (i.e. is coherent in meaning). The definition I've given is more often known by the name *Unification,* especially in the theories of LFG and HPSG. In the long run, these two definitions often converge on the same thing, so I've blended the name from Chomskyan grammar with the definition from LFG and HPSG. The theoretical approach described in this book is also a blend.

Since we have a match, we can use the C-MERGE rule to join these together into a DP:

(3)

This structure is licensed by Full Interpretation (henceforth FI), because *cats* meets the INTERNAL requirements of *these*, because cats is an N; it is +count; and it is plural.

Exercise **Q1** ▢ In your own words, explain why the DPs in (4) are unacceptable.

(4) (a) *these cat

(b) *that cats

Q2 ▢ Keeping in mind your answer to Q1, and using (1) and (2) as models, write out the feature structures for *that* and *cat*.

12.2 Expressing complements

Definition ***Complement:***[2] the word or phrase that is C-MERGED with the head as required by the head's INTERNAL feature.

Discussion With *these cats*, the word *these* is the head, and the word *cats* is a complement because it is selected for by the INTERNAL feature of *these*.

Exercise **Q3** ✎ In each of the following sentences there is an underlined word. Assume this is the head of a phrase. Circle the words that are the complement of that head.

(5) (a) <u>The</u> cat ate the tuna.

(b) The cat ate <u>the</u> tuna.

(c) The cat <u>ate</u> the tuna.

(d) John went <u>to</u> the store.

Q4 ✎ The verbs in the following sentences have slightly more complex internal features (look back at unit 8 to see what they are). Identify the complements to the verb in each of these sentences. Some verbs may have more than one complement. (In sentence (h), there are two verbs; identify the complements to both of them.)

(e) Calvin gave the tuna to Pangur.

(f) Calvin gave Pangur the tuna.

---

[2] Note that this word is spelled complement not compliment. Complements "complete," they don't "compliment," hence the spelling.

(g)   I <u>put</u> the book in the box.

(h)   I <u>think</u> that Calvin <u>likes</u> tuna.

Comment In this unit, we will be limiting ourselves to the merger of complements. We will deal with adjuncts and the elements that appear in the EXTERNAL feature (called specifiers) in later units.

Discussion Notice that because more than one thing can appear in the value of an INTERNAL feature (e.g. the value of the internal feature for *put* is <DP, PP>), we can have more than one complement.[3] For our purposes, this means that we have a tree structure such as (6):

(6)

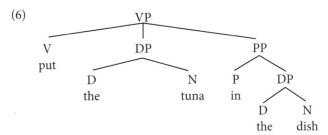

Let's break this apart into smaller steps. We'll start on the right side at the bottom with *the* and *dish*. *The* requires an N due to its INTERNAL feature. We merge them together, and put a label (DP) on top that matches the head.

(7)

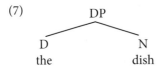

Next, the internal preposition *in* requires a DP complement, so we merge the DP in (7) to give the PP in (8):

(8)

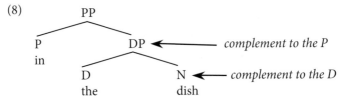

---

³ Such structures are not universally accepted; there are many theories that posit more complicated structures for ditransitive verbs. See for example chapters 6, 7 and 14 of Carnie (2006) for a detailed textbook explanation.

Now, forming a separate constituent, we C-MERGE the D *the* with the N *tuna*.

(9)

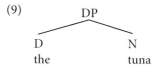

Finally, the verb *put* requires a DP and a PP, so we take the trees in (8) and (9) and C-MERGE them together with the verb to give the tree in (6) above.

Exercise **Q5** 📖 Using (6) as a model and looking at the INTERNAL features that you came up with in unit 9, draw the trees for the following verb phrases:

 (a) gave the tuna to the cat

 (b) gave the cat the tuna

 (c) ask the time

Discussion Thus far we've looked at determiners taking N complements, prepositions taking DP complements and verbs taking DP and PP complements, but other kinds of complementation exist as well. Consider the verb *destroy*. *Destroy* requires a DP complement:

(10) (a) Calvin destroyed the couch.

 (b) *Calvin destroyed.

There is a noun that is closely related to *destroy*: *destruction*. Just as we can destroy a couch, we can talk about *the destruction of the couch*. *The couch* is the object in (10a), but it also seems to serve a similar function in *the destruction of the couch*. This suggests that *of the couch* might be a complement of the noun *destruction*. What is different about the complements of nouns (and, as we'll see, adjectives) is that they are always optional:

(11) (a) the destruction of the couch

 (b) the destruction

The INTERNAL feature of a noun like *destruction* allows an optional PP complement which is always marked with an *of*. This is indicated by the parentheses around the PP:

(12) [INTERNAL (PP$_{of}$)]

With this in mind, let's run through the derivation of (11a). Let's start by merging *the* and *couch*:

(13)

Next we merge this with *of*:

(14)

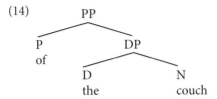

This PP can serve as the value of the INTERNAL feature of *destruction*. Since the head is a noun, the label of the whole constituent is NP (for "noun phrase")

(15)

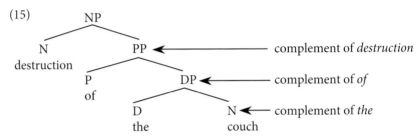

Finally we C-MERGE this NP as the complement of *the* giving the DP:

(16)

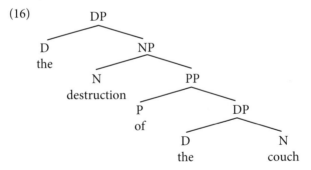

Exercise **Q6** 📖 The verb *fear* requires a DP complement:

(17) (a) The child fears the tigers.

(b) *The child fears.

The adjective *afraid* is similar in meaning to the verb *fears*. Given the data below, what is the value of the INTERNAL feature for the adjective *afraid*?

(18) (a) The child is afraid of the tigers.

(b) The child is afraid.

Q7 📖 Using your answer to Q6 immediately above and using (16) as a loose model, draw the tree for the VP *is afraid of the tigers*. You may assume that the verb *is* has the following INTERNAL feature [INTERNAL {AdjP/DP/VP}].

Challenge Not all instances of adjectives allow complements. For example, it is impossible in English to say *the afraid of tigers child*. Can you think of an explanation for this? (Warning, this is a hard question, so don't be frustrated if you can't come up with an answer – it has been a challenge for linguists for fifty years. But maybe you'll be the one to solve it!)

12.3 The Principle of Headedness

Exercise **Q8** 📖 You may not have noticed it, but I tried to slip one by you in drawing the tree for (16). I made one C-MERGE that wasn't correctly licensed by an INTERNAL feature. Can you figure out where I played fast and loose? (Hint: have a look at the values given for the INTERNAL features of determiners as in (1), then look carefully at what I actually merged with the leftmost determiner in (16). You might also look at the nature of all the complements of determiners shown in all the trees before (16).)

Notation ***Principle of Headedness***: in any circumstance where a SUBCAT feature mentions a category, one may substitute in a phrase headed by that category and vice versa (e.g. you can freely substitute NP for N, and N for NP; DP for D and D for DP, VP for V, V for VP, etc.).

Exercise **Q9** 📖 Explain how the Principle of Headedness allows for sentences such as *I saw those*.

Discussion Just as we substituted a phrase (NP) for a simple word (N) in (16), we can substitute a word (D) for a phrase (DP) in the INTERNAL feature of the verb *saw*, as in the sentence *I saw those*. The tree for this VP is given in (19).

(19)

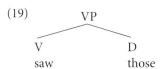

The tree for a VP in a sentence such as *I saw those cats* is given in (20):

(20)

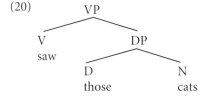

125

Because of the Principle of Headedness, both these structures are allowed when the verb's subcategorization info includes the feature [INTERNAL DP].

Exercise **Q10** 📖 Draw the tree for the verb phrase *is afraid*.

Q11 📖 Given the assumption necessary for the tree you drew in Q7 that the internal feature of *is* is [INTERNAL {AdjP/DP/VP}], is the tree you just drew for Q10 a violation of Full Interpretation? Why or why not?

Exercise **Q12** 📖 Draw the tree for the VP *gave it to him*. You can base your tree on (6), but pay special attention to the categories of *it* and *him*. Notice that these are nouns, not DPs.

Q13 📖 Do the pronouns in your tree cause a violation of FI? Does the Headedness Principle help here? Why or why not?

Comment While pronouns aren't of category D, they do bear the [SUBCAT +D] feature. As a matter of convention, we will allow +D nouns to appear wherever Ds or DPs appear.

12.4 Null determiners

Exercise **Q14** 📖 Next consider the following sentences: *I love Calvin*; *I love sugar*; *I love beans*. Assume that the internal feature for the verb *love* is [INTERNAL DP]. Does the headedness principle permit these sentences? Would the solution we gave for pronouns work here? Why or why not? (You may want to go back and look at unit 7 and the features proposed there.)

Discussion In unit 7, we argued that pronouns, proper nouns and mass nouns were different subcategories of the category N. Pronouns cannot appear with determiners or adjectives, but proper nouns and mass nouns can under certain circumstances. Similarly, we distinguish mass nouns as having the property that they can only appear with certain determiners (*much* and never *many*). The implication of this for our formal analysis is that we cannot use the headedness principle or the +D feature to account for the fact that we can have bare nouns appearing in DP positions. A different solution must be found.

Let us start with the observation that there are determiners that distinguish between mass and count nouns. The quantifier *many* appears only with count nouns, the quantifier *much* appears with mass nouns. We can express this with the following partial feature structures:

(21) (a) *many*

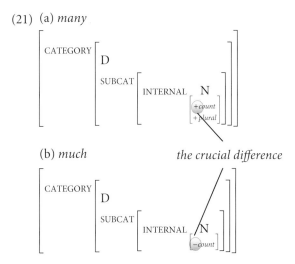

(b) *much*   *the crucial difference*

Determiners such as *these, the* and *those* are like *many* in that when they are used with a noun, the noun can only have a count interpretation. This means that they will have a feature structure like that of *many*, where the internal feature is specified for $N_{[+count]}$. Notice crucially, however, that these determiners don't have an equivalent that is used with mass nouns; there are no equivalents to *much*. Mass nouns appear at first to be simply unmarked with a determiner in most circumstances (e.g. *I don't have water*).

Consider for the moment the possibility that there are determiners in English that have no phonetic content (i.e. they are silent). To many people starting syntax this seems like a silly idea: "Words we can't hear? Ridiculous!" However, the idea has currency among professional grammarians, as there is a fair amount of evidence that null words might exist. If we look crosslinguistically, for example, we see that in languages such as Spanish or Italian, the subject pronoun of a sentence is typically omitted. One might analyze these missing nouns as really being there, but simply being silent. We saw another case in unit 10, where I claimed that present and past tense in English are represented with null T heads ($\varnothing_{pres}$ and $\varnothing_{past}$). Another example, closer to the case at hand, is Irish Gaelic. Irish has a word for *the*, but no word for the indefinite determiner *a*:

(22) (a)   an   teach

the house

"the house"

(b)   teach

house

"a house"

127

Allowing ourselves to be mildly Anglocentric for the moment, the absence of an indefinite determiner is very surprising. The determiner *a* adds something meaningful to an English noun, so how could Irish express the same idea without such a functional item? Not everyone agrees with this idea, but the obvious solution is to claim that Irish does have an indefinite determiner but this word is silent.

If you will at least accept this hypothesis tentatively, then the solution to our problem of proper nouns, mass nouns and plurals is straightforward: these all appear with null (Ø) determiners:

(23) (a)

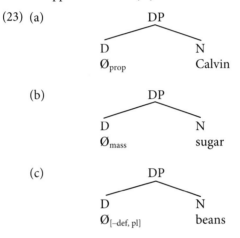

    (b)

    (c)

Since these are DPs, they will meet the [INTERNAL DP] requirement of the verb *love*.

Notation With this in mind, let's sketch out some partial feature structures for these various determiners. First, I'll give you representations for *a* and *the*. Here we use the feature SEM for semantics again that we saw in unit 10 on auxiliaries. *The* is a definite determiner (it is used to mark that the noun refers to some particular element); *a* is an indefinite determiner. We'll use the value ±*def* as values of SEM to represent this.

(24) (a) *the*

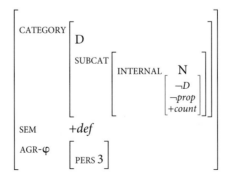

(b)   *a*

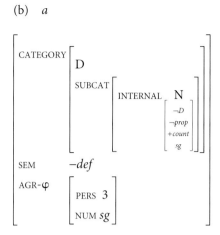

At first blush, these look pretty complicated, but in fact they are straightforward. Each bit represents some information about these determiners we need to know. The ±*def* values of the SEM feature tell us about the definiteness of the determiners. The AGR-φ features tell us that these always appear on nouns that are third person (this is because only pronouns can show up in the first and second person). There is one big difference between the two entries: *a* is marked for being singular, but *the* has no specification for number. This is because *the* can be used with both plural and singular nouns (*the cat, the cats*), but *a* can only be used in the singular (*a cat, *a cats*), so there is no NUM specification for *the*. The real work is done in the INTERNAL feature. In the feature structure for *the*, the internal feature requires an N (or NP because of the principle of headedness), which is not a pronoun (¬D), not a proper noun (¬*prop*), but is a count noun (+*count*). The feature structure for *a* has the same restrictions, but with the additional proviso that the noun must be singular.

Let's now try to write similar structures for our null determiners. The feature structure for the silent determiner that appears with proper nouns is given in (25):

(25) Ø*prop*

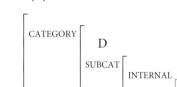

This differs from the feature structure for *the* in exactly one way: it requires that the complement N be a proper noun. Thus, this null determiner is only used before proper nouns.

Exercise **Q15** 📖 Using (25) as a model draw the feature structure for the null determiners that appear with mass nouns ($\emptyset_{mass}$) and the ones that appear with indefinite plural count nouns ($\emptyset_{[-def, plural]}$). With the last one, be careful to represent the number requirement both in the AGR-φ feature and in the restriction on the N with the INTERNAL features.

Exercise **Q16** 📖 Draw the trees for the following VPs. Pay careful attention to whether the complements to the verb are bare determiners, full DPs, pronouns (N_{+D}) or null determiners with mass/proper/plural noun complements.

(a) give John these

(b) put roses on it

(c) ate tuna

(d) began the destruction of the city

Summary In this unit we've covered a lot of ground:
- Syntactic trees are created using an operation called C-MERGE.
- C-MERGE takes one element (the head) and combines it with something that satisfies the INTERNAL features.
- The elements that satisfy the INTERNAL subcategory feature are called complements. This unit has focused on the merger of complements.
- Heads and phrases built from those heads can be interchanged when satisfying the SUBCAT features through C-MERGE. This is known as the Principle of Headedness.
- Pronouns are of subcategory +D, and are allowed to stand anywhere a determiner is (by stipulation).
- Some determiners don't require complements (e.g. *these, those*).
- Mass nouns, proper names and indefinite plurals make use of special null determiners.

In the next unit, we work some more on complements, returning to our earlier discussion of English auxiliaries and affix hopping. We run through these as a detailed exploration of complements. In the units that follow, we then turn to two other kinds of elements that undergo different versions of the merge operation: adjuncts and specifiers. This will allow us to draw trees for complete sentences.

Suggested further reading

- Adger (2003), chapter 4
- Carnie (2006), chapter 3
- Chametzky (1996)
- Chomsky (1995)
- Hornstein, Nunes and Grohman (2005), chapters 6 and 9
- Huddleston and Pullum (2005), chapter 4
- Kim and Sells (2008), chapter 4
- Larson (2010), unit 22
- Lobeck (2000), chapter 11
- Sag, Wasow and Bender (2005), chapter 4
- Speas (1990)
- Stowell (1981)

Answers to questions

Q1 Sentence (4a) is ungrammatical because there is a mismatch between the number required by *these* (plural) and the number of *cat* (singular). The same holds true of (4b) except that *that* is singular and *cats* is plural. These sentences are predicted to be ungrammatical because of FI, which requires there to be a match in features when required.

Q2 *that*

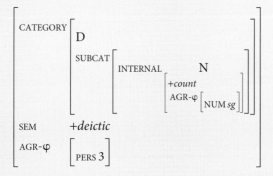

(NOTE: you were not expected to include the [SEM +*deictic*] feature here. It's included just for completeness.)

cat

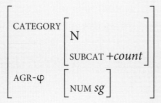

Q3 (a) cat, (b) tuna, (c) the tuna, (d) the store

Q4 (e) *the tuna* and *to Pangur*; (f) *the tuna* and *Pangur*, (g) *the book* and *in the box* (h) for think: *that Calvin likes tuna*; for likes: *tuna*

Q5 (a)

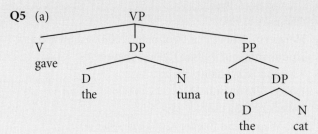

(b)

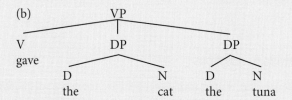

(c)

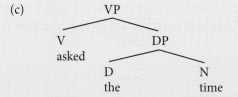

Q6 [INTERNAL (PP$_{of}$)]

Q7

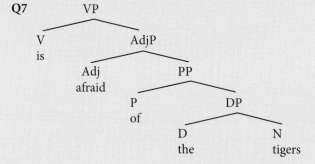

Q8 In all instances up to (16), the element C-MERGED with D was a simple N. N is the value of the internal feature seen in (1). But in the element C-MERGED with the leftmost determiner in (16) is an NP (noun *phrase*), not a simple N. This should be a violation of Full Interpretation (FI) because the value of the internal feature is not correctly met.

Q9 The verb *saw* requires a DP because of its INTERNAL feature. *Those* is a bare determiner with no complement, so it is not a DP. However, the principle of headedness allows us to substitute a D for a DP in a SUBCAT feature. (We must also claim that the N in the INTERNAL feature of *those* is optional: [INTERNAL (N)].)

Q10

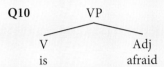

```
        VP
      /    \
    V        Adj
    is       afraid
```

Q11 This is not a violation of FI because the principle of headedness allows us to substitute the bare Adj for the AdjP in the value of the INTERNAL feature of *is*.

Q12

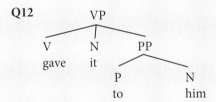

```
         VP
      /  |    \
    V    N      PP
    gave it    /    \
              P       N
              to      him
```

Q13 We have two violations of FI here. GAVE requires <DP, PP>. *It* is not a DP. Similarly, *to* requires a DP and *him* is an N, not a DP nor a D head.

Q14 The headedness principle does not help us here, because *Calvin, sugar* and *beans* are nouns (N) and the feature specifies a DP (or D). We can't appeal to the +D feature because there are a number of reasons to believe that proper nouns, pronouns, plural nouns and mass nouns are all different subcategories.

Q15 (a) Ø$_{mass}$

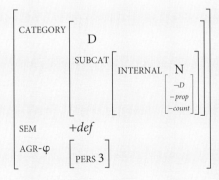

$$
\begin{bmatrix}
\text{CATEGORY} & \begin{bmatrix} \text{D} \\ \text{SUBCAT} \begin{bmatrix} \text{INTERNAL} \begin{matrix} \text{N} \\ {\scriptstyle \neg D} \\ {\scriptstyle -prop} \\ {\scriptstyle -count} \end{matrix} \end{bmatrix} \end{bmatrix} \\
\text{SEM} \quad +def \\
\text{AGR-}\varphi \quad \begin{bmatrix} \text{PERS 3} \end{bmatrix}
\end{bmatrix}
$$

(It would also be acceptable not to specify a value for prop because proper nouns are all count nouns, so –*count* entails –*prop*.)

(b) Ø_{plural}

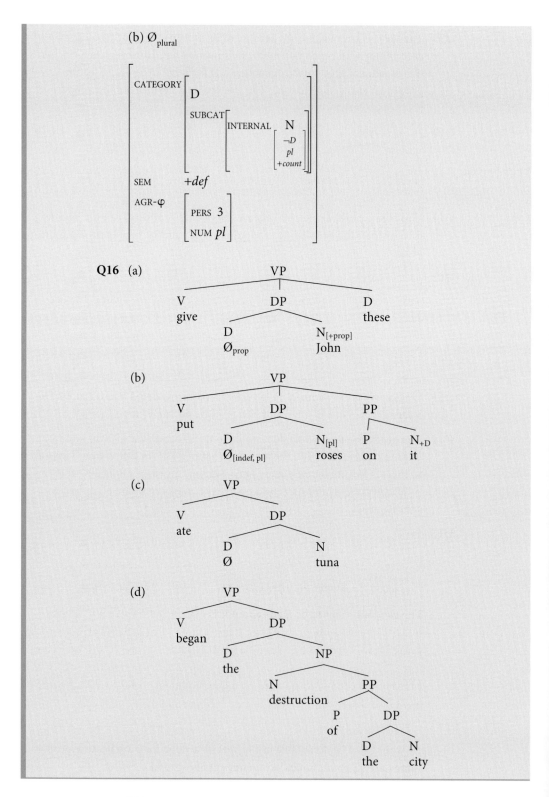

Q16 (a)

(b)

(c)

(d)

UNIT 13 COMPLEMENTS: A CASE STUDY

> **Objectives:**
> - Practice using the rule C-MERGE with a particular application to auxiliary verbs and tense.
> - Learn more about phonologically null T.
> - Practice making TP structures and stacked VP structures.

Comment   In this unit, the goal is to practice C-MERGE with modals and auxiliaries. We will concentrate on *have* and *be* auxiliaries here and one version of the *do* auxiliary.

13.1 Passive auxiliaries

Notation   To get you going, let's start with the passive auxiliary be_{pass}. Let us look at what kinds of things can *follow* the be_{pass} (shown here in its past tense form *was*).

(1) (a) The cake was eaten.   (main verb in participial form)

    (b) The cake was given to the soldier.   (VP: main verb in participial form with a complement[1])

    (c) *The cake was been eaten.   (*another passive auxiliary)

    (d) *The cake was been eating.   (*a progressive auxiliary)

    (e) *The cake was have eaten.   (*a perfective auxiliary)

    (f) *The cake was will/willen eat.   (*a modal auxiliary)

The generalization to be made about this data is that passive be_{pass} can be followed by only main verbs or VPs headed by main verbs (as allowed by the Principle of Headedness). These verbs must bear participle inflection. This is encoded in the partial feature structure for the auxiliary in the form of an INTERNAL feature. Where there is a restriction on the value of V, such that it must be a main verb and that V must be a participle. (2a) gives you the bare

---

[1] One of the complements of the verb is missing here (in fact it's showing up as the subject); this is because the verb is passive. We'll return to this in later units.

form for be_{pass}. (2b) shows you the same but for the preterite (past tense) form was_{pass}.

(2) (a) be_{pass}

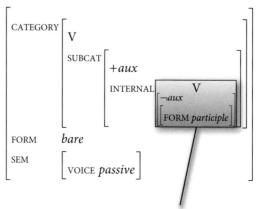

$$\left[\begin{array}{l} \text{CATEGORY} \left[\begin{array}{l} \text{V} \\ \text{SUBCAT} \left[\begin{array}{l} +aux \\ \text{INTERNAL} \left[\begin{array}{l} \text{V} \\ \neg aux \\ \text{FORM } participle \end{array}\right] \end{array}\right] \end{array}\right] \\ \text{FORM} \quad bare \\ \text{SEM} \quad \left[\text{VOICE } passive\right] \end{array}\right]$$

the crucial restrictions on the complement

(b) was_{pass}

$$\left[\begin{array}{l} \text{CATEGORY} \left[\begin{array}{l} \text{V} \\ \text{SUBCAT} \left[\begin{array}{l} +aux \\ \text{INTERNAL} \left[\begin{array}{l} \text{V} \\ \neg aux \\ \text{FORM } part \end{array}\right] \end{array}\right] \end{array}\right] \\ \text{FORM} \quad preterite \\ \text{SEM} \quad \left[\text{VOICE } passive\right] \\ \text{AGR-}\varphi \left[\begin{array}{l} \text{NUM } sg \\ \text{PERS } \neg 2 \end{array}\right] \end{array}\right]$$

If we want to C-MERGE was_{pass} with *eat*, the latter has to be in its participial form. The partial feature structure for *eaten* is given in (3).[2]

(3) *eaten*

$$\left[\begin{array}{ll} \text{CATEGORY} & \text{V} \\ \text{FORM} & participle \\ \text{SEM} & eat \end{array}\right]$$

---

[2] I'm leaving aside the INTERNAL and EXTERNAL features of *eaten* here for the moment. We'll return to this later.

This feature structure matches the INTERNAL features of was_{pass}: it is in the participial form and it isn't an auxiliary. As such, it can combine with was_{pass} via the rule of C-MERGE. The result of this is the tree in (4).

(4)

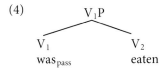

Notation   A few words are in order about (4). First, note that there are two Vs here. We need some notation to keep track of which of these is the head of the VP. To do this I've marked one of the verbs with the subscript $_1$ and the other with $_2$. The VP is listed as V_1P, which tells us that V_1 is the head.

Exercise   **Q1** 📖 Using (2) as your model, draw the feature structure for is_{pass} (remember that is_{pass} bears third singular AGR-φ features).

Q2 📖 Using (3) as your model, draw the feature structure for *finished* (as a participle).

Q3 📖 Using (4) as your model, then draw the tree for the VP *is finished*.

13.2 Progressive auxiliaries

Exercise   Consider the following data about the progressive be_{prog}:

(5)   (a)   The cat was leaving.   (main verb in gerund form)

        (b)   The cat was eating the tuna.   (VP: main verb in gerund form and complement)

        (c)   The tuna was being eaten.   (passive auxiliary in gerund form)

        (d)   *The cat was being eating.   (*another progressive auxiliary)

        (e)   *The cat was having eaten.   (*a perfective auxiliary)

        (f)   *The cat was willing eat.   (*a modal auxiliary)

Q4 ✏ Like the passive be_{pass}, the progressive be_{prog} allows both main verb and VPs headed by main verbs (5a and b) (but in their gerund form rather than participial form) but it also allows one *additional* form as a complement. Which one? ....

Q5 📖 Using (2) as your model, draw the feature structure for be_{prog}.

Q6 📖 Draw the feature structure for was_{prog}.

Q7 📖 Draw the feature structure for is_{prog}.

Be careful about the following things: make sure you have the SEM feature for the progressive. Change the restriction on the INTERNAL feature so that it allows main verbs and passive auxiliaries, but not any other V category (hint: use the ¬ notation and refer to one of the SEM features). Also for is_{prog} make sure you have AGR-φ features for third person singular.

Notation   The following is the feature structure for the gerund form of the passive auxiliary $being_{pass}$. This is the form of be_{pass} found in passive sentences like *The bread was being eaten.*

(6) $being_{pass}$

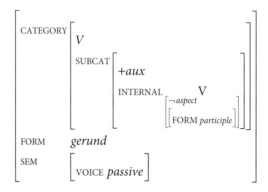

Exercise   Q8 📖 Using (3) and (6) as models, draw the tree for the gerund *eating* (as in *Calvin is eating*). Note: for the purposes of this question, you do not have to include any SUBCAT features, but you can if you like.

Exercise   Q9 📖 Draw the trees for the VPs in the following sentences (you can ignore the subject DPs, just draw the VP including the object DPs if any):

(a)   Calvin was eating.

(b)   Calvin was eating tuna. (*Be careful, tuna is a mass noun, which means there is a null determiner on it!*)

(c)   The tuna was eaten.

(d)   The tuna was being eaten.

13.3 Perfective auxiliaries

Exercise   Consider the following data about the perfect $have_{perf}$:

(7)   (a)   The cat had eaten.   (main verb – participle)

     (b)   The cat had eaten the tuna.   (VP: main verb – participle and complement)

     (c)   The tuna had been eaten.   (passive auxiliary in participial form)

(d)   The cat had been eating.   (progressive auxiliary in participial form)

(e)   *The cat had having eaten.   (*another perfective auxiliary)

(f)   *The cat has willen eat.   (*a modal auxiliary)

Q10 ➥ Like the progressive *be*$_{prog}$, the perfective *have*$_{perf}$ allows main verbs, VPs headed by main verbs, and passive VPs (7a–c) as complements, but it also allows one more form than the progressive.
Which one? ....

Q11 📖 Using (2) as your model, draw the feature structure for *have*$_{perf}$. Be careful about the following things: make sure you have the SEM feature for the perfect. Also, change the restriction on the INTERNAL feature so that it allows main verbs passives and progressives, but not any other V category (hint: use the ¬ notation).

Q12 📖 Using (2) as your model, draw the feature structure for *had*$_{perf}$.

Q13 📖 Using (2) as your model, draw the feature structure for *has*$_{perf}$. Keep in mind that *has* is only used with third-person singular subjects.

Notation   We need a few more feature structures here. Note that for both *be*$_{prog}$ and *be*$_{pass}$, we're going to have to have participial forms (*been*$_{prog}$ and *been*$_{pass}$). The feature structure for *been*$_{pass}$ will differ from (6) above in that it will have a [FORM *participle*] feature instead of a [FORM *gerund*] feature. The feature structure for *been*$_{prog}$ will be the same as your answer to Q5, except with a [FORM *participle*] feature instead of the [FORM *bare*] feature.

(8)   (a)   *been*$_{pass}$

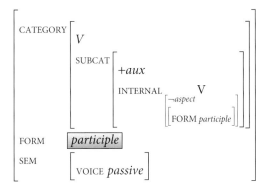

139

(b) *been*_{prog}

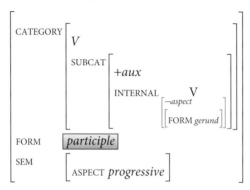

Exercise **Q14** 📖 Draw the trees for these complex VPs (ignore the subject DP):

(a) Calvin had eaten.

(b) Calvin had eaten tuna.

(c) The tuna had been eaten.

(d) Calvin had been eating.

(e) The tuna had been being eaten.

Comment Take a careful look at the tree in the answer to Q14(e) in the answer key below. Here we have the maximal set of verbs that can C-MERGE together. The passive *being*_{pass} can only take a main verb (or VP) as its complement. This is the bottom level of the tree (V_3P). At the level of V_2P, we have *be*_{prog} taking a passive V_3P as its complement. Finally, at V_1P, we have the perfect *have*_{perf} taking the progressive V_2P as its complement. Because of the restrictions on each of these verbs' internal features, this is the maximum number of auxiliaries that can appear in a main clause.

13.4 Modals

Discussion Next we turn our focus to modals and other instances of the category T. Let's start with the modal *should*:

(9) (a) The cat should eat. (main verb in bare form)

(b) The cat should eat the tuna. (VP: main verb in bare form and complement)

(c) The tuna should be eaten. (passive auxiliary in bare form)

(d) The cat should be eating. (progressive auxiliary in bare form)

(e) The cat should have eaten. (perfective auxiliary in bare form)

(f) *The cat should will eat. (*another modal auxiliary)

Essentially, modals can take any kind of V as a complement, but cannot take another T category (9f). As we discussed in unit 10, modals are of category T, not of category V. The complement of a modal is always in its bare form. We represent this with the following feature structure:

(10) *should*

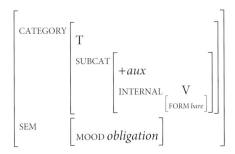

The tree for the TP (9b) is given in (11).

(11)

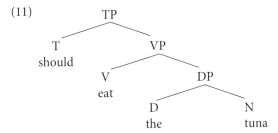

Exercise   Look at the following data:

(12) (a)   The cat will eat.   (main verb)

(b)   The cat will eat the tuna.   (VP: main verb and complement)

(c)   The tuna will be eaten.   (passive auxiliary)

(d)   The cat will be eating.   (progressive auxiliary)

(e)   The cat will have eaten.   (perfective auxiliary)

(f)   *The cat will should eat.   (*another modal auxiliary)

Q15 📖 Write out the feature structure for the word *will*. Use (10) as a model.

Q16 📖 Draw the trees for these complex TPs:

(a)   Calvin will eat.   (future tense)

(b)   Calvin will eat tuna.   (future tense)

(c)   The tuna will be eaten.   (future passive)

(d)   Calvin will be eating.   (future progressive)

141

(e)   Calvin will have eaten.   (future perfect)

(f)   The tuna will be being eaten.   (future progressive passive)

(g)   The tuna will have been eaten.   (perfect passive)

(h)   Calvin will have been eating.   (future perfect progressive)

(i)   The tuna will have been being eaten.   (future perfect progressive passive)

13.5 Tense

Discussion   Recall our discussion of the feature structures for the null tense nodes in unit 10. The feature structure for $\emptyset_{past}$ requires that the verb be in its preterite form; the structure for $\emptyset_{pres}$ requires that the verb be in its present tense form (which varies depending upon the person and number of the subject).

(13) $\emptyset_{past}$

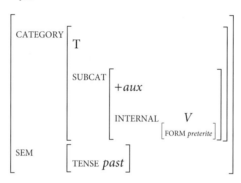

(14) $\emptyset_{pres}$

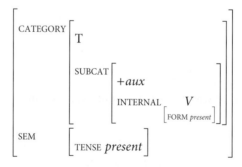

We'll return to the question of how we deal with the different forms of the present tense verb later in unit 16, once we have dealt with the mechanism of tagging.

142

Exercise **Q17** 📖 Draw the trees for the following TPs. Keep in mind that you have to have a null tense in all of them. You can leave the subject DP (*Calvin* or *the tuna*) out of your tree.

(a) Calvin ate.   (past tense)

(b) Calvin ate tuna.   (past tense)

(c) The tuna was eaten.   (past passive)

(d) Calvin was eating.   (past progressive)

(e) Calvin had eaten.   (past perfect)

(f) The tuna was being eaten.   (past progressive passive)

(g) The tuna had been eaten.   (past perfect passive)

(h) Calvin had been eating.   (past perfect progressive)

(i) The tuna had been being eaten.   (past perfect progressive passive)

13.6 *Do*, *does* and *did*

Discussion English has the peculiar property that in certain circumstances, present and past tense inflection on a verb is replaced by the auxiliary *do* or its variants *does* and *did*. Typically, we find *do* in three situations:

The first is when we negate a verb that has no other auxiliary (in other words, when we have only a null T ($\emptyset_{past}$ or $\emptyset_{pres}$) and a main verb in its preterite or past tense form):

(15) (a) Reggie chased the ball.

(b) Reggie did not chase the ball.

When we have negation (*not*), the past tense inflection appears on the auxiliary *did*, not on the verb (which appears in its bare form). We'll refer to this usage as *do*$_{neg}$ (and of course its inflected forms *did*$_{neg}$, *does*$_{neg}$).

The second case is when we want to emphasize the occurrence of the event described by the verb, or when we want to emphasize when the event happened or when we want to contrast the event.

(16) (a) Jean: Reggie chased the ball?

Bob: Oh, he *did* chase the ball indeed!

(b) Jean: I think Reggie is chasing the ball.

Bob: Not any more, but he *did* chase the ball!

(c) Jean: Did Reggie catch the mouse?

Bob: No, but he *did* catch a lizard.

We'll refer to this usage as *do/did/does*$_{emph}$ ("emph" stands for emphatic).

143

Finally, we have the set of forms that are used in questions seen in (17):

(17) (a) Did Calvin eat the beef waffles?

   (b) What did Calvin eat?

Let's refer to this last case as *do/did/does*$_Q$ (Q for questions). This last case is quite hard to deal with, because the auxiliary has inverted with the subject. We'll return to this third case in unit 22. In the present unit, we'll only deal with *do/does/did*$_{emph}$ and *do/does/did*$_{neg}$.

Exercise Consider only the negative cases of *do*. *Do* is followed by the negator *not*, which is followed by a verb.

Q18 ✆ What form does that following verb always take? (i.e. is it present? Is it preterite? Is it bare? Is it a participle? Is it a gerund?) ....

Notation We need two feature structures to account for the negative uses of *do*. The first is for *do/did/does* itself. The feature structure for *did*$_{neg}$ is given in (18). You'll notice that this auxiliary is of category T and selects for a complement that is of category Neg ([INTERNAL *Neg*]).

(18) *did*$_{neg}$

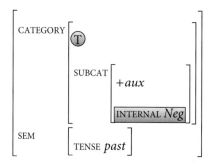

Next we need structure for the word *not*.

(19) *not*

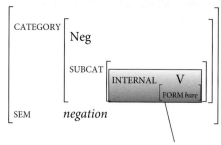

This feature structure selects for a complement that is a bare verb.

Exercise   **Q19** 📖 Using (18) as a model, draw the feature structures for *does*$_{neg}$.

Q20 📖 Draw the tree for the TP *did not eat*.

Challenge   The *not* that follows *did/does/do*$_{neg}$ requires that the following verb be in its bare form. What are we to make of the *not* words in the following?

(20)   (a)   is not eating

(b)   has not eaten

(c)   was not eaten

How can we account for the fact that *not* is followed by a participial form in (20b and c) and the gerund in (20a)? Hint: you don't really have the tools to solve this problem yet, but as you move along, you'll learn about movement and tagging. In the meantime, try to be creative and see if you can solve this problem.

Exercise   Next we turn to *do*$_{emph}$.

Q21 📖 Using (18) as a model, but being very careful about the INTERNAL feature, draw the feature structures for *did*$_{emph}$.

Q22 📖 Draw the tree for the TP *DID*$_{emph}$ *eat*.

Summary   In this unit, we've practiced applying the C-MERGE to one fairly intricate set of data involving English auxiliaries. We saw how the INTERNAL feature is used to restrict what can appear as the complements to various auxiliaries, thus deriving the order they must appear in as well as the form of their complements.

Suggested further reading

- Carnie (2006), chapter 9
- Huddleston and Pullum (2005), chapter 3
- Kim and Sells (2008), chapter 8
- Lobeck (2000), chapters 4, 5, 6, 7, 8 and 9
- van Gelderen (2010), chapter 6

Answers to questions

Q1 Is_{pass}

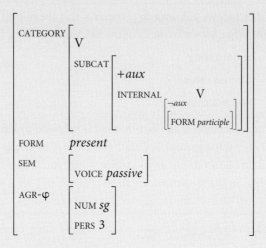

Q2 *finished (participle)*

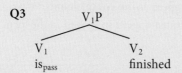

Q3

```
            V₁P
          /     \
       V₁        V₂
     is_pass    finished
```

Q4–7 Be_{prog} also allows the passive auxiliary as a complement. Note that three forms are excluded: modals, perfective auxiliaries and other progressive auxiliaries. Modals are excluded by making reference to the category V (modals are category T). The perfective and progressive auxiliaries are excluded by requiring that the value of the INTERNAL feature is $V_{[\neg ASPECT]}$ (any verb that does not bear an ASPECT FEATURE).

146

Q5 *be*$_{prog}$

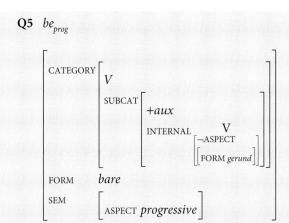

Q6 *was*$_{prog}$

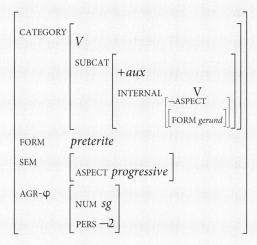

Q7 *is*$_{prog}$

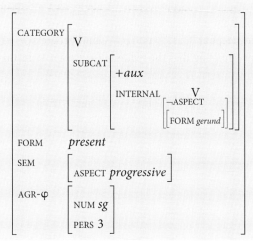

Q8 *Eating*

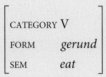

$$\begin{bmatrix} \text{CATEGORY} & \text{V} \\ \text{FORM} & \textit{gerund} \\ \text{SEM} & \textit{eat} \end{bmatrix}$$

Note: The verb *eat* has both INTERNAL and EXTERNAL SUBCAT features. We're just leaving those off for simplicity's sake.

Q9 (a)

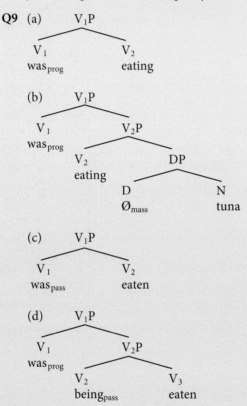

(b)

(c)

(d)

Q10 *Have*$_{perf}$ also allows the progressive auxiliary. This can be marked one of a number of ways. The easiest way would be: V$_{\neg perf}$ (any verb that does not bear a [ASPECT *perfect*] feature). Modals are ruled out as complements because they are not of category V.

Q11 *have*$_{perf}$

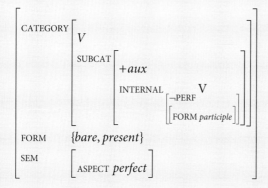

Note: *have* is both the *bare* FORM of the verb and the FORM of the verb found in the present tense in all cases except where there is a third-person singular subject. If you listed either of these, you were on the right track.

Q12 *had*$_{perf}$

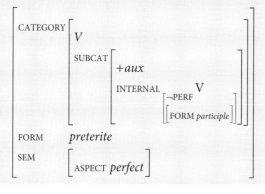

Q13 *has*$_{perf}$

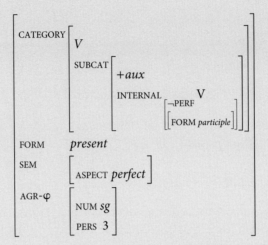

Note: *Has* is only found in the present tense (it is never the bare form). It also is limited to third person singulars.

Q14 (a)

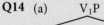

(b)

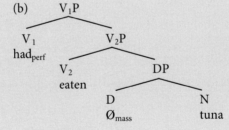

(c)

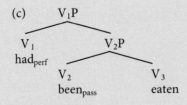

(d)

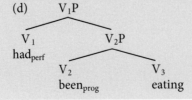

(e)

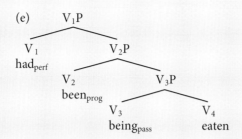

Q15 *will*

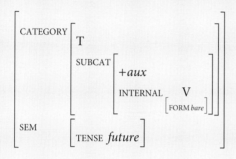

$$\begin{bmatrix} \text{CATEGORY} & \begin{bmatrix} \text{T} \\ \text{SUBCAT} \begin{bmatrix} +aux \\ \text{INTERNAL} & \text{V} \\ & \begin{bmatrix} \text{FORM } bare \end{bmatrix} \end{bmatrix} \end{bmatrix} \\ \text{SEM} & \begin{bmatrix} \text{TENSE } future \end{bmatrix} \end{bmatrix}$$

Q16 (a)

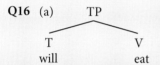

(b)

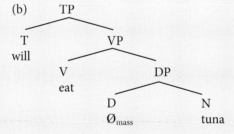

(c)

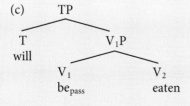

(d)

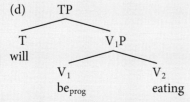

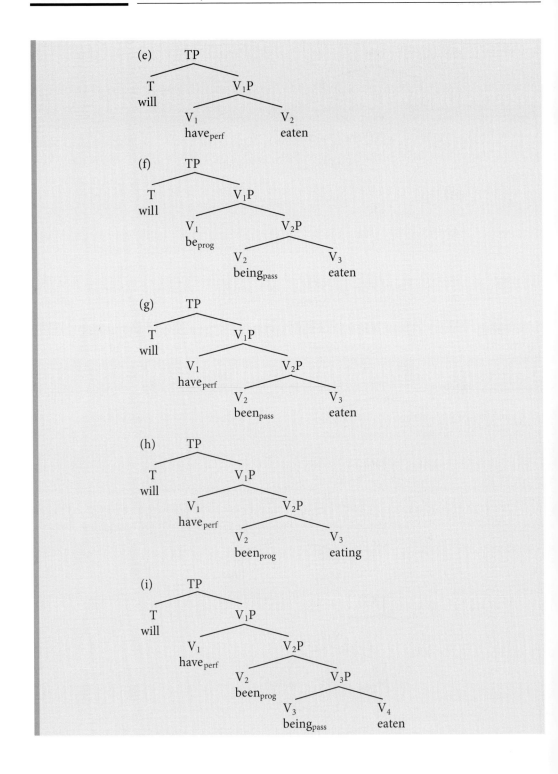

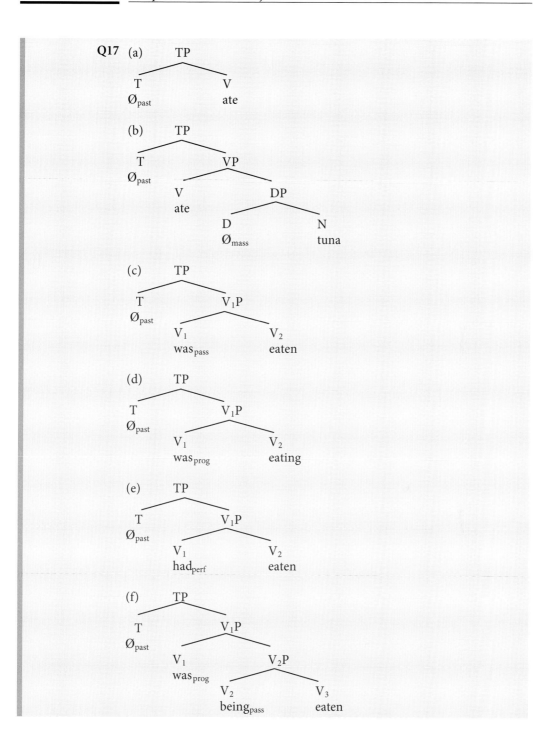

Q17

(a)
```
        TP
       /  \
      T     V
    Ø_past  ate
```

(b)
```
        TP
       /  \
      T     VP
    Ø_past  /  \
          V      DP
          ate    /  \
               D      N
             Ø_mass  tuna
```

(c)
```
        TP
       /  \
      T     V₁P
    Ø_past  /  \
          V₁     V₂
        was_pass eaten
```

(d)
```
        TP
       /  \
      T     V₁P
    Ø_past  /  \
          V₁     V₂
        was_prog eating
```

(e)
```
        TP
       /  \
      T     V₁P
    Ø_past  /  \
          V₁     V₂
        had_perf eaten
```

(f)
```
        TP
       /  \
      T     V₁P
    Ø_past  /  \
          V₁      V₂P
        was_prog  /  \
                V₂      V₃
              being_pass eaten
```

(g)

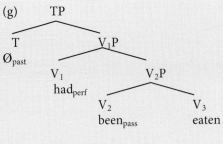

(h)

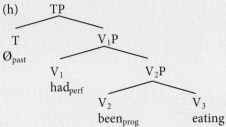

(i)

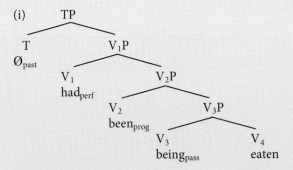

Q18 When combined with *do, not* is always followed by a verb or auxiliary in the bare form.

Q19 *does*ₙₑg

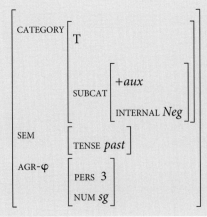

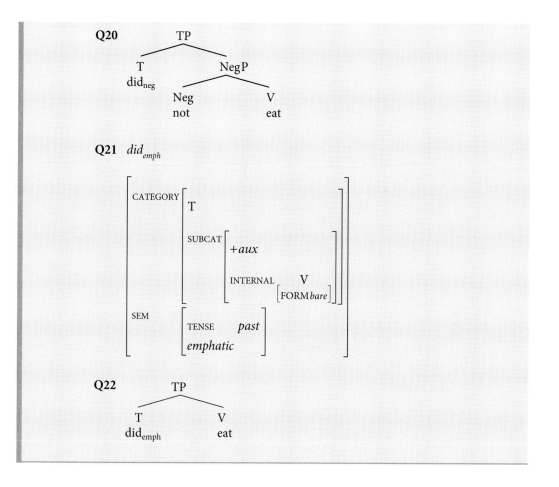

Q20

TP

T
did_neg

NegP

Neg
not

V
eat

Q21 *did_emph*

CATEGORY [T]

SUBCAT [+aux]

INTERNAL V [FORM bare]

SEM

TENSE past
emphatic

Q22

TP

T
did_emph

V
eat

UNIT 14 SPECIFIERS: VP AND TP

Objectives:

- Learn about the EXTERNAL feature and the specifiers of VP.
- Apply the operation MOVE to get DPs from the specifiers of VP into the specifiers of TP.
- Learn about CASE as a motivation for movement.

Comment In the last few units, we looked at the way in which the INTERNAL features and the MERGE rule gave us complements. Next, we turn our attention to EXTERNAL features. These introduce the arguments that are traditionally called "subjects." Although we'll also use EXTERNAL features to account for the position of possessive nouns.

14.1 Specifiers

Definition The **specifier** is an argument that is required by the EXTERNAL feature.[1] These are arguments that typically end up being the subject of the sentence (1) or the possessor in a complex DP (2) which is marked with the *'s* ending:

(1) The cat ate all the tuna.   *Subject of a sentence*

(2) The cat's plate of tuna.   *Possessive marked DP (using 's)*

Exercise **Q1** ✏ Identify whether the underlined DPs in the following sentences and DPs are specifiers or complements relative to the boldfaced **head**. Circle the correct answer.

(a) The box **of** tissues fell into the bath.	Compl.	Specifier
(b) The box of tissues **fell** into the bath.	Compl.	Specifier
(c) The box of tissues fell **into** the bath.	Compl.	Specifier
(d) Calvin's **book** of articles caused a sensation.	Compl.	Specifier
(e) Calvin's book of articles **caused** a sensation.	Compl.	Specifier

---

[1] This is the modern usage of the term "specifier." In older work, other elements took on the role of the specifier including determiners and intensifiers. Current work eschews this usage, but if you look at older books on syntax, you will almost certainly come across the term being used that way.

156

(f) Calvin's book **of** articles caused a sensation   Compl.   Specifier

(g) Calvin's book of articles **caused** a sensation   Compl.   Specifier

Discussion Specifiers are introduced to satisfy a head's EXTERNAL feature. Take, for example, the verb *kiss*. Recall from unit 8 that *kiss* has the following feature structure:

(3) *kiss*

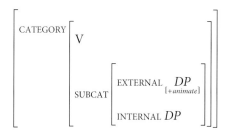

The INTERNAL feature tells us that *kiss* must be C-merged with a DP that signifies the entity who is kissed. If we apply C-MERGE to *kiss* and a DP like *the cat*, we get a tree like (4):

(4)

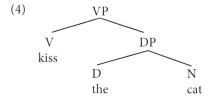

Definition When we do a MERGE operation that satisfies the requirements of a feature we say that feature is **checked**. The merging of *the cat* with *kiss* "checks" the INTERNAL feature of the head *kiss*.

Definition **SPECIFIER-MERGE (S-MERGE)** combines two (or more) items together into a constituent as required by the EXTERNAL features of one of the items. The constituent is given the label of the head.

Discussion The Principle of Full Interpretation requires that all features are compatible. The feature structure for *kiss* seen above in (3) also contains the EXTERNAL feature that requires a DP that is animate (only animate things can kiss). We need to check this feature as well. We do this by merging a constituent that meets the EXTERNAL requirements of the verb, thus checking that feature. Since the verb *kiss* requires an animate DP, we merge one like *the man*. S-MERGE results in another VP label above the one created by the MERGE with the complement:

(5)

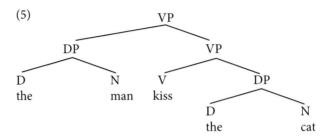

The resultant structure is still a VP.

Ordering Note that if we look at trees from the bottom to the top, the C-MERGE process has to apply before the S-MERGE rule. We will stipulate this ordering.

14.2 Movement

Discussion All the modifiers or arguments of the head *kiss* are part of the VP headed by *kiss*. This is part of a general pattern whereby modifiers and arguments of a head form a constituent with that head (recall this from unit 10).

There are two serious problems with the tree in (5), however. Most importantly, the tree in (5) actually has the subject in the wrong position. The other problem has to do with the feature [+*animate*]. We'll deal with the positional problem in this unit and the problem with the feature in unit 16.

In the tree in (5), the DP *the man* is the specifier of the verb *kiss*. This is because it satisfies the EXTERNAL feature of *kiss*. However, notice what would happen if we were to merge this VP with a T node like *will*:

(6)   TP

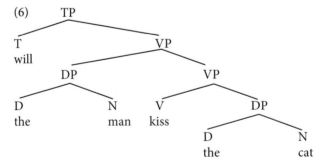

Assuming that our intended sentence is a statement, not a question, the only possible order here is unacceptable. (It is OK as a question, but that's beside the point):

(7) Will the man kiss the cat. (*as a statement)

The grammatical system we've developed here predicts that this is the only possible order! It incorrectly predicts that the acceptable form *The man will kiss the cat* will be unacceptable. There is no obvious way to S-MERGE the DP *the man* as a specifier to the V to check the verb's EXTERNAL feature, yet have it appear to the left of T categories. The situation gets even worse when we start using stacked VPs representing voice and aspect. Since the DP must be merged to satisfy the main verb's EXTERNAL feature, our grammar actually predicts (incorrectly) that the subject will appear to the right of all these auxiliary verbs:

(8)   *Will have been being the cat kissed.

You might think that the sensible answer to this question is to say that EXTERNAL arguments are not merged as part of the VP, but instead are the result of an external feature on the T category *will*. But notice that auxiliaries like *will* do not impose restrictions on the animacy of the subject, and animate subjects are required even when an auxiliary is present. The selection of the animacy of the subject is a property of the EXTERNAL feature of the **main** verb. Nevertheless, these EXTERNAL arguments appear to the left of auxiliaries. In order to explain this, we'll have to appeal to a new kind of rule: a rule of movement. We'll claim that external arguments start in the specifier of VP but then move to and surface in a position immediately to the left of tense auxiliaries and modal verbs. This position is the specifier of the T head (the specifier of TP).

Notation There are two interchangeable devices to indicate movement. The first notation involves drawing the tree putting elements in the places where they start (in this case in the specifier of the VP), then drawing an arrow pointing to the place where the word ends up:

(9)

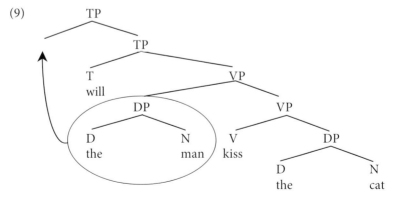

The other notation is to draw the moved element in the position it appears in on the surface, and leave a special notational symbol *t* (for "trace") in the position where the word started:

(10)

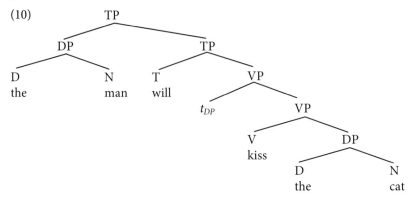

The two notations can even be mixed. In the following tree, I've used the trace notation, but indicated the movement with an arrow:

(11)

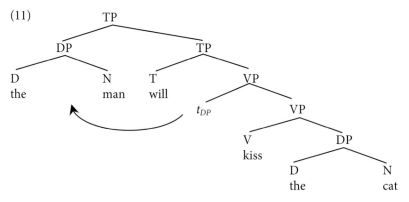

These notations say exactly the same thing. In this book, I'll mainly use the first notation unless drawing all the arrows will make the diagram incomprehensible, or I want to emphasize a single movement, in which case I will use the mixed notation.

Exercise **Q2** 📖 For each of the following sentences undo the movement of the subject DP. If there is a null T node (such as $\emptyset_{past}$ or $\emptyset_{pres}$), indicate its position as well!

      e.g. The tuna had been eaten. → $\emptyset_{past}$ had been the tuna eaten.

(a)   The cat should eat the tuna.

(b)   The cat ate the tuna.

(c)   The cat had eaten the tuna.

(d)   The cat had been eating the tuna.

Q3 📖 Using (9) as a model, draw the trees for the underlying forms you developed for Q2 (a–d) above. Be sure to start the subject DP in the specifier of the most deeply embedded VP (the VP of the main verb).

14.3 Case

Discussion   Movement is a powerful device, and we want to restrict the situations in which it occurs, so that the operation can't apply blindly and randomly move stuff around.

Observe that we have moved the subject into the specifier of TP. This was motivated by the empirical fact that in English the subject appears immediately before any T elements (such as *will*). This proposal predicts that it is a special property of T that motivates the movement of the subject DP into this position. So in order to limit DP movement, we should look for some special property that ties DPs to Tense.

Let's start with pronouns. As we observed way back in the early part of this book, pronouns exhibit a variation called **case**. Pronouns that appear in the subject position take nominative case (*I, he, she, we, they*); pronouns that appear in any other position (other than possessives) take accusative case (*me, him, her, us, them*). In fact, nominative case actually seems to be restricted to the subject position of tensed clauses. In English, infinitives are marked with a special tense marker *to*. The subjects of infinitive verbs in English, when they are allowed at all, must take accusative case.

(12) (a)   *I* left

(b)   Bill wants [*me* to leave].

Nominative case on pronouns is a property tied to Tense. Only finite verbs (those that are in present, past or future tense) take a nominative subject.

Of course, in English, only pronouns show overt case morphology. But we've already seen cases where semantically relevant material is silent (such as null determiners and null T words). Consider the possibility that all nouns in English bear case features, they just don't realize that case overtly as a suffix. Given that in other languages (such as Latin, for example) all nouns express case, this possibility is not entirely out of the range of possibility.

Definition   **Abstract Case** is the name given to the case features associated with a particular DP, whether they are realized morphologically or not. It is a tradition to distinguish abstract Case from morphologically marked case by capitalizing the first letter of Case when we are talking about the abstract variety. Abstract nominative Case is a property of the subjects of tensed clauses; accusative is the Case on objects; and possessive is the Case marked with *'s* in English.

Exercise **Q4** ✏ Identify the abstract Case taken by the underlined DP in each of the following sentences. Nom stands for nominative Case, Acc stands for accusative Case and Poss stands for possessive (or genitive) Case.

(a)	<u>The cat</u> ate the dog's tuna.	Nom	Acc	Poss
(b)	The cat ate <u>the dog</u>'s tuna.	Nom	Acc	Poss
(c)	The cat ate <u>the dog's tuna</u>.	Nom	Acc	Poss
(d)	<u>He</u> ate her tuna.	Nom	Acc	Poss
(e)	He ate <u>her</u> tuna.	Nom	Acc	Poss
(f)	He ate <u>it</u>.	Nom	Acc	Poss

Discussion We see from other languages such as German where determiners express case (13), that determiners are elements that bear case. We'll assume the same is true here.

(13) (a) der   Nominative masculine "the"

  (b) den   Accusative masculine "the"

  (c) dem   Dative masculine "the"

  (d) des   Possessive masculine "the"

Notation CASE is a feature found on determiners and +D elements. Its values include *nom, acc* and *poss*.

Challenge We've proposed a feature called FORM for verbs and a feature called CASE for nouns. Could you collapse these two features into one single feature? Why or why not?

14.4 Movement motivated by case

Discussion Let's start again with pronouns. The feature structure for a pronoun such as *he* is:

(14) *He*

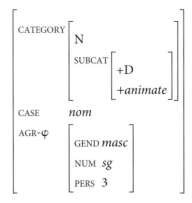

Let's propose that the feature structure for T categories such as *will, should, Ø_{past}* or *Ø_{pres}* will contain the requirement that the EXTERNAL feature contain a restriction that it be occupied by an element with a [CASE *nom*] feature:

(15) *will*

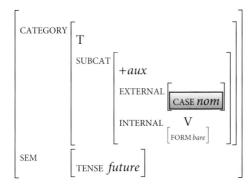

Recall the lexical entry for *kiss*:

(16) *kiss*

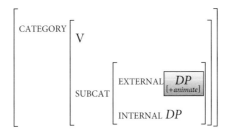

Notice that *kiss* does not have any specification for CASE, but it does require a DP that is +*animate*. *Will*, by contrast, doesn't make any semantic restriction on animacy in its external feature, but does require that its specifier be in nominative Case. *He* satisfies both these requirements. However, note that *he* can't simultaneously satisfy both requirements! It is only one word and these two requirements are of different heads. Movement is the solution to this conflict. Movement only occurs where a word simultaneously has to satisfy multiple requirements of different categories. In this case, full interpretation requires that *he* first satisfies the [+*animate*] DP (or +D) requirement of the verb *kiss*. To do this we S-MERGE the pronoun as the specifier of the VP to check the EXTERNAL feature of the verb:

(17)

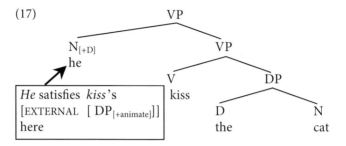

This structure is merged as a complement to *will*, and satisfies the V requirement of the INTERNAL feature of *will*.

(18)

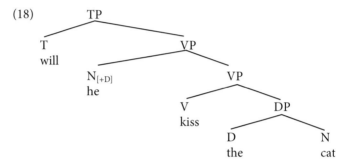

But *will* also requires a specifier, crucially one with nominative Case, so we move (or perhaps a better term is **remerge**) the pronoun *he*.

(19)

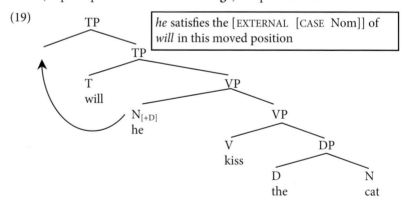

This results in the surface string with the correct order (20).

(20) He will kiss the cat.

Exercise **Q5** 📖 Draw the feature structure for *the* when it is used for abstract nominative Case. Hint: use the feature structure you developed for *the* back in unit 12 as a starting point, then modify it using (14) as a model to add the Case feature.

Q6 📖 Can you use the same feature structure for the *the* in *Calvin ate the tuna*? Why or why not?

Discussion   Merging a DP in one place and then moving to its final position might seem like a particularly arcane way to get subject arguments into the correct position. You might be wondering why we don't just draw them up there in the first place. On a theoretical level, it allows us to ensure that S-MERGE always links items that are related by some feature. However, there is empirical evidence for this as well. Consider the quantifier *all*, which can take another DP as a complement:

(21)

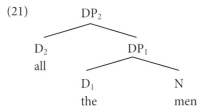

What is interesting about this determiner is that it can appear between the T node and the main verb:

(22) (a)   All the men will go.

(b)   The men will <u>all</u> go.

All modifies *the men*, even though it is split from *the men* by the auxiliary. Notice that the position where *all* appears in (22b) is precisely the position that the subject DP is predicted to start in if it were S-merged in the VP. We might hypothesize that the tree in (21) is S-merged into the specifier position of the VP:

(23)

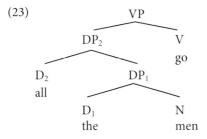

After the T C-merges with the VP, the lower DP$_1$ moves to the specifier of TP position to check the abstract nominative Case features.

(24)

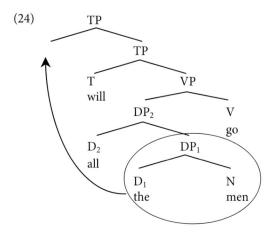

This results in the right order for (22b). This phenomenon is known as **quantifier float**, and is evidence for the idea that subject DPs start off in the specifier of V and move to the specifier of TP.

Exercise **Q7** 📖 Using (24) as a model, draw the tree for *The cats all ate the tuna.* Keep in mind that you will have to use a $\emptyset_{past}$ T node.

Challenge Hypothesize on why it is possible to move the whole complex DP *all the men* if *the men* is the DP bearing the CASE feature. How would you go about proving your hypothesis?

Exercise **Q8** 📖 Using the following data from Irish, make an argument supporting the claim that subjects start out (and finish) in the specifier of VP (i.e. subjects in Irish do not move to the specifier of TP). Assume that *tá+ag* are just like *be*$_{prog}$+gerund in English, except that *ag* is a prefix on the main verb.

(25) Tá an cat ag-ithe na héisc.

　　　Is the cat ing-eat the fish

　　　"The cat is eating the fish."

Summary In this unit, we've examined how subjects of VPs are introduced into the tree. Because they are required by a verb's EXTERNAL feature, they are S-merged as specifiers of the VP. Empirical evidence for this position comes from floated quantifiers in English and the position of subjects in Irish, as seen in Q8. In order to account for why subjects typically appear further to the left in English, we proposed that subject DPs move from the specifier of VP to the specifier of TP in order to "check" their nominative Case. Nominative Case is a property of a variety of Tense categories (but not all!). T categories, such as *will* and $\emptyset_{pres}$, have an external feature that requires an element with nominative Case. In order to satisfy this requirement, the DP in the specifier of the VP is moved into the specifier of TP to check this feature.

Suggested further reading

- Carnie (2006), chapters 6, 7 and 10
- Chomsky (1995), chapter 4
- Hornstein, Nunes and Grohman (2005), chapter 4
- Kim and Sells (2008), chapter 5
- Koopman and Sportiche (1991)
- Radford (2004), chapters 7 and 8
- Roberts (1997), chapter 2
- Sportiche (1988)
- http://en.wikipedia.org/wiki/Specifier

Answers to questions

Q1 (a) C; (b) S; (c) C; (d) S; (e) S; (f) C; (g) C

Q2 (a)   Should the cat eat the tuna.   (note, not a question!)

(b) $\emptyset_{past}$ the cat ate the tuna.

(c) $\emptyset_{past}$ had$_{perf}$ the cat eaten the tuna.

(d) $\emptyset_{past}$ had$_{perf}$ be$_{prog}$ the cat eating the tuna.

Q3 (a)

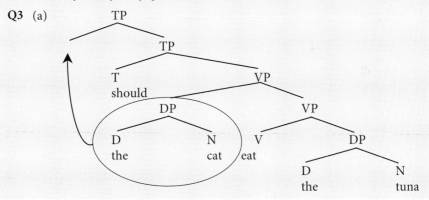

Q3 (b)

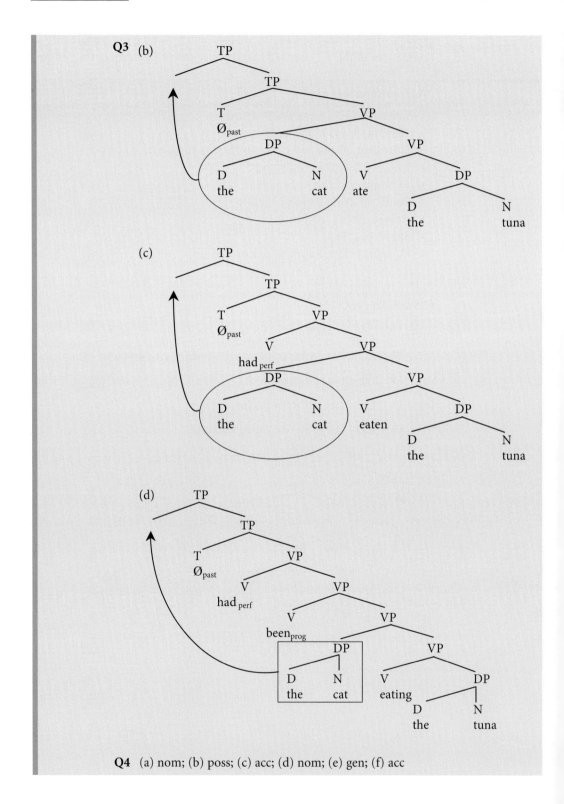

(c)

(d)

Q4 (a) nom; (b) poss; (c) acc; (d) nom; (e) gen; (f) acc

Q5 *the*_{nom}

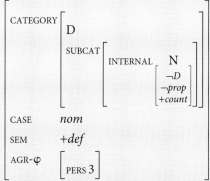

$$\begin{bmatrix} \text{CATEGORY} & \begin{bmatrix} \text{D} \\ \text{SUBCAT} \begin{bmatrix} \text{INTERNAL} & \begin{bmatrix} \text{N} \\ \neg D \\ \neg prop \\ +count \end{bmatrix} \end{bmatrix} \end{bmatrix} \\ \text{CASE} \quad nom \\ \text{SEM} \quad +def \\ \text{AGR-}\varphi \quad \begin{bmatrix} \text{PERS } 3 \end{bmatrix} \end{bmatrix}$$

Q6 Right now, nothing prevents you from using this feature structure in that position. However, since we know that pronouns in this position bear accusative case, it's likely that we'll want a different feature structure for the *the* in object position, one that has a [CASE *acc*] feature. This will parallel the differently cased determiners of German.

Q7

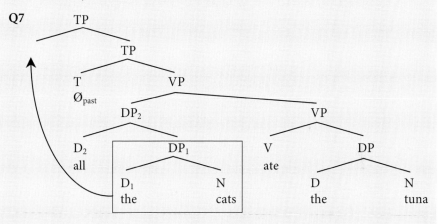

Q8 In Irish the subject follows auxiliaries like *Tá*, but precedes the main verb. This is the same position as floated quantifiers in English. It appears as if Irish does not require that DPs check their CASE features in the specifier of DP (or perhaps they lack abstract CASE).

UNIT 15 SPECIFIERS: NP AND DP

Objectives:

- Learn about the EXTERNAL feature and the specifiers of NP.
- Examine the behavior of the 's possessive marker in English.
- Apply the operation MOVE to get DPs from the specifiers of NP into the specifiers of DP.
- Learn about possessive Case as a motivation for movement.
- Learn about possessive pronoun readjustment rules.

15.1 Subjects of DPs

Comment   In the last unit we looked at DPs in the specifiers of VPs and how they moved to the specifier of TP. The topic of this unit is the closely related phenomenon of specifiers in NPs and DPs.

As we have observed before, there are parallels between verbs and nouns in terms of their arguments. This is particularly true when the verb and the noun are morphologically related.

(1)   (a)   The cat ate the tuna.

(b)   the cat's eating of the tuna

Just as *the cat* is the EXTERNAL argument of *eat* in (1a), we can argue that *the cat* in (1b) is the EXTERNAL argument of the nominal *eating*. The feature structure then for a noun like *eating* looks like (2). The main difference between this and the verbal structure is that with nouns the arguments are typically optional. (Note that this noun *eating* is a gerund here.) We'll mark this nominal usage of the gerund with the category N instead of V. The parentheses on the values of the INTERNAL and EXTERNAL features indicate that the argument is optional.

(2)   *eating*_N

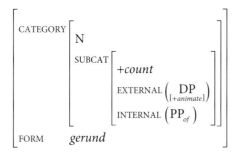

Exercise   **Q1** 📖 Write out the feature structure for the verb *destroy* and the noun *destruction* based on the following data. Do not try to give a FORM feature; concentrate instead on the nature of the CATEGORY features.

(a)   The army destroyed the city.

(b)   the army's destruction of the city

(c)   The wind destroyed the city.

(d)   the wind's destruction of the city

Comment   Next, let's consider if anything else can be an EXTERNAL argument with nouns.

Exercise   **Q2** 📖 Your task is to compare the distribution of clear subjects of nouns like those in (a) with possessives (b). What does this tell us about EXTERNAL arguments with nouns? Is there any difference in terms of structure between (a) and (b)?

(a)   the army's destruction of the city

(b)   the cat's can of tuna

Q3 📖 Based on your answer to Q2, write out the feature structure for the noun *can* in (b) (Hint: it's going to look a lot like your feature structure for *destruction*.)

15.2 Possessive *'s*

Comment   Next let's turn our attention to the suffix *'s*. This suffix is puzzling for a number of reasons, not the least of which is that it doesn't attach to the noun it seems to modify. In fact, it appears at the end of the noun phrase, even when that noun phrase ends in some category other than a noun.

(3)   (a)   [the man]'s hat

(b)   [the man from California]'s hat

(c)   [the man I believe in]'s hat

(d)   [the man who talks too quickly]'s hat

(e)   [the man who is afraid]'s hat

(f)   [the man who left]'s hat

In (3b), 's is found at the end of the word *California*, but it isn't California's hat, but the man's hat, even if he is from California! Sentences (3c–f) show an even more disturbing pattern, the 's attaches to a preposition (3c), an adverb (3d), an adjective (3e) and even a verb (3f). 's appears to behave differently than any other suffix in English, which always attaches to a head noun.

Exercise If the possessor DP is in the specifier of the NP as we've hypothesized, this predicts that we should be able to C-MERGE this complex NP with a D like *a* giving a DP:

(4)

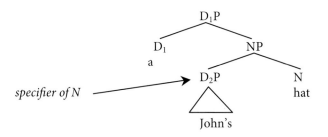

specifier of N

Notation: I've used a triangle to simplify the diagram here. The triangle implies that the usual structure under it is present even though it isn't spelled out. *You should avoid using triangles in your own trees.*

However, this results in an unacceptable form:.

(5)   *a [John]'s hat

Q4 📖 Is the phrase *a man's hat* a counterexample to this claim? (Hint: what noun is *a* modifying? Is it *man* or *hat*? So which N does *a* C-MERGE with?)

Definition **Complementary distribution**: Two elements are in complementary distribution if they cannot appear at the same time. For example, in English, unaspirated stop consonants like /p/ can appear after /s/ and aspirated stops like /pʰ/ can appear anywhere except after /s/. These two sounds are in complementary distribution. When two elements are in complementary distribution, it entails that they are members of the basic category.

Discussion The fact that 's and *a* cannot co-occur on the same noun (that is, they are in complementary distribution) suggests that they are both part of the same class: determiners. If this is the case, then the tree for a DP like *John's hat* might look more like (6) (based loosely on Abney 1987):

(6)

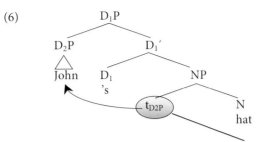

John starts out as the specifier of *hat*. It does so, so that it can satisfy the EXTERNAL feature of *hat*:

(7) *hat*

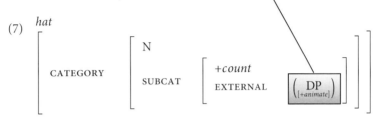

It then moves to the specifier of D$_1$P as indicated by the arrow in (6).

Exercise **Q5** 📖 Why does the DP move? Try to explain the movement by proposing a feature structure for *'s*.

Exercise **Q6** 📖 Draw the tree for sentence (3b), using the tree in (6) as a model, but don't use a triangle!

Exercise **Q7** 📖 Look carefully at the tree you have drawn for Q6. This kind of analysis explains the data in (3), where *'s* comes after words like *California*. Explain why trees like the one you drew for Q6 allow the *'s* to follow words that are not the actual possessor (such as *California* in (3b)).

Exercise In unit 14, exercise Q8, you were asked to argue that subjects in Irish stayed in the specifier of the VP, and did not raise to the specifier of TP. In this exercise, you are asked to make a similar argument about the possessors in Hungarian.[1]

Q8 📖 Consider the following data. Draw a tree for (8); base it on the tree above in (6), but put the possessor in the specifier of NP instead of DP, and don't indicate movement. Ignore the ending on *hat*, it is irrelevant to the question.

(8) az én kalapom

the I hat.1SG

"my hat"

---

[1] Data from Szabolcsi (1994).

Exercise **Q9** 📖 Propose a feature structure for the Hungarian determiner *az*.

Exercise Hungarian has another possessive construction, seen in (9).

(9) Marinak a   kalapja

Mary   the hat.3sG

"Mary's hat"

Q10 📖 Is this construction more like the English *'s* construction or more like the Hungarian *az* construction?

Q11 📖 Draw the tree for (9).

Q12 📖 Draw the feature structure for the Hungarian determiner *a*.

Comment In the Hungarian example in (8), we see both a pronoun *én* and the determiner *az*. In English, we don't get both a determiner and a pronoun, we only get a special possessive determiner. For example, we don't get *he's* but *his*. To account for this we'll appeal to morphological readjustment rules, as we did to account for variation in the way the *-en* suffix surfaces in English participles. Let's assume that pronouns move just the way other nouns do. So the tree for *his hat* starts out as *'s he hat*. Then movement of *he* occurs to satisfy the case requirement on the EXTERNAL feature of *'s*.

(10)

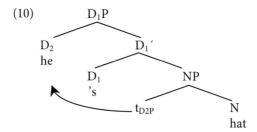

This results in the string *he's hat*. A morphological readjustment rule of *he's* → *his* applies giving the surface form *his hat*. The morphological readjustment rules for English are:

(11) me's → my

you's → your

he's → his

her's → her

it's → its (this one is just orthographic)

us's → our

them's → their

Exercise   **Q13** 📖 Draw the tree for *my hat.*

Challenge   Provide an account of the possessive pronouns *mine, your, his, hers, ours, theirs* that show up in sentences like *She read her book and I read mine.* There are many possible solutions here, but I suggest you try one with a special null noun ($\varnothing_N$) that means something like "thing possessed." This null noun will obligatorily take a pronominal possessor. You'll also need a readjustment rule to get this possessor to turn into *mine, hers,* etc.

Summary   In this unit, we extended the notion of specifier from subjects to any element introduced by an EXTERNAL feature, including possessors in DPs. We claimed that possessive *'s* is a determiner, because it is in complementary distribution with other determiners. Claiming this also explains why it follows any modifiers of the possessor. In parallel to the discussion in the previous unit, we argued that possessors start in the specifier of the N, in order to satisfy the EXTERNAL feature of the N. The possessor then moves to the specifier of the *'s* determiner for case reasons. We also saw some crosslinguistic variation in the position of the possessor; in Hungarian with the determiner *az,* it stays in the specifier of the NP. Finally, in order to explain the absence of *'s* with pronouns, we appealed to some morphological readjustment rules.

Suggested further reading

- Abney (1987)
- Adger (2003), chapter 7
- Carnie (2006), chapters 6, 7 and 10
- Harley (2006), chapter 6
- Huddleston and Pullum (2005), chapter 5
- Koopman and Sportiche (1991)
- van Gelderen (2010), chapter 9
- http://en.wikipedia.org/wiki/Specifier

Answers to questions

Q1 The only difference between these and the corresponding entries for *eat* and *eating* is that non-living things can destroy but not eat. Therefore, there is no +*animate* on the external argument.

(a)   *destroy*

$$\begin{bmatrix} \text{CATEGORY} & \begin{bmatrix} V \\ \text{SUBCAT} & \begin{bmatrix} \text{EXTERNAL} & \text{DP} \\ \text{INTERNAL} & \text{DP} \end{bmatrix} \end{bmatrix} \\ \text{FORM} & \textit{bare} \end{bmatrix}$$

(I've left the SEM feature off here, but you could include it.)

(b)   *destruction*

$$\begin{bmatrix} \text{CATEGORY} & \begin{bmatrix} N \\ \text{SUBCAT} & \begin{bmatrix} +\textit{count} \\ \text{EXTERNAL} & (\text{DP}) \\ \text{INTERNAL} & (\text{PP}_{of}) \end{bmatrix} \end{bmatrix} \end{bmatrix}$$

Q2 True possessive nouns appear in exactly the same position as the subject nouns we identified before: they appear before the head noun and are marked with the 's marker. This suggests that possessive nouns are also EXTERNAL arguments.

Q3 *can*

$$\begin{bmatrix} \text{CATEGORY} & \begin{bmatrix} N \\ \text{SUBCAT} & \begin{bmatrix} +\textit{count} \\ \text{EXTERNAL} & (\text{DP}) \\ \text{INTERNAL} & (\text{PP}_{of}) \end{bmatrix} \end{bmatrix} \end{bmatrix}$$

Q4 No, it is not a counterexample. The *a* here modifies *man* (so is part of the DP *[a man]*, not *hat*. *Hat* has no obvious determiner on it, even in this example.

Q5 *'s*

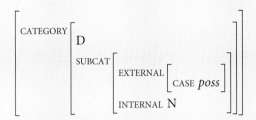

This feature structure requires that *'s* have an element in its specifier with a poss case. The DP raises to this position to satisfy this requirement. Note that other determiners (e.g. *a, the*) do *not* have this requirement, which explains why they don't follow a noun.

Q6

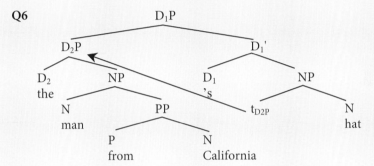

Q7 Because the possessor DP (D_2P) is in the specifier of the D_1P headed by *'s*, everything inside that constituent will precede the *'s* determiner, including things that follow the head noun in D_1P

Q8

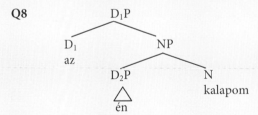

Q9 *az*

$$\left[\begin{array}{l} \text{CATEGORY} \left[\text{D} \right] \\ \text{SUBCAT} \left[\text{INTERNAL N} \right] \end{array} \right]$$

Note that there is no EXTERNAL feature for Hungarian *az*, which means the possessor of *kalapom* does not raise to the specifier position of D_1P.

Q10 It is more like the English *'s* construction. The possessor DP seems to have raised into the specifier position of the *'s* DP.

Q11

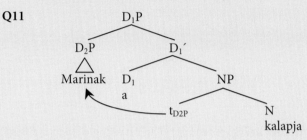

Q12 *a (Hungarian)*

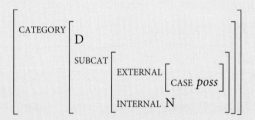

(This is identical to the entry for English *'s*.)

Q13

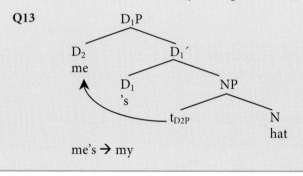

me's → my

UNIT 16 TAGGING

> **Objectives:**
> - Learn about using tags to pass semantic features up to a functional head.
> - Learn about using tags to pass AGR-φ features up to a functional head.
> - Learn about using tags to force movement.

16.1 Head agreement: animacy in DPs

Comment Consider the following feature structure for the verb *kiss* and the pair of sentences in (2).

(1)   *kiss*

$$
\begin{bmatrix}
\text{CATEGORY} & V \\
\text{SUBCAT} & \begin{bmatrix} \text{EXTERNAL} & DP_{[+animate]} \\ \text{INTERNAL} & DP \end{bmatrix}
\end{bmatrix}
$$

(2)   (a)   The man kissed the cat.

     (b)   #The table kissed the cat.

Exercise **Q1** 📖 The entry for *kiss* requires that the DP that is the specifier has to be *+animate*. Look carefully at the DPs in (2). There are two words in the DP in (2a): *the* and *man*. Which of these elements is *+animate*?

Q2 📖 Why might the source of the animacy for this DP be a problem for the theory as we've articulated it so far?

Comment The phenomenon we are talking about here is sometimes called **feature passing**. Typically, feature passing takes certain features of some lexical head (like the N *man* in (2a)), and makes them the features of the functional head that C-MERGES with that lexical head. So, for example, the N *man* passes its *+animate* feature over to the determiner, which heads the DP. Similarly, the N *table* passes up the *−animate* features associated with it. This means that the DP *the man* is *+animate* by virtue of this feature passing.

179

Notation We indicate feature passing using a device known as a **tag**. Tags mark identity in values in feature structures. Tags are typically numbers written inside of a box. The identity of two numbers means that the values of the features are identical. We will indicate this in the lexical entry for *the*.

(3) *the*

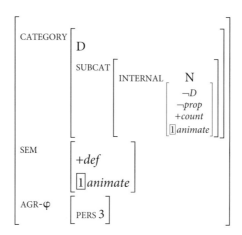

This is quite a complicated feature structure, so let's break down the bits of this structure and then look at the use of the tag $\boxed{1}$. *The* is of category D. It indicates definiteness (+*def*), and it is always third person (PERS 3). The INTERNAL feature here says that the noun that is the complement of *the* may not be a proper noun (¬*prop*) or a pronoun (¬D), but it must be a count noun (+*count*). Finally, we have the ±*animate* feature. You'll notice that there are two $\boxed{1}$s in this feature structure. One of these is in the list of restrictions on the complement noun in the INTERNAL feature. The other is associated with the semantics (SEM) of the determiner itself. The fact that both cases of ±*animate* have a $\boxed{1}$ in front of them means that whatever value comes from the complement noun will also be the value for the determiner itself. So if the noun comes in with a −*animate* (e.g. *table*), the determiner will have an identically valued −*animate* feature. Similarly, if the noun is +*animate* (e.g. *man*), then the determiner will also be +*animate*.

Exercise Consider the DPs in (4); remember that *kiss* requires an animate subject.

Q3 📖 Does the indefinite determiner *a* behave the same way as *the*?   Y   N

(4) (a)   A man kissed the cat.

(b)   *A table kissed the cat.

Q4 📖 Draw the feature structure for the indefinite determiner *a*. (Hint: start with the feature structure in example (24b) in unit 12, then make some modifications modeled on (3) above.)

16.2 Number–feature tagging

Exercise Consider the following sentences.

(5) (a) The man paints beautifully.

(b) The men paint beautifully.

Notice that the verb in (5a) takes the form *paints* with a singular EXTERNAL DP but when the EXTERNAL DP is plural, we get the form *paint* (5b). From this we can conclude that it isn't only the noun *men* that is plural, but the whole DP that is in the subject position.

Q5 ▢ Draw a feature structure for *the* that shows feature passing of [NUM pl]. To do this question start with the feature structure in (3), making sure that you retain the ⑴ for animacy. Use the tag ⑵ to indicate the value of the NUM feature for *the*. Note that NUM is an AGR-φ feature, not a SEM feature.

Notation You may have noticed that sometimes the value of a feature is written before a feature (e.g. +*animate*) and sometimes it is written after [NUM pl]. This is just a notational quirk. ± values are traditionally written before the feature, but other values (e.g. *sg, pl*, etc.) are written after. In fact the two notations are just variants of one another. If you preferred you could also write +*animate* as [ANIMATE +]. These mean the same thing. (Tags can be similarly distributed before or after the feature.) In this book, I've stuck with the convention that ± values are written before the feature, but if you prefer a more symmetrical notation you should feel free to use the one where the value follows the feature.

Another important thing to note is that the particular number used in the tag is entirely arbitrary. You can use any number, as long as the same number is used identifying the values for any given feature in your feature structure. Use a different number for each feature you are tagging.

Exercise In Q5 above, you drew a feature structure with tagging to indicate feature passing of the value of the NUM feature from the noun to the determiner.

Q6 ▢ Do you need to revise the feature structure for the indefinite determiner *a* that you drew in answer to Q4? If you do, then draw the feature structure indicating the tagging. If you don't, then explain why not.

Q7 ▢ In unit 12, we developed a feature structure for the deictic determiner *these*. Do we need any tags to pass on the NUM feature value with these? If we do, then draw the feature structure indicating the tagging. If we don't, then explain why not.

Q8 📖 Sticking with the deictic determiner *these*, do you need to revise the feature structure to pass the ±*animacy* feature? If you do, then draw the feature structure. If you don't, then explain why not.

Comment We've now solved the problem raised by the lexical entry in (1). This entry required that the external argument be animate. But the animacy was not indicated on the determiner itself but on the noun inside the DP. We got around this by passing the feature values from the noun to the determiner using a tag. Then we showed the utility of tags for percolating another feature up to the determiner *the*: the NUM feature.

16.3 Using tags to trigger movement

Comment Consider our lexical entries for a T node like *will* and a verb like *kiss*:

(6) *will*

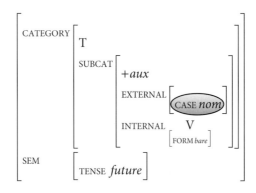

(7) *kiss*

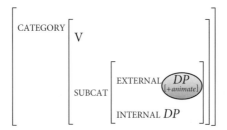

In unit 13, we argued that it was the circled EXTERNAL feature that triggered the movement of a DP from the specifier of the VP to the specifier of the TP. For a sentence like *Mary will kiss the cat*, the DP starts as the external argument of *kiss* where, after feature passing of the +*animate* value from the N to the Null D, it satisfies the EXTERNAL feature of KISS. The VP [$_{VP}$ [$_{DP}$ Ø$_{prop}$ *Mary*] [$_{VP}$ *kiss* [$_{DP}$ *the cat*]]] has been C-MERGED with *will* (satisfying

182

will's INTERNAL feature). At this point in the derivation of the sentence the tree looks like (8):

(8)

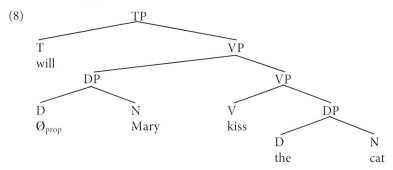

To satisfy the EXTERNAL feature of *will*, we move (or remerge) *Mary* into its specifier:

(9)

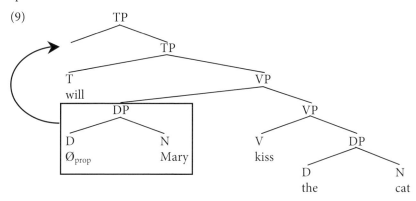

Exercise Now consider the following sentence:

(10) *He will Mary kiss the cat.

This is, of course, not a good sentence of English. But consider the properties of this sentence.

Q9 ✆ Is *he* plausibly in the specifier of the TP?   Y   N

Q10 ✆ What requirement does the EXTERNAL feature of *will* impose on its specifier? ....

Q11 ✆ Is *he* in the nominative case?   Y   N

Q12 ✆ Is *Mary* plausibly in the specifier of the VP?   Y   N

Q13 ✆ What requirement does the EXTERNAL feature of *kiss* impose on its specifier? ....

Q14 ✆ Is *Mary* animate?   Y   N

Q15 ✆ Does our theory predict that sentence (10) will be grammatical or ungrammatical? (circle 1)   grammatical   ungrammatical

Discussion The system we have developed thus far has nothing in it to prevent two different DPs (e.g. *he* and *Mary*) from satisfying the two distinct external requirements imposed by *will* and *kiss* respectively in (10). Tags allow a way out of this. We can specify for each T node that its EXTERNAL feature must be identical to the external feature of its complement, using tags.

(11) *will*

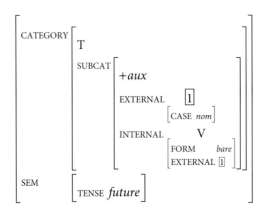

This feature structure says that whatever element satisfies the EXTERNAL feature of the verb also satisfies the EXTERNAL feature of *will*.

Exercise **Q16** 📖 Draw the feature structure for past tense $\emptyset_{past}$ using tags. Use (11) as a model.

Exercise **Q17** 📖 Do we also need to add tags to the stacked auxiliary verbs like $have_{perp}$ be_{prog} etc.? Draw the feature structure for had_{perf} and $have_{perf}$ as found in *I should have eaten*.

Q18 📖 What about *not*? Does it require tags? If not explain why. If so, draw the feature structure.

Challenge The property of movement of a DP to the specifier of TP holds for all T heads in English (but not, for example, the T heads of Irish). Above we stipulated this property in each lexical entry for each T. Can you think of a better way to capture the generalization that this is a property of all T heads in English? Is there a way to make a general statement (rule or constraint) that captures this property?

16.4 Local (cyclic) movement

Comment Because each word (both verbs and negation) between the verb and the tense node and the verb itself has to tag the EXTERNAL feature of the next predicate down, it follows that each and every single specifier between the verb and the T must be (temporarily) occupied by the subject as it works its way up the tree. Take, for example, the sentence in (12).

(12) He must not have been sleeping.

He starts out satisfying the external feature of sleeping. It must start here because the verb *sleep* imposes the restriction of +*animate* on the subject. So the tree structure at this step is as shown in (13):

(13) (a)

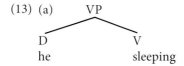

Next, we C-MERGE this to *been*ₚᵣₒ𝓰. This auxiliary expresses progressive aspect and selects for a V that is a gerund, giving us (13b):

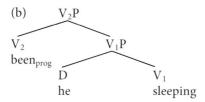

The EXTERNAL feature of *been*ₚᵣₒ𝓰 also is tagged to be identical to the EXTERNAL feature of its complement. So *he* moves to form the specifier of V₂P.

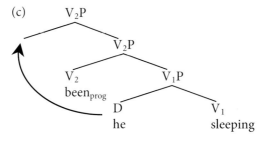

Each subsequent merging in the tree involves such a movement:

(d)

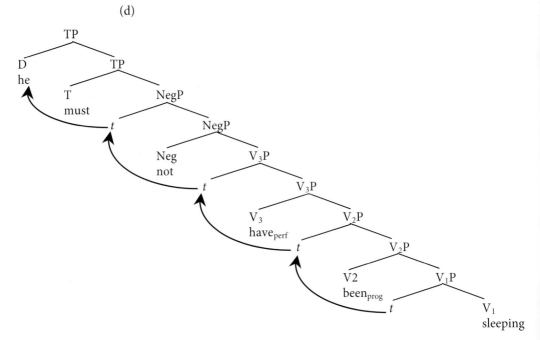

Definition Each movement in (d) is a **local** movement. Each of these small movements is motivated by the fact that any given verb may only see into the feature structure of its complement. So in order for the EXTERNAL argument of *sleeping* to end up as the EXTERNAL argument of *must*, it has to do these little hops through each of the intermediate specifiers. Movement like this that proceeds through short hops is known as **local** or **cyclic** movement.

Exercise **Q19** 📖 Using (13d) as a model, draw the tree for *She had been dancing*. (Be careful here, as the auxiliary *had* is in its preterite form.)

Challenge In sections 16.1 and 16.2 above, we used tagging to force "agreement" between both NUM and ±*animate* features of the D and the N. One possible extension of tags would be to use them to explain why we get agreement between subjects and verbs as well. So, for example, we might tag the AGR-φ features of the verb so that they have to be the same as those on the DP that satisfies the verb's external feature. Is this the best way to do subject–verb agreement? Consider both data from a language like English, where often a single verb form (e.g. *paint*) is used with a wide variety of persons and numbers of subjects: *I paint, you paint, we paint, they paint* (but *he/she/it paints*), and data from languages where verbs inflect more precisely to agree

186

with their subject noun. For example, in the past tense the Polish verb *pisać* takes the following forms:[1]

(14)

	Singular		Plural
	Masculine	**Feminine**	
1	pisałem	pisałam	pisaliśmy
2	pisałeś	pisałaś	pisaliście
3	pisał	pisała	pisali

Do we want to have a general statement about agreement using tagging? Or should we have simple stipulations in each form (saying, for example, that a verb *pisałem* must have an external argument that is first person singular masculine)? There is no right answer to this question. The solution may turn on whether you want to have separate feature structures for the roots of words (e.g. *pisa-*) and their inflections (*-łem*) or if you want to only have feature structures for whole words (*pisałem*).

Summary In this unit, we've introduced the new notation of tagging. We've used tagging for a number of purposes. One is to pass particular features (like animacy and number) from heads up to the specifier of the category that is on top of them. Another is to force movement of an element to satisfy multiple features.

Suggested further reading

- Bobaljik (2008)
- Kim and Sells (2008), chapters 4 and 6
- Sag, Wasow and Bender (2003), chapter 2

Answers to questions

Q1 *man*

Q2 *The* is the determiner head of the DP; *the* is not marked for animacy but its complement is! However, the lexical entry for a verb like *kiss* requires that the determiner be marked for animacy, even though *the* is clearly neither *+animate* nor *−animate*.

Discussion Typically speaking, the properties of a phrase (such as category, etc.) are the properties of its head. But in the case of *the man*, the animacy of the DP seems to come from the animacy of the complement N. We need some

---

[1] Feldstein (2001).

mechanism for ensuring that some features of the complement here get passed up to be the features of the whole phrase.

Q3 Yes

Q4 *a*

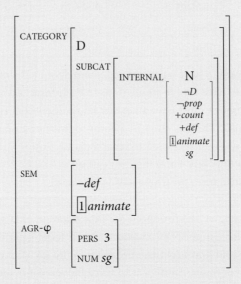

Q5 *the*

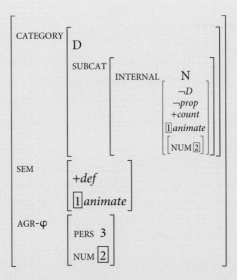

Q6 No, you do not need to change it. The indefinite determiner *a* is only ever used with singular nouns (**a men*). In addition, the feature structure given above in Q4 specifies that *a* is used with singular nouns. Note the requirement that the complement of *a* is specified as singular, as is *a* itself (in its AGR-φ feature).

Q7 No, you do not. *These* is only ever used with plural nouns (**these man*), as is specified in both its AGR-φ and in the restriction on the properties of the noun that is its complement (i.e. in the INTERNAL feature).

Q8 Yes, this does merit a revision of the version in unit 12. *These men* is animate, but *these tables* is not. This is indicated with the tag:

these

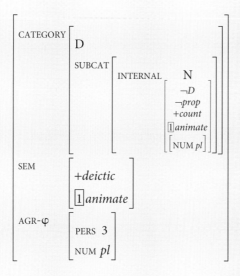

Q9 Yes

Q10 nominative case

Q11 Yes

Q12 Yes

Q13 +*animate*

Q14 Yes

Q15 The sentence is predicted to be grammatical because all the requirements imposed by the EXTERNAL features are met.

Q16 $\emptyset_{past}$

$$\begin{bmatrix} \text{CATEGORY} & \begin{bmatrix} \text{T} \\ \text{SUBCAT} & \begin{bmatrix} +aux \\ \text{EXTERNAL} & \boxed{1} \\ & [\text{CASE } nom] \\ \text{INTERNAL} & \begin{bmatrix} \text{V} \\ \text{FORM} & preterite \\ \text{EXTERNAL} & \boxed{1} \end{bmatrix} \end{bmatrix} \end{bmatrix} \\ \text{SEM} & [\text{TENSE } past] \end{bmatrix}$$

Q17 Yes you do, because verbs can be stacked on top of one another, and the feature structure for the T can only see the features of the top-most complement. However, the DP subject is required by the EXTERNAL feature of the most deeply embedded V. Each stacked V has to tag the EXTERNAL feature of the verb below it.

had$_{perf}$

$$\begin{bmatrix} \text{CATEGORY} & \begin{bmatrix} \text{V} \\ \text{SUBCAT} & \begin{bmatrix} +aux \\ \text{EXTERNAL} & \boxed{1} \\ & [\text{CASE } nom] \\ \text{INTERNAL} & \begin{bmatrix} \text{V} \\ -\text{PERF} \\ \text{FORM} & participle \\ \text{EXTERNAL} & \boxed{1} \end{bmatrix} \end{bmatrix} \\ \text{FORM} & preterite \\ \text{SEM} & [\text{ASPECT } perfect] \end{bmatrix}$$

have$_{perf}$ *(bare form as in* I should have eaten*)*

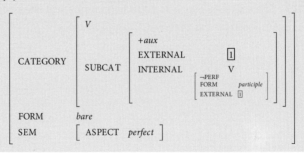

$$\begin{bmatrix} \text{CATEGORY} & \begin{bmatrix} \text{V} \\ \text{SUBCAT} & \begin{bmatrix} +aux \\ \text{EXTERNAL} & \boxed{1} \\ \text{INTERNAL} & \begin{bmatrix} \text{V} \\ -\text{PERF} \\ \text{FORM} & participle \\ \text{EXTERNAL} & \boxed{1} \end{bmatrix} \end{bmatrix} \\ \text{FORM} & bare \\ \text{SEM} & [\text{ASPECT } perfect] \end{bmatrix}$$

Discussion   Here there is no CASE restriction on the external argument of *have*. This is because this is not the final landing place for the DP. *Have* here is not the tensed verb, so it does not require nominative case of its subject. In the sentence *I should have eaten*, the verb that requires a nominative case subject is *should*.

Q18   Yes, *not* must also tag the EXTERNAL feature of its complement.

not

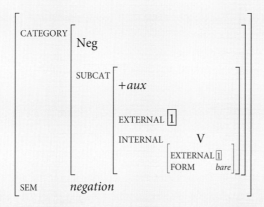

Q19

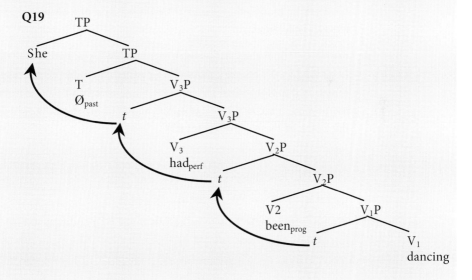

Discussion   The tricky part of this one is the fact that we have a phonologically null T node, but we still need to move *she* into the specifier of the TP so that *she* satisfies $\emptyset_{past}$'s CASE requirements, even though this movement doesn't change the surface order of words that are pronounced.

191

UNIT 17 MERGE: ADJUNCTS

> **Objectives:**
> - Learn how to identify the optional modifiers called adjuncts and distinguish them from complements and specifiers.
> - Introduce the feature MOD.
> - Learn how to attach adjuncts through ADJOIN.
> - Practice drawing trees with adjuncts.
> - Understand ambiguity in the position of adjuncts.

17.1 Informally identifying adjuncts

Comment The units in this group have been about cases where MERGE was applied based on a head's INTERNAL or EXTERNAL features. The elements that were merged with the head are complements or adjuncts. However, often a head can be modified by material that is not part of a head's INTERNAL or EXTERNAL features.

Exercise **Q1** 📖 Consider the verb phrases in the following sentences of English. Look back at the lexical entries you wrote in unit 9 for the verbs. Are the underlined prepositional phrases (PPs) and adverbs that modify these verbs mentioned in the INTERNAL features? Semantically speaking, which head does each of these elements modify?

(a) I [$_{VP}$ rubbed it [$_{PP}$ <u>with a cloth</u>] [$_{Adv}$ <u>thoroughly</u>]].

(b) Susan [$_{VP}$ arrived [$_{Adv}$ <u>quickly</u>]].

(c) I [$_{VP}$ kissed Calvin [$_{PP}$ <u>on the lips</u>]].

Comment We find similar effects with adjectives modifying nouns as in (1a) and intensifiers modifying adjectives:

(1) (a)   the furry cat

    (b)   very furry

The adjective *furry* modifies *cat*, but the entry for *cat* does not specify (or require) it. Similarly, the adverb *very* modifies *furry*, but it isn't required.

Definition Modifiers of a head that are not introduced by an INTERNAL or EXTERNAL feature are known as **adjuncts**. Adjuncts typically add optional clarificatory information.

Discussion   There are a number of tests to help you identify whether modifiers are complements or adjuncts and we'll look at a couple of these at the end of this unit. For the moment, however, here are a couple of simple heuristics (i.e. quick and dirty tricks) that allow you to distinguish these notions:

- If the head is an N and the modifier is a PP headed by *of*, then the PP is a complement to the N: *a book <u>of poems</u>*.
- If the head is an N and the modifier is a PP headed by any other preposition, then the PP is an adjunct to the noun: *a book <u>with a red cover</u>*.
- If the head is an N and the modifier is an Adj or AdjP, then the Adj or AdjP is an adjunct to the noun: *the <u>red</u> book*.
- If the head is an Adj or Adv and the modifier is an intensifier, then the intensifier is an adjunct to the Adv or Adj: *<u>very</u> big*.
- If the head is a P and the modifier is a D or DP, then the DP is complement to that D: *with <u>the books</u>*.
- If the head is a D and the modifier is an N or NP, then the N or NP is a complement to the D: *the <u>man</u>*.
- With verbs, you have to pay careful attention to the internal feature. If the verb is ditransitive (either <DP, PP> or <DP, DP>), then the two DPs or the DP and the PP are both complements to the verb: *send <u>the package to Mary</u>*. If the verb is transitive, then the first DP after the V is the complement. If the verb is intransitive then the V has no complement.
- Any other PP, DP or AdvP modifying the verb is an adjunct.
- VPs are almost always complements to either T or an auxiliary V.

There are some other cases not listed here (including embedded clauses), but this is a start.

This is quite a list! For some people it is easiest to keep these basic rules of thumb in mind. However, as scientists, we need a less stipulative approach to the question. We'll return to more scientific and explanatory tests later in this unit.

Exercise   **Q2** ✏ Using the rules of thumb listed above, decide if the underlined phrases in the following sentences are adjuncts or complements to the boldfaced heads.

(a)   Reggie **ate** <u>the tuna</u> with a fork quickly.   C   A

(b)   Reggie **ate** the tuna <u>with a fork</u> quickly.   C   A

(c)   Reggie **ate** the tuna with a fork <u>quickly</u>.   C   A

(d)   Reggie ate **the** <u>tuna</u> with a fork quickly.   C   A

(e)   Reggie ate the tuna **from** <u>the plate</u> quickly.   C   A

(f)   Reggie ate the tuna with **a** <u>fork</u> quickly.   C   A

(g)	the **binder** <u>of notes</u> with the ripped cover	C	A
(h)	the **binder** of notes <u>with the ripped cover</u>	C	A
(i)	the binder **of** <u>notes</u> with the ripped cover	C	A
(j)	the binder of notes **with** <u>the ripped cover</u>	C	A
(k)	the binder of notes with **the** <u>ripped cover</u>	C	A
(l)	the binder of notes with the <u>ripped</u> **cover**	C	A

Discussion Now we turn to the question of how adjuncts are merged into trees. Consider the difference between two types of adjuncts: adjectives and adverbs. Adjectives can modify Ns, but no other categories.

(2) (a) the big cat

(b) *Susan smuggled the tuna big./*Susan big smuggled the tuna.

(c) *big afraid

(d) *big quickly

etc.

By contrast, Advs modify Vs, Adjs, Advs and Ts, but no other categories.

(3) (a) John danced skillfully. (V)

(b) very afraid (Adj)

(c) very quickly (Adv)

(d) John will leave tomorrow. (T)

(e) *the skillfully dancing (*N)

(f) *skillfully those (*D)

(g) *skillfully in (*P)

etc.

It seems as though these modifiers choose the category of the elements they can modify. Note, however, that there are more subtle restrictions within the class of adverbs. For example, the intensifier *very* only modifies adverbs and adjectives, and never verbs or tenses (*She very danced, *I will leave very*); similarly, adverbs such as *tomorrow* seem only to modify T and adverbs like *skillfully* only modify verbs.

Definition In traditional terminology, adverbs such as *skillfully* are called **manner adverbs**, adverbs like *tomorrow* are **temporal adverbs** and adverbs like *very* are **intensifiers**.

194

17.2 The feature MOD

Notation We will need two modifications to our feature system to capture adjuncts. The difference between adjectives and adverbs seems to lie in what type of category they attach to. This is almost subcategory-like. So one minor change we'll make in our system is that we'll combine both adjectives and adverbs into a single category we'll call "A." We'll distinguish between adjectives and adverbs by referring to a new feature: MOD. MOD is a SUBCAT feature and is used to indicate what elements an adjunct can modify. So, for example, a partial feature structure for the adverb *skillfully* is as follows:

(4) *skillfully*

$$
\begin{bmatrix}
\text{CATEGORY} & \begin{bmatrix} A \\ \text{SUBCAT} & \begin{bmatrix} \text{MOD } V \end{bmatrix} \end{bmatrix}
\end{bmatrix}
$$

This says that the manner adverb *skillfully* is part of the category A (adjectives and adverbs), but belongs to the subtype that modifies only verbs.

The adverb *tomorrow* has a different feature structure. It modifies only tenses (T):

(5) *tomorrow*

$$
\begin{bmatrix}
\text{CATEGORY} & \begin{bmatrix} A \\ \text{SUBCAT} & \begin{bmatrix} \text{MOD } T \end{bmatrix} \end{bmatrix}
\end{bmatrix}
$$

Exercise **Q3** 📖 Intensifiers only modify other A categories. Give a partial feature structure for *very*. Use (5) as a model. Keep in mind you'll have to change the value of the MOD feature.

Exercise **Q4** 📖 Try your hand now at drawing the feature structure for the adjective *big*. Use (5) as a model.

Notation Notice that this system – with a single category covering both adjectives and adverbs (A) and using the MOD feature to distinguish between them (and among adverbs) – provides a more elegant and cohesive account of the categories. As we'll see below, this MOD feature will allow us to also capture the fact that these elements always behave like adjuncts. From this point forward, we will use A and the MOD feature when describing adjectives and adverbs rather than the Adj and Adv categories we've been using up to now.

17.3 The operation ADJOIN

Comment While adjuncts subcategorize for the category of the element they modify (using the MOD feature), it's clear that the category of the phrase that results from merging an adjunct with some element is the category of the head that the adjunct is merged with. So, for example, if you merge an adjective with a noun, the result is a noun phrase (NP), not an adjective phrase.

This is the opposite of merge of complements, where the thing that has the internal SUBCAT feature "projects." With adjuncts, the thing with the MOD SUBCAT feature does *not* project.

(6) (a) complement structure   (b) adjunct structure

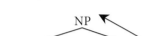

NP	NP

N	PP	A	N
[INTERNAL P]		[MOD N]	

In (6a), the element with the INTERNAL feature (the N) is the head of the NP. In (6b) the thing with the MOD feature (the A) is *not* the head of the NP.

Definition **ADJOIN**: combine two (or more) items together into a constituent, to satisfy a MOD feature. The combined category is given the label of the non-head.

e.g.   ADJOIN for MOD feature

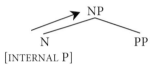

A   N   →   NP
big   dog

[MOD N]   A   N
                      big   dog

Comment As a reminder: **C-MERGE** combines two (or more) items together into a constituent to satisfy INTERNAL and **S-MERGE** combines two (or more) items together into a constituent to satisfy EXTERNAL features. In both cases, the word bearing the feature gives its category to the phrase.

e.g.   C-MERGE for INTERNAL feature

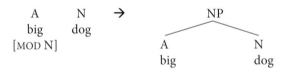

V $N_{[+D]}$ →   VP
kissed   him

[INTERNAL D]   V $N_{[+D]}$
                          kissed   him

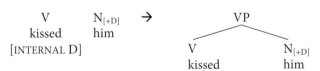

e.g. S-MERGE for EXTERNAL feature

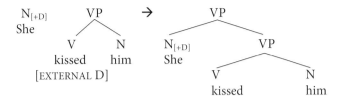

Challenge Above we've proposed three rules: ADJOIN, C-MERGE and S-MERGE. Why haven't we proposed a single rule of combination that does the work of all these rules? How might you distinguish between the hypothesis where there is one rule and one where there are three? Is there an empirical way to distinguish these possible hypotheses? Can you choose among the options on grounds of scientific elegance or similar criteria?

Exercise Q5 📖 Using the trees above as models, draw the trees for the examples below. Assume the feature structure for *quickly* is identical to the feature structure for *skillfully* given above in (4). Assume that the feature structure for *quick* is identical to the feature structure for *big*. Don't forget about null determiners and *'s*!

(a) danced skillfully

(b) danced a jig

(c) danced a jig skillfully

(d) quickly danced

(e) quickly danced a jig

(f) danced a quick jig

(g) John's uncle

(h) the big uncle

(i) John's big uncle

(j) John will dance the jig skillfully tomorrow.

Comment Look at the trees you drew for (a), (d), (h) and (j). Note that the adjective adjunct *big* in (h) and the adverb adjunct *quickly* in (d) come before the head they modify, but the adverb adjuncts *skillfully* and *tomorrow* follow their head. So, adjuncts can either follow their head or precede it.

Challenge *Part 1:* Is the same true for complements and specifiers? Can they both precede and follow their heads? Consider forms like *linguistics professor* (cf. *professor of linguistics*). Can the specifier ever follow the head? *Part 2:* Is there any mechanism in our grammar for encoding these orderings? Can you think of a way to do it?

17.4 Adjunct PPs

Comment It is possible to have an item that has both a MOD feature and an INTERNAL feature. Take, for example, the sentence in (7):

(7) He opened the jar with a screwdriver.

The preposition *with* takes its own complement (*a screwdriver*), yet at the same time it acts as an adjunct on *open*. As such, *with* will require both a MOD feature and an INTERNAL feature.

(8) *with* (to be revised)

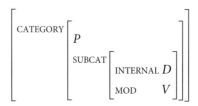

This feature structure says that *with* takes a DP complement and it acts as an adjunct on verbs. Applying the C-MERGE rule to *with* + [$_{DP}$ a screwdriver] gives you the tree in (9), where the DP is checking the internal feature of *with*.

(9)

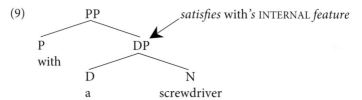

To satisfy the MOD feature of *with*, we can attach it as an adjunct to the VP *opened the jar*. As with all adjunction structures, the thing being modified projects its category:

(10)

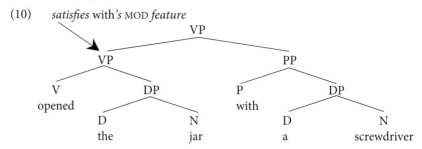

198

Exercise **Q6** 📖 Consider the first noun phrase in the sentence below:

(a) The man with binoculars is creepy.

What does the PP *with binoculars* modify here? Adapt the feature structure for *with* given above in (8) to account for the modification relation shown in this sentence.

Q7 📖 Draw the tree for the DP *the man with the binoculars*.

Comment The preposition *of* is different from other prepositions. It marks complements and not adjuncts. PPs marked with *of* are usually complements.

Exercise **Q8** 📖 Does the feature structure for *of* include a MOD feature? Why or why not?

Q9 📖 Draw the feature structure for *of*.

17.5 Ambiguity and adjuncts

Exercise The following sentence is ambiguous:

(a) Reggie saw the man with the binoculars.

Q10 📖 What are the two meanings for this sentence?

Q11 📖 Draw the trees showing the two meanings. Keep in mind that *with the binoculars* is going to be adjoined to two different parts of the tree reflecting the two different things it can modify in this sentence.

Comment Because the lexical entry for *with* allows either an N or a V as the value of the MOD feature, then in cases like the sentence above, the PP can attach either to the N or the V, creating an ambiguity in interpretation.

Exercise In this exercise, we consider a different kind of ambiguity. The adverb *quickly* is unambiguous in its MOD feature, it only targets verbs. Yet the sentence below is ambiguous.

(a) Reggie said that Bill left quickly.

Q12 📖 What are the two meanings for this sentence?

Q13 📖 Explain why this ambiguity is possible even though the feature structure isn't ambiguous like *with*.

Q14 📖 Draw the trees showing the two meanings.

17.6 Distinguishing complements and adjuncts

Comment In the first section of this unit, you were given some quick heuristics for distinguishing complements from adjuncts. In this section, we look at some more rigorous tests for making this distinction.

199

Comment By stipulation, the mechanism for merging adjuncts must apply after all the complements are merged. A consequence of this is that adjuncts cannot appear between a complement and a head because the head and the complements will form a smaller constituent than the structure containing the adjunct. This is consistent with the data. To investigate this, we'll look first at PP modifiers of nouns. Many nouns can take complements. In unit 15, we saw an example, where the noun *destruction* can take a complement such as *of the city*. This PP is a complement because it parallels the complement required by the verb *destroy*. Let's contrast the behavior of this PP with the adjunct *by the Huns*.

(11) (a)   the destruction of the city   by the Huns

                              complement adjunct

      (b)   ?*the destruction by the Huns of the city

                         adjunct   complement

For most speakers of English, the second sentence is noticeably degraded, and for many even flat out unacceptable. Other examples show the same thing:

(12) (a)   the book of poems with the red cover   *head< complement<*
                                                     adjunct

      (b)   *the book with the red cover of poems   *head< adjunct<*
                                                      complement

The same effect is even stronger with the complements and adjuncts of verbs. A complement such as the DP *the man* must appear closer to the head *hit* than the adjunct *with the stick*.

(13) (a)   I hit the man with the stick.   *head < complement < adjunct*

      (b)   *I hit with the stick the man.   *head < adjunct < complement*

Definition We can thus formalize the distinction using the following test:

(14) The adjacency test for adjuncts:[1] if you have both a complement and an adjunct, the complement must appear adjacent to the head.

Exercise **Q15** ✏ Using the adjacency test in (14) above, determine if the underlined Adverbs and PPs are complements to the boldfaced head. Circle either "Complement" or "Adjunct."

   (a)   I **scrambled** the eggs <u>with a fork</u>.   Complement?   Adjunct?

   (b)   Calvin **ate** <u>the tuna</u> from the dish.   Complement?   Adjunct?

---

[1] This test works only for languages like English. Some languages, such as French, don't fully follow this pattern. We'll return to this in later units.

(c)	Calvin **ate** the tuna <u>from the dish</u>.	Complement?	Adjunct?
(d)	Pangur saw the **student** <u>of linguistics</u> with long hair	Complement?	Adjunct?
(e)	Pangur saw the **student** of linguistics <u>with long hair</u>.	Complement?	Adjunct?
(f)	Pangur **saw** <u>the student of linguistics</u> with a telescope	Complement?	Adjunct?
(g)	Pangur **saw** the student of linguistics <u>with a telescope</u>	Complement?	Adjunct?

Exercise **Q16** 📖 Consider the data below. How is this data different from that in Q2 above? What are we to make of the status of the two PPs modifying these verbs? Are they complements or adjuncts? (Hint: look back at unit 8 and look at the INTERNAL feature for the verb *arrive*.)

(a) Pangur arrived [$_{pp}$ at the vet] [$_{pp}$ on Friday].

(b) Pangur arrived [$_{pp}$ on Friday] [$_{pp}$ at the vet].

(c) Pangur left [$_{pp}$ for the weekend] [$_{pp}$ from the bus terminal].

(d) Pangur left [$_{pp}$ from the bus terminal] [$_{pp}$ for the weekend].

Definition *The reordering test for adjuncts*: if two modifiers can be freely reordered, then both modifiers are adjuncts.

Discussion This test is related to the one above: complements are merged before adjuncts. If you have multiple complements, their order is specified in the list that appears in the internal feature. For example, the fact that the DP must precede the PP with the verb *put* (*I put the book on the table* vs. **I put on the table the book*) is due to the fact that the value of the internal feature for *put* is <DP, PP>. The mechanism for merging adjuncts operates a little differently, and it applies relatively freely. This means that while complements appear closer to the head than adjuncts and are strictly ordered, adjuncts have more freedom in their ordering. This can be seen in the examples in (15) where all the underlined elements are adjuncts to the boldfaced head and can be reordered with respect to one another.

(15) (a) The **book** <u>with the red cover</u> <u>in French</u>.

(b) The **book** <u>in French</u> <u>with the red cover</u>.

(c) I **hit** the man <u>with the stick</u> <u>on Friday</u>.

(d) I **hit** the man <u>on Friday</u> <u>with a stick</u>.

Needless to say, complements cannot be reordered with adjuncts:

(16) (a) *I hit with the stick the man on Friday.

    (b) *I hit with the stick on Friday the man.

    (c) *I hit on Friday the man with the stick.

    (d) *I hit on Friday with the stick the man.

Exercise **Q17** ✏ Using the reordering test (note: you will need to change the order of elements in the following sentences to do this!), determine if the underlined phrase is an adjunct or a complement with respect to the boldfaced head.

(a) Reggie **caught** the tuna with a spear
    in the ocean.   complement?   adjunct?

(b) Reggie **caught** the tuna with a spear
    in the ocean.   complement?   adjunct?

(c) Reggie **caught** the tuna with a spear
    in the ocean.   complement?   adjunct?

(d) Fiona **ran** quickly to the phone   complement?   adjunct?

(e) Fiona **ran** quickly to the phone   complement?   adjunct?

NB: For the next three examples be sure that you do NOT drop the preposition to *before the attendant when you reorder the sentence!*

(f) Jean **gave** her shoes to the attendant quietly complement?   adjunct?

(g) Jean **gave** her shoes to the attendant quietly complement?   adjunct?

(h) Jean **gave** her shoes to the attendant quietly complement?   adjunct?

Comment There are a number of other tests for distinguishing between complements and adjuncts. See Carnie (2006) for a more extensive discussion of such tests.

Comment To review our discussion thus far in this unit, the main theoretical difference between a complement and an adjunct has to do with the fact that adjuncts are not mentioned in the INTERNAL feature of the head they modify. Empirically, this cashes out in terms of the ordering (and reorderability) of the two types of modifiers: if there is a complement, it must be closer to the head than any adjuncts. Adjuncts also show more flexibility in their reordering with respect to one another.

Summary In this unit, we've looked extensively at the distinction between complements and adjuncts. We saw how these different elements can be distinguished. Adjuncts are introduced using the MOD feature and the ADJOIN rule. The ADJOIN rule causes the item that doesn't have the MOD feature and projects it up to the phrasal level. We also looked at how to draw trees with adjuncts, and looked at ambiguity in structure.

Suggested further reading

- Carnie (2006), chapter 6
- Chomsky (1995), chapter 4
- Hornstein (2009)
- Hornstein, Nunes and Grohman (2005), chapter 6
- Huddleston and Pullum (2005), chapter 4
- Larson (2010), units 15, 16 and 18
- Lobeck (2000), chapters 12 and 13
- Radford (1988), chapter 4
- Rubin (2003)
- Sag, Wasow and Bender (2003), chapter 5

Answers to questions

Q1 The value of the INTERNAL features of *rub* and *kiss* is DP; *arrive* has no value for this feature. However, each of the underlined phrases modifies the verbal head, even though they are PPs and Advs.

Q2 (a) C; (b) A; (c) A; (d) C; (e) C; (f) C; (g) C; (h) A; (i) C; (j) C, (k) C; (l) A

Q3 *very*

$$\left[\begin{array}{l} \text{CATEGORY}\ \left[\begin{array}{l} A \\ \text{SUBCAT}\ \left[\text{MOD}\ A\right] \end{array}\right] \end{array}\right]$$

Q4 *big*

$$\left[\begin{array}{l} \text{CATEGORY}\ \left[\begin{array}{l} A \\ \text{SUBCAT}\ \left[\text{MOD}\ N\right] \end{array}\right] \end{array}\right]$$

Q5 (a)

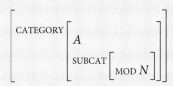

```
        VP
       /  \
      V     A
   danced  skillfully
```

(b)

```
        VP
       /  \
      V     DP
   danced  /  \
          D    N
          a    jig
```

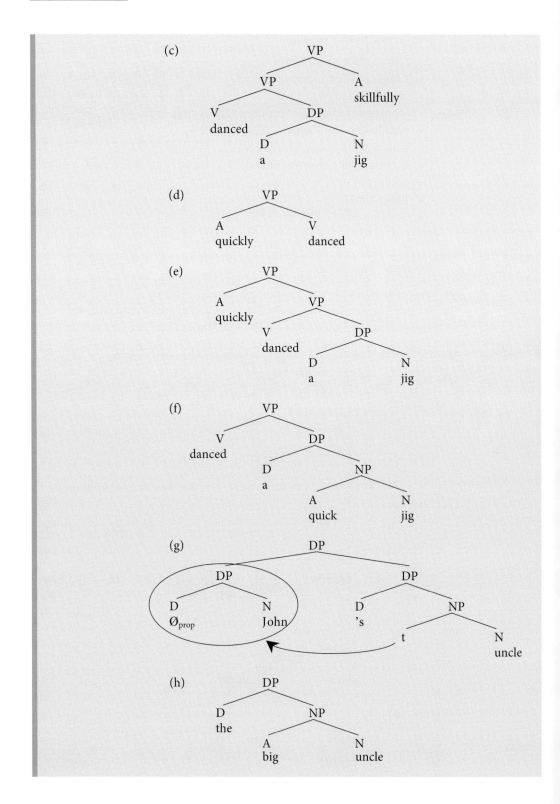

(i)

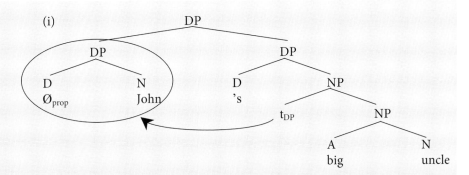

Comment   This tree could also have been drawn with the adjunct above the specifier; since the trace is silent, we don't know its relative order to the adjective:

(i)

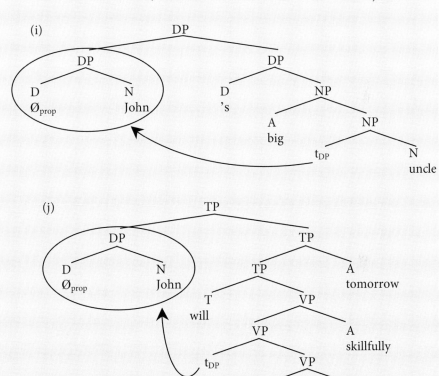

(j)

Comment The TP for this tree could also have been drawn with the specifier lower and the adjunct higher. Our system has no way to distinguish these options.

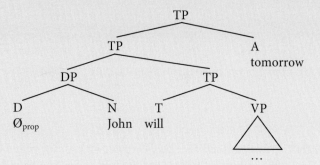

Comment Similar to (i) above, the relative height of the adverb *skillfully* and the trace is also ambiguous. So the VP for (j) could also have been drawn as:

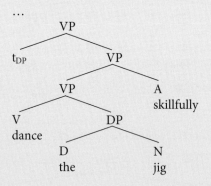

Q6 The entry has to be modified so that the MOD feature can modify either a verb or a noun.

with

$$
\begin{bmatrix}
\text{CATEGORY} \begin{bmatrix} P \\ \text{SUBCAT} \begin{bmatrix} \text{INTERNAL } D \\ \text{MOD} \quad \{V \, / \, N\} \end{bmatrix} \end{bmatrix}
\end{bmatrix}
$$

Q7

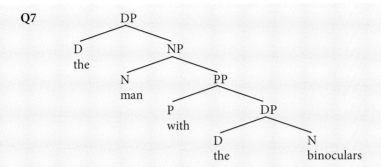

Q8 No, since *of* never marks adjunct it does not need a MOD feature. It is always brought into the tree by virtue of the INTERNAL feature of some other head, such as the noun.

Q9 *of*

$$
\begin{bmatrix}
\text{CATEGORY} \begin{bmatrix} P \end{bmatrix} \\
\text{SUBCAT} \begin{bmatrix} \text{INTERNAL } D \end{bmatrix}
\end{bmatrix}
$$

Q10 This sentence can mean either (i) that by using the binoculars he saw the man, or (ii) that he just saw a man who was holding binoculars.

Q11 The tree for the interpretation where Reggie is using the binoculars:

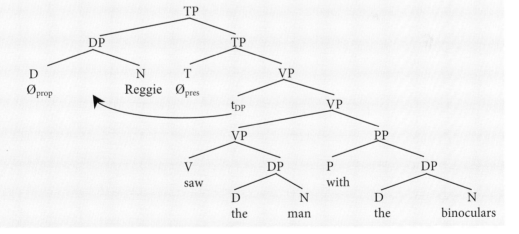

The tree for the interpretation where the man is holding the binoculars:

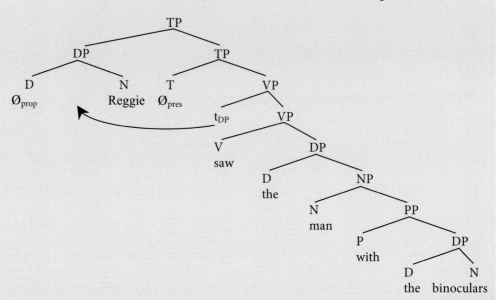

Q12 The adverb *quickly* can refer either to the act of saying or the act of leaving.

Q13 This is possible because there are two verbs in the sentence. Even though *quickly* can only modify verbs, it has two to choose from.

Q14 The tree for the meaning where *quickly* modifies *said* is the following:

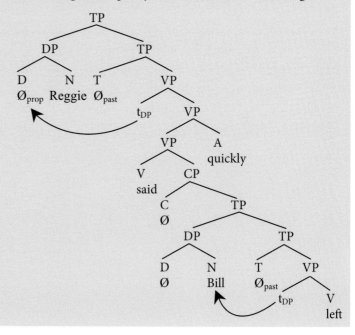

The tree for the meaning where *quickly* modifies *left* is the following:

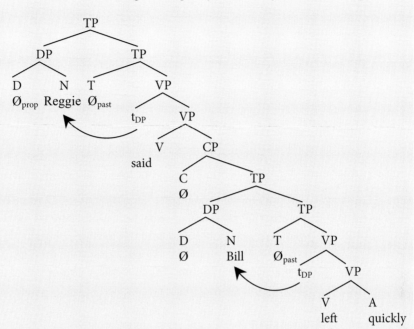

Q15 (a) adjunct; (b) complement; (c) adjunct; (d) complement; (e) adjunct, (f) complement; (g) adjunct

Q16 These sentences may be a surprise to you since either order of the PPs is OK. However, if you look at the lexical entry of the verb *arrive*, you'll see that it has no INTERNAL feature, so this verb takes no complements. The same is true for the verb *leave*. As a consequence, both the PPs in these sentences are adjuncts.

Q17 (a), (f) and (g) are complements; all the rest are adjuncts.

UNIT 18 DRAWING TREES

Objectives:

- Learn methods for drawing trees.
- Practice tree drawing.

This unit differs significantly from other units in this book. Instead of fleshing out the details of syntactic analysis, here we focus on the practical matter of providing constituent tree analysis. I'm going to work through a couple of examples for you in detail, providing you with the opportunity to practice along the way. The unit ends with a bunch of sentences you can practice tree drawing on.

18.1 Example 1

In the system that we've developed in this book, the exact shape of the constituent structure for a given sentence is a consequence of the lexical entries for the words that compose it. The words determine which items combine, and how they combine. Therefore, we're going to have to look at the SUBCAT features of each of the words we're looking at.

In principle, we could start building constituents anywhere in this sentence, but as a practical matter it's good to have some starting points to work from. As observed in the previous unit complements are always closest to their head. What this means, in terms of trees, is that they are the most deeply embedded (and lowest in the tree). If you look at the trees in previous units, you'll see that the trees are generally most deeply embedded on the right side. So even though we say sentences from left to right, when drawing trees it's usually easier to start on the right hand side of the sentence and make several passes from right to left constructing the tree upwards. More experienced linguists often draw trees downwards, and you're welcome to do that if you prefer. However, in my experience, newcomers to tree drawing do best if they work their way up the tree.

It's also important to start with the categories that are the most deeply embedded. As a heuristic, try starting by building APs first, then DPs, NPs and PPs, then the VP and then the TP and CP categories.

We'll start with the relatively simple sentence given in (1):

(1)   The very young singer often loses his book of music on the subway.

We'll start with adjectives and adverbs. There is one adjective (*young*) and one modifying adverb (*very*) here. *Very* modifies *young*, so let's construct this AP first. Neither element takes a complement. The lexical entry for *very* is:

(2)   *very*

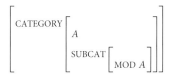

This entry says that *very* acts as an adjunct on another A category. Because we have the MOD feature here, the adjoin rule is used, which means the adjective *young* projects to create the AP category:

(3)

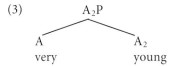

Recall that the subscripted number is used to indicate that the A *young* is the head of this AP, not the A *very*.

We'll return to the tree in (3) shortly and combine it with other material, but now let's start constructing all the DPs, NPs and PP categories. Starting at the right edge, we have the noun *subway*. This noun doesn't take any complements or specifiers and it isn't modified by anything, so we don't need to construct an NP category around it. It does, however, serve as the complement of the D head *the*. Recall from unit 12 that the lexical entry for *the* is:

(4)   *the*

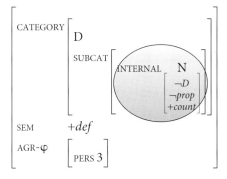

This entry requires that the D take a non-pronominal, non-proper count noun complement. *Subway* meets this criterion. Therefore, they can be combined, with *subway* checking the determiner's INTERNAL feature.

(5)

This DP functions as the complement of the P on:

(6) *on*

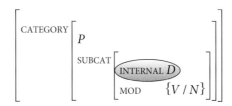

By the Principle of Headedness, we count DPs as if they are Ds. So the DP in (5) is the complement to this P, satisfying the INTERNAL feature.

(7)

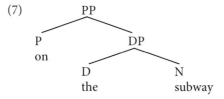

We haven't yet satisfied the MOD features of this preposition, but will do so when we merge the PP in (7) with the VP that it modifies.

Next let's work on *of music*. First, and very importantly (!), note that even though the PP in (7) immediately follows the noun *music*, and PPs generally can act as adjuncts on nouns, in this circumstance it does *not*. *On the subway* modifies the verb *lose*, not *music*. Because these phrases are adjacent, it's very tempting to the beginning syntactician to tuck this PP into the NP *music*; resist that temptation. The N *music* isn't modified by anything and doesn't take a complement, so it stands on its own. Another tempting mistake is to leave off the determiner, but recall from unit 11 that there is a null determiner here:

(8) Ø*mass*

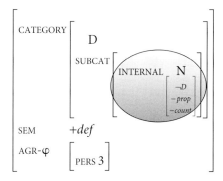

So we have the following DP:

(9)

In unit 17, we discussed how the lexical entry for *of* is slightly different from that of other prepositions in that it has no MOD feature. However, crucially it does have a complement feature:

(10) *of*

$$\begin{bmatrix} \text{CATEGORY} & \begin{bmatrix} P \\ \text{SUBCAT} & \begin{bmatrix} \text{INTERNAL } D \end{bmatrix} \end{bmatrix} \end{bmatrix}$$

Therefore, this P takes the DP [Ø*mass* *music*] as a complement.

(11)

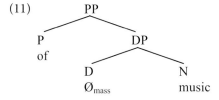

You'll recall that *of* has no MOD feature because it always marks complements and never adjuncts.

Moving on to the next N to the right, the noun *book* is considerably more complex than the ones we've seen up to this point. In this sentence, *book* has both a specifier (the "he" that becomes *his* later) and a complement, which is the PP in (11). These are licensed in the lexical entry for book:

(12) *book*

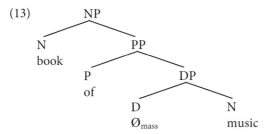

By stipulation, we always apply the rule of C-merge before we apply the rule of S-MERGE. Therefore, we'll deal with the INTERNAL feature first.

(13)

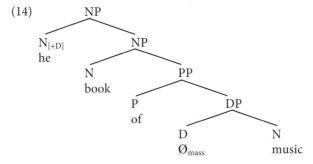

Next, we apply the S-MERGE rule. The pronoun *he* is of category N, but it has the subcategory of +D, which allows it to appear in D/DP positions and thus satisfy the EXTERNAL feature of *book*.

(14)

Of course, this is not what the final DP is; we need to change *he* into *his*, but this can only happen after we merge the possessive determiner *'s*. Here we have to revise the feature structure we've seen before to include tagging, thus ensuring both that the whole DP bears the right number ① and animate features ②, but also that the specifier of the DP is the same as the specifier of its complement NP ③.

(15) *'s*

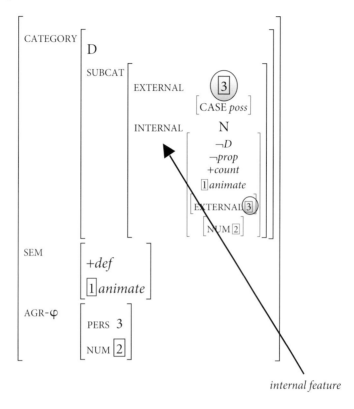

internal feature

First, we C-MERGE (14) as the complement to *'s* to check the determiner's INTERNAL feature. By the Principle of Headedness, the NP can stand in for the N in (15).

(16)

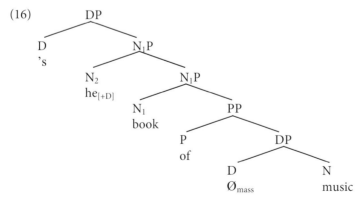

Next, we have to deal with the external feature of the determiner. The ③ tags circled in (15) trigger movement (or remerging) of the specifier of the NP into the specifier of the 's.

(17)

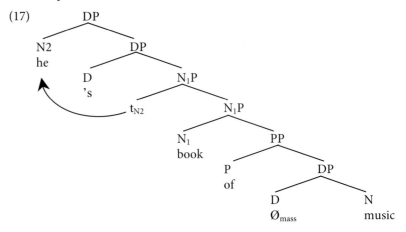

He+'s become *his* by a morphological readjustment rule (see unit 16). WHEW! That was tricky! However, we're not done yet.

One more NP to go before we do the VP and the TP. This is the subject NP *the very young singer*. Recall from several pages ago that we have already constructed the AP for *very young* (see (3) above). The noun *singer* doesn't take any complements, so we're free to attach this AP as an adjunct. The lexical entry for *young* is:

(18) *young*

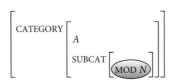

We can thus use the ADJOIN rule adjoining the tree in (3) to the noun, thus checking the circled MOD feature in (18). This gives us the NP in (19):

(19)

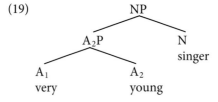

This NP can serve as the complement of the D head *the*, giving (20):

(20)

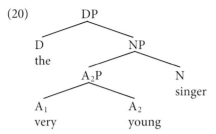

We've now finished all the NPs and PPs. In the example we're looking at here, there are no PPs modifying N heads, but keep in mind that PPs can also modify NPs as adjuncts. Our next task is to construct the VP. As a matter of convention, we always attach complements first, then adjuncts, and then finally specifiers. So let's start with the complement of the verb, which is the complex DP given in (17). This DP satisfies the internal feature in the (abbreviated) lexical entry for *lost* given in (21) and giving the tree in (22) by virtue of C-MERGE:

(21) *lost*

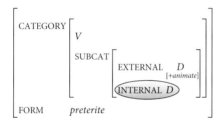

(22)

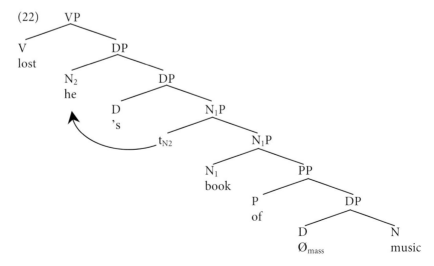

Next, we attach adjuncts. The preposition *on* has a MOD feature that lets it adjoin to a V (see (6) above). Although in most circumstances it doesn't matter, I suggest that in general you ADJOIN adjuncts before you do any S-MERGER because there are a few cases where doing it in the reverse order will give you an incorrect ordering of words.

(23)

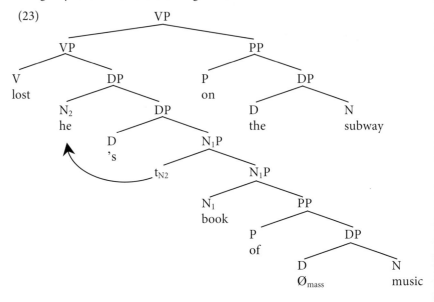

Finally, we have to S-MERGE a DP to check the verb's EXTERNAL feature. This DP must be +*animate*. The animacy of the D is inherited from its N complement by tagging, as discussed in unit 16. The DP in (20) meets this criterion.

(24)

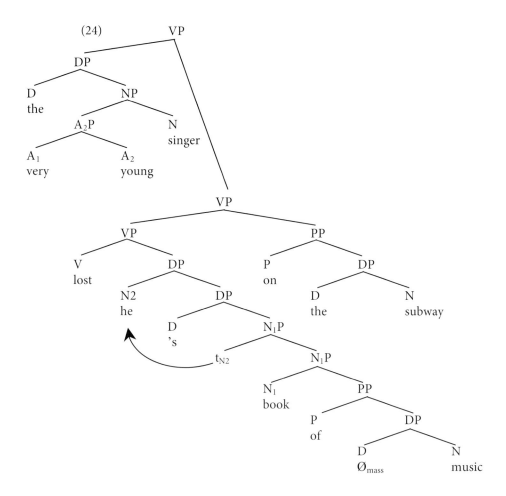

Although this gives us the correct surface string order for the sentence, it fails to include the T node necessary to license the preterite verb. The lexical entry for this is taken from unit 16:

(25)

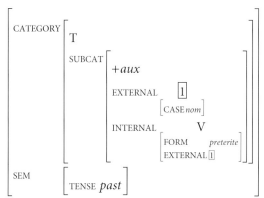

The complement to this T is the VP in (24). Note that the verb is preterite in form, matching up with the internal requirement in (25). The external feature of this T requires that the specifier of the VP be moved (remerged) into the specifier of the TP. The reasons for this move would be more obvious if we had an overt T head like *will*, but we assume it happens here too. Both the C-MERGER of T with the VP and the movement into the specifier are represented in (26):

(26)

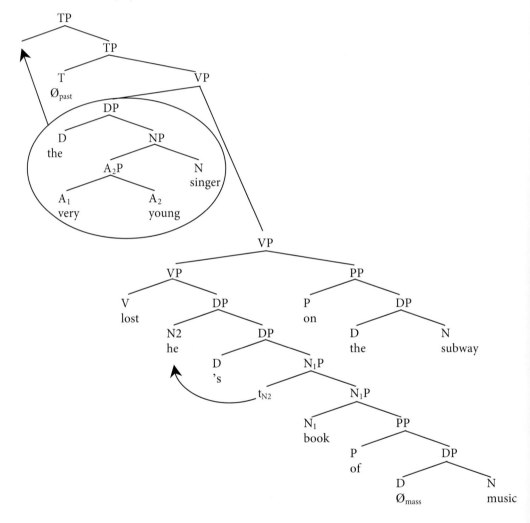

18.2 Example 2

As a matter of contrast with (1), consider how we might tree the sentence

(27) The very young singer lost <u>the book of music by Beethoven</u> in the subway.

This sentence is nearly identical to that of example (1), but differs in one crucial way. In this structure, the PP next to *music* modifies *music*, not *lost*. So the adjunction of this PP happens much lower in the tree. In particular, we have the DP *the book of music by Beethoven*. This is treed in (28). The rest of the tree would be identical to that in (26).

(28)

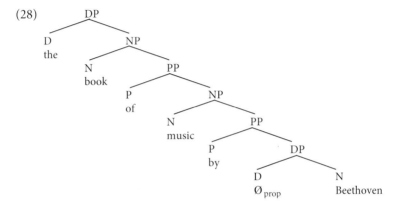

18.3 Example 3

Next let's tree a sentence with an embedded clause:

(29) John said that the very young singer lost the music in the subway.

When drawing a sentence with an embedded clause, always start by drawing the tree for that embedded clause first. In this case, the embedded clause is identical to the clause we drew in example (1). I won't torture you by running through that again. This TP is a complement to the complementizer *that*, which takes statements as complements. We'll be returning to sentence types and complementizers in later units, but for now just assume that all complementizers have an [INTERNAL T] feature. I'm going to cheat with this tree and use a triangle for the TP, but when you are drawing trees, you shouldn't use this short cut:

(30)

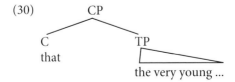

221

This CP is a complement to the verb *say*:

(31)

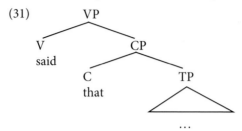

The rest of the derivation is similar to example (1). We S-MERGE the specifier of the VP (the animate proper DP *John*), then merge Ø$_{past}$, then move *John* to the specifier of the TP:

(32)

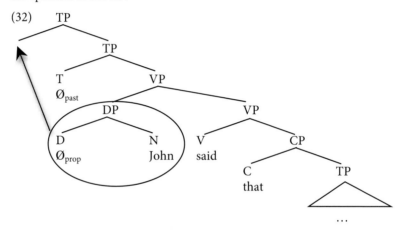

18.4 Summary

Below, you have an exercise with five sentences with various kinds of tree drawing to do. For each of these sentences you'll probably want to write out the lexical entries for each of the words if we haven't seen them already. Think carefully about what modifies what, and what elements are required by what other elements when you are constructing these entries. Once you have the entries, give the tree a go. Try your best; as usual, the answers follow in the grey box at the end of the unit.

Exercise **Q1** 📖 Draw the trees for the following sentences:

(a)   Helen likes a good bite from an apple.

(b)   Lynn despises the drawing of trees.

(c)   That the University imposed budget cuts infuriated the Dean.

(d)   The very grumpy old man found a package of letters in the trash yesterday.

(e)   He always said that the drinking of liquor on weekdays cleared his mind.

Suggested further reading

- Carnie (2006), chapters 5 and 6
- Larson (2010), unit 8

Answers to questions

Q1

(a)

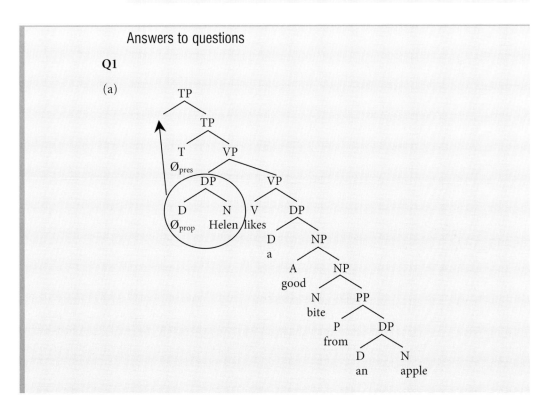

(b)

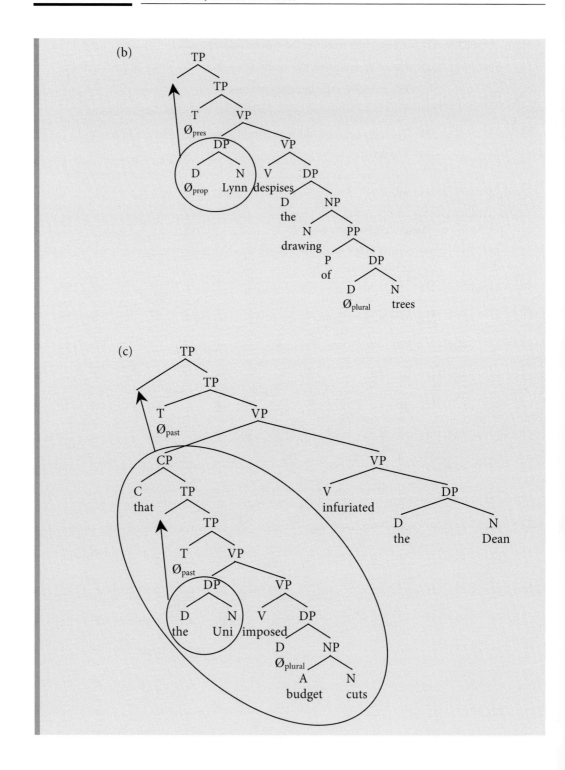

(c)

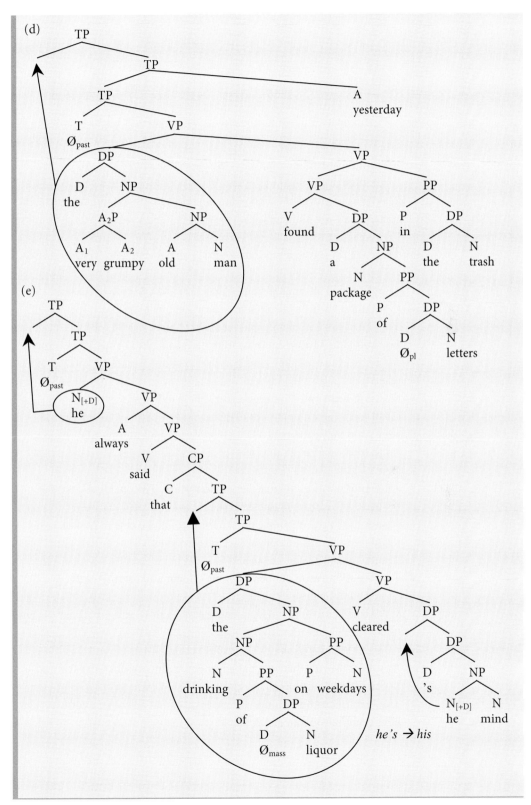

(d)

(e)

he's → his

GROUP 3 REVIEW

The following were the major ideas introduced in group 3:

- Constituents are words or groups of words that behave as single units.
- There are several tests for constituency including the stand-alone test, the replacement test and displacement.
- Tree structures represent constituency.
- There are three major types of constituent: complements, specifiers and adjuncts.
- Complements are attached due to the INTERNAL feature of a head.
- C-MERGE is the rule that attaches complements to heads.
- We practiced attaching complements in DPs, NPs, PPs, VPs and TPs. We saw how SUBCAT features in combination with the C-MERGE rule explain the order of modals, auxiliaries and verbs.
- Specifiers are attached because of the EXTERNAL feature of a head.
- S-MERGE is the rule that attaches specifiers to heads.
- Subjects are generated in the specifier of the VP, then moved for case reasons to the specifier of TP. This explains quantifier positioning in English and the position of subjects in VSO languages like Irish.
- The operation MOVE takes an item already in the tree and moves it to a different position to satisfy a second feature. The operation MOVE is triggered by tags, often to mark specific features such as Case.
- Possessive DPs also involve movement and, in the case of pronominal possessives, special morphological rewrite rules.
- Complementary distribution shows us that 's is actually a determiner.
- Tagging allows us to explain both movement and certain required agreement relations.
- We learned how to distinguish complements from adjuncts using various tests including reordering and adjacency.
- Adjuncts are introduced by the feature MOD.
- ADJOIN is the rule that attaches adjuncts. It differs from C-MERGE and S-MERGE in that the resultant structure is a projection of the non-head.
- The Principle of Full Interpretation ensures that all the features of heads have been fully satisfied.

- The Principle of Headedness allows a phrase to stand in the place of a specified head. So if a SUBCAT feature requires a D, then a DP can be used, etc.
- Some words and categories are null (i.e. have no phonological content). We know they are there because they have semantic effects, and are required for the combinatoric system to work correctly.

4 Movement and control

UNIT 19 PASSIVES

Objectives:
- Review the identification of passives vs. actives.
- Look at the feature structure of the passive auxiliary $be_{passive}$.
- Figure out why the doers of actions appear to be optional in passives.
- Determine the feature structure for the preposition by_{agent}.
- Draw the trees for the passive sentences.

19.1 Review

Comment Recall from unit 9 our discussion of voice. Voice refers to the perspective on the action. Active sentences highlight the doer of an action, passive sentences have the item that is acted upon as the subject of the sentence. Consider:

(1) (a) Calvin ate the beef waffles.   *active*

    (b) The beef waffles were eaten (by Calvin).   *passive*

In an active sentence, the doer of the sentence (*Calvin*) appears in the subject (first) position and the thing acted upon (*the beef waffles*) appears in the object position. Recall that in English, the passive voice is marked with a *be* auxiliary and the participial form of the verb: *The beef waffles <u>were eaten</u>*. The formula for a passive is BE + PARTICIPLE (contrast this with the perfect, where the participle is combined with the verb *have*). Active sentences bear no special marking.

Exercise **Q1** ✍ To remind yourself how to identify passives from actives, mark which sentences are passive and which ones are active:

    (a) Pangur ate the tuna.   Active   Passive

    (b) Drywall was put up just before the holidays. Active   Passive

    (c) Thomas drank the milk.   Active   Passive

    (d) Jennifer smelled the milk.   Active   Passive

    (e) Art put up the drywall.   Active   Passive

    (f) The piano will be played.   Active   Passive

231

Discussion Recall from unit 13 that passive *be* (be_{pass}) can only be followed by a main verb in its participial form. This was seen in the following data:

(2) (a)   The cake was eaten.   (main verb in participial form)

(b)   *The cake was been eaten.   (*another passive auxiliary)

(c)   *The cake was been eating.   (*a progressive auxiliary)

(d)   *The cake was have eaten.   (*a perfective auxiliary)

(e)   *The cake was willen eat.   (*a modal auxiliary)

Based on this data, we came up with the following lexical entry for be_{pass}:

(3) be_{pass} (first try)

$$
\begin{bmatrix}
\text{CATEGORY} & V \\[4pt]
& \text{SUBCAT} \begin{bmatrix} +aux \\ \text{INTERNAL} \begin{bmatrix} V \\ \neg aux \\ [\text{FORM} \quad participle] \end{bmatrix} \end{bmatrix} \\[4pt]
\text{FORM} & bare \\
\text{SEM} & [\text{VOICE} \quad passive]
\end{bmatrix}
$$

The value of the INTERNAL feature requires that it be a main verb ($\neg aux$) and that is in its participial form (typically ending in *-en* or *-ed*).

19.2 The INTERNAL feature

Comment The lexical entry in (3) can't be right though: it fails to say anything about the EXTERNAL argument. Auxiliary verbs in general use tagging to indicate that the subject of the embedded verb is the same as the subject of the auxiliary. Recall from unit 16 the following lexical entry for perfective *have*:

(4) $have_{perf}$

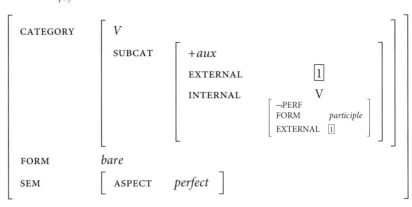

232

In (4) the external feature is tagged as being identical to the external feature of its complement. This means that the EXTERNAL argument of the main verb (e.g. "eat") will become the EXTERNAL argument of *have* (like *John* in *John has eaten*).

Exercise **Q2** 📖 Tagging the two external arguments, as in (4), won't work for passives. Why not? To help you answer this question, compare the pairs of sentences in (5); pay careful attention to which argument of the verb ends up as the subject of the sentence in the passive:

(5) (a) Pangur ate the tuna.

  (b) The tuna was eaten.

  (c) Sam gave the gift to Dean.

  (d) The gift was given to Dean.

  (e) Tom danced a waltz.

  (f) A waltz was danced.

Discussion We need to tag the EXTERNAL argument of the passive *be* with the INTERNAL argument of its complement:

(6) *be*~*pass*~ (second try)

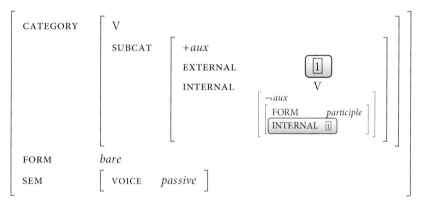

19.3 The EXTERNAL feature

Exercise **Q3** 📖 Think about the EXTERNAL argument of the verb *eat*. This verb requires that we have an animate "eater" in the sentence. Which of the following two passive sentences does the lexical entry in (6) predict will be grammatical?

  (a) The cheese was eaten.

  (b) The cheese was Tom eaten.

Q4 📖 Explain why.

Q5 📖 Is the sentence actually grammatical?

Comment We need some way to suppress the external argument in passives. We will do this by requiring that the FORM feature of the external argument of the complement verb is null. This means that the only thing that can be the external argument of a passive is a null element (we will return to the cases with *by* phrases shortly). The lexical entry for *be*~*pass*~ is:

(7) *be*~*pass*~ (final version)

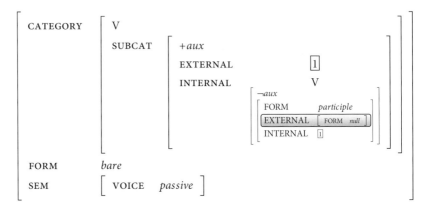

Exercise Q6 ▢ Using (7) above as a model, and referring back to the feature structures in unit 13, write up the feature structure for *is*~*pass*~.

Q7 ▢ Write up the feature structure for *was*~*pass*~.

Q8 ▢ Write up the feature structure for *being*~*pass.*~

Q9 ▢ Write up the feature structure for *been*~*pass*~.

Challenge Draw the feature structures for *were*~*pass*~ and *are*~*pass*~. Keep in mind that these feature structures have to work both for all the plurals (*we, you* (pl), *they*), but also for singular *you*. This is the tricky part!

19.4 PRO: the null pronoun

Definition In the feature structure in (7), we refer to an element with the feature [FORM *null*]: this is a pronoun with no phonological content. We've seen many null elements before (usually written as Ø); these all bear this feature. The element we're going to use as the silent subject in passive constructions is called PRO. We're also going to use PRO in a kind of sentence called a "Control Construction," which we'll discuss in the next unit. For the moment, the feature structure for PRO that we'll use is given in (8):

(8)   PRO

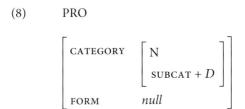

In the case of a verb like *eat*, this can satisfy the EXTERNAL feature, so we get a tree like (9). In this tree, the object *the cheese* has C-merged to satisfy the INTERNAL feature of *eaten*, and PRO S-MERGES to satisfy the EXTERNAL feature.

(9)

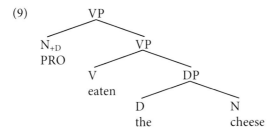

We then MERGE this structure with some passive form of the verb *be*. We'll use the past tense form *was*$_{pass}$ here:

(10)

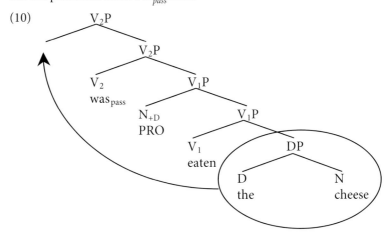

There are two things going on in this VP. (a) The verb *was*$_{pass}$ selects a complement whose external feature is null. This is accomplished by PRO, in the specifier of V$_2$P. (b) The tag in the EXTERNAL feature of *was*$_{pass}$ triggers the movement of the DP into the specifier of *was*$_{pass}$.

For completeness sake, let's C-MERGE this structure with Ø$_{past}$, whose tagged CASE feature will trigger the subsequent movement of *the cheese* into the specifier of TP.

(11)

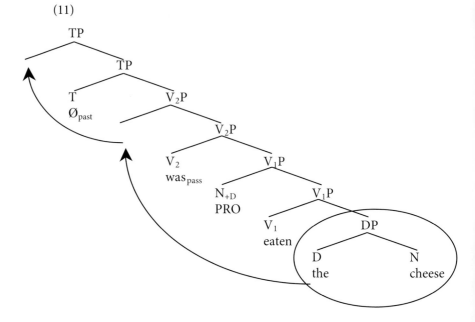

Exercise **Q10** 📖 Using (11) above as a model, draw the trees for the following sentences. Keep in mind that some of these will require extra VPs and extra steps of movement.

   (a)   The cheese will be eaten.

   (b)   The cheese is eaten.

   (c)   The cheese has been eaten.

Challenge   One detail of PRO is problematic. PRO is required in passives, but it can't appear in active sentences (otherwise we'd get sentences like *has eaten the cheese*, where PRO is the subject). Why can't PRO show up in normal active sentences? A hint to solving this problem: consider the possibility that PRO, because it is silent, doesn't bear any CASE feature.

19.5 *By-phrases*

Comment   In passives, the "doer" of the action is often optionally marked by a phrase starting with the preposition *by*, as in (12):

(12) The cheese was eaten by the mouse.

This PP bears all the hallmarks of an adjunct: it can be separated from the head by another element (13a); it can be reordered (13b) with other adjuncts.

(13) (a)   The cheese was eaten quietly by the mouse.

(b)   The cheese was eaten by the mouse quietly.

This tells us that these PPs are attached into the tree using the rule of ADJOIN. ADJOIN happens precisely when a modifier has the feature MOD. Therefore, we're going to want to come up with a feature structure for *by* that includes this feature. Such a structure would look like (14):

(14) *by*$_{agent}$

$$
\begin{bmatrix}
\text{CATEGORY} & P \\
& \text{SUBCAT} \begin{bmatrix} \text{INTERNAL} & D_i \\ \text{MOD} & \begin{bmatrix} & V \\ \text{EXTERNAL} & \begin{bmatrix} \text{FORM} & null \end{bmatrix}_i \\ \text{FORM} & participle \end{bmatrix} \end{bmatrix}
\end{bmatrix}
$$

This P takes a complement of category D (which corresponds to the DP representing the doer of the action). It modifies (MOD) a participle V that has a null EXTERNAL argument. This ensures that this *by*-phrase always modifies a passive verb.

Notation   There is one additional item in the feature structure that you have not seen before. This is the "index" $_i$ found on both the D_i and the [FORM *null*]$_i$. This element indicates that the DP serving as the complement of *by* must refer to the same person as the doer of the action represented *by* PRO. When two items in a feature structure or tree bear the same index (i, j, k, etc.) they are said to be **coindexed**. When two items are coindexed, it means that they refer to the same individual. The complement of the preposition (*by the mouse*) must be the same individual as the person represented by the PRO. So PRO must refer to the mouse!

Exercise   Q11 📖 Draw the tree for *The cheese was eaten by the mouse.*

Summary   In this unit, we've looked at passives in more detail than in previous units. We reviewed how to identify passives. Then we looked at the fact that the subject of a passive is the same as the object in an active. We accomplished this by tagging the EXTERNAL argument of *be*$_{pass}$ with the INTERNAL argument of the next verb down. Next, we turned to the lack of an overt "doer" in passive sentences. This was accomplished by requiring that the EXTERNAL argument of the embedded verb had to be null (the EXTERNAL argument is PRO). We also looked at the *by* preposition which introduces optional "doer" arguments, which are coindexed with the PRO.

Suggested further reading

- Adger (2003), chapter 6
- Baker, Johnson and Roberts (1989)
- Carnie (2006), chapter 10
- Collins (2005)
- Goodall (1993)
- Haegeman (1994), chapter 6
- Hornstein (1999)
- Huddleston and Pullum (2005), unit 15
- Jaeggli (1986)
- Kim and Sells (2008), chapter 9
- Kroeger (2004), chapter 3
- Radford (1988), chapter 8; (2004), chapter 8
- Sag, Wasow and Bender (2003), chapter 10
- Tallerman (2005), chapter 7

Answers to questions

Q1 (a) active; (b) passive; (c) active; (d) active; (e) active; (f) passive

Q2 Tagging the two EXTERNAL arguments won't work here because the subject (EXTERNAL argument) of the passive is the INTERNAL argument of the main verb.

Q3–5 The lexical entry predicts that sentence (b) would be the right one, because there is nothing in this lexical entry that gets rid of the "eater" (*Tom*). So the EXTERNAL argument of *eat* can be expressed (and would show up as the specifier of *eat*), giving way to the strange and ungrammatical sentence in (b).

Q6 is_{pass}

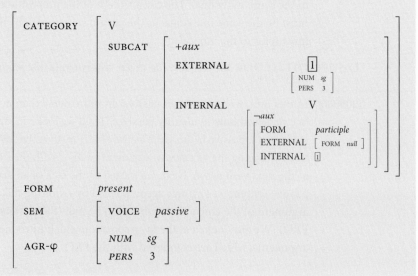

Q7 *was*~pass~

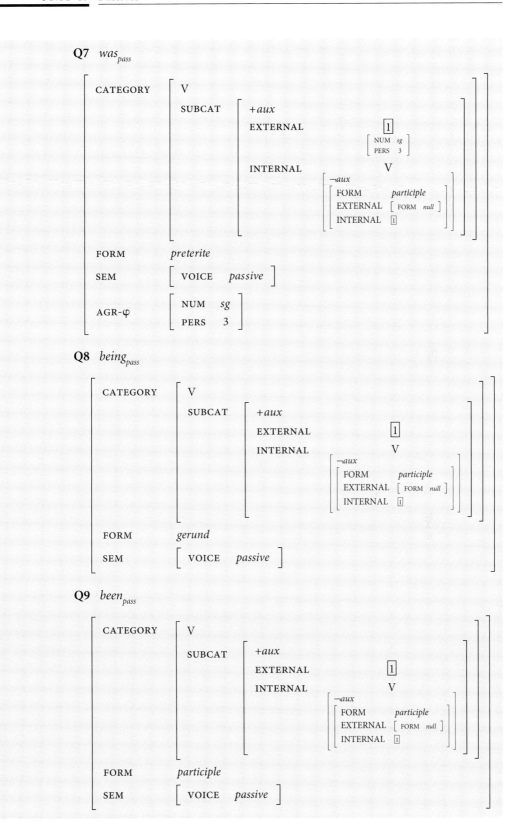

Q8 *being*~pass~

Q9 *been*~pass~

Q10 *(a)*

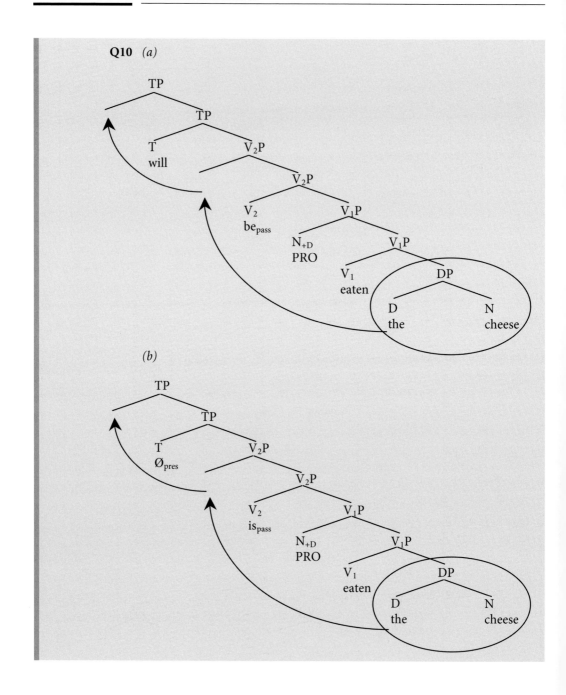

(b)

(c)

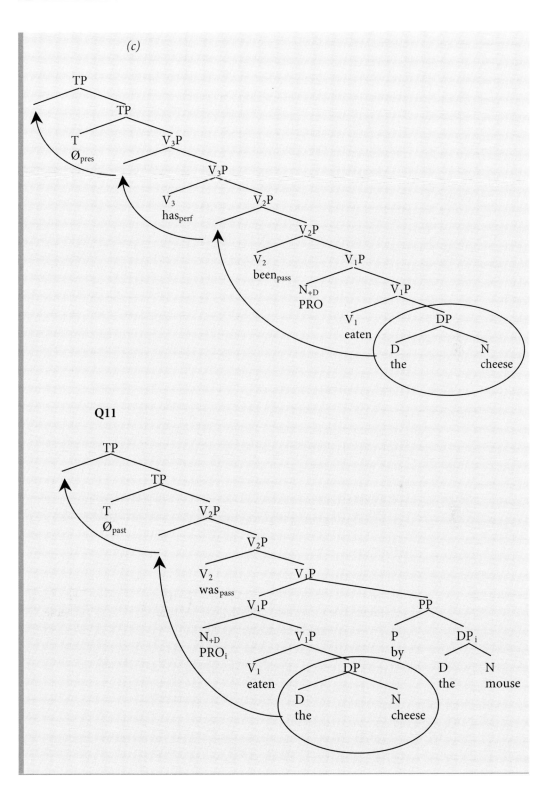

Q11

UNIT 20 NON-FINITE CLAUSES 1: CONTROL CONSTRUCTIONS

> **Objectives:**
> - Distinguish finite from non-finite clauses.
> - Develop a feature structure and trees for sentences with non-finite *to*.
> - Learn about the copula and structures for predicates like *is reluctant* and *is eager*.
> - Learn to distinguish attributive and predicative usages of adjectives.
> - Use PRO to represent the implied argument.
> - Formulate the feature structures for control predicates.
> - Draw trees for control constructions.

20.1 Non-finite clauses

Comment In units 8 and 18, we looked briefly at embedded clauses (which were CPs), which were the complement to certain verbs. The clauses we've looked at so far have all been tensed. In this unit, we're going to look at a very specific kind of embedded clause that lacks a tense. These clauses are called non-finite clauses.

Definition A **non-finite clause** is a clause that does not morphologically express the tense relations of past, future or present nor has a modal auxiliary like *should, can, must,* etc. A clause that does mark one of those relations is called a **finite clause**.

Discussion In many languages, non-finite clauses are marked by using a special verb form called the **infinitive**. For example, in French, verbs marked with the *-ir* or *-er* endings are infinitives. English does not technically have an infinitive. Instead, in most non-finite clauses,[1] in English, we use the bare form of the verb coupled with a special modal/T element in *to*, as seen in the pair below:

(1) (a) I think [that John left].   *finite clause*

(b) I asked [John <u>to leave</u>].   *non-finite clause*

---

[1] Although not all of them! There are cases where non-finite clauses exist with a gerund (e.g. *Pangur hates [eating spam]. [Doing his homework] bothered John*), or with a bare verb form (e.g. *I've never seen [John eat peanuts] before*). For reasons of length, we're only going to treat infinitives marked with *to* in this book.

242

Exercise **Q1** ✆ Using the pattern in (1) as a guide, determine if the embedded clauses in the following sentences are finite or non-finite. Be careful, the word *to* is only a marker of a non-finite clause when it is not in front of a DP or noun! Circle the correct answer.

(a)	I think that George left.	*finite*	*non-finite*
(b)	I think that George should leave.	*finite*	*non-finite*
(c)	I want George to leave.	*finite*	*non-finite*
(d)	I believe George left.	*finite*	*non-finite*
(e)	I believe George to have gone.	*finite*	*non-finite*
(f)	I think George went to the store.	*finite*	*non-finite*
(g)	I asked George to go to the store.	*finite*	*non-finite*

Comment In finite clauses, a subject is obligatory. In many non-finite clauses the subject is either optional and implied or obligatorily absent, as seen in (2):

(2) (a) I want George to leave.

  (b) I want to leave.

In (2b), the non-finite clause has no subject parallel to the *George* in (2a). Instead, there is an implied subject that is the same as the pronoun *I*.

When the subject of an infinitive is a pronoun and is actually present, it takes accusative case as in (3):

(3) I want <u>him</u> to leave.

Exercise **Q2** ✆ Using the patterns in (2) and (3) as guides, determine if the embedded clauses in the following sentences are finite or non-finite.

(a) I asked him to leave.

(b) I asked that he leave.

(c) I asked to leave.

(d) I saw him leave.

(e) Susan seems to have gone.

(f) It seems that Susan left.

20.2 The structure of non-finite clauses

Discussion Focusing on the structure of non-finite clauses marked with *to*, let's consider what the featural composition of this word is, and what the trees for a non-finite construction might look like. Let's start by figuring out what category *to* belongs to.

Exercise **Q3** 📖 In what ways is the *to* in infinitives like the preposition *to* in sentences like *I went to the store* and in what ways is it different? Think carefully about what kinds of elements must follow the preposition *to* and what the meaning of the preposition *to* might be. Are these the same as the *to* in non-finite clauses?

Discussion This suggests that we have at least two *to*s in English. One is a preposition *to_p*, the other is the marker of non-finite clauses. So we know it isn't the preposition, but what is it?!

Exercise **Q4** 📖 Recall that modal auxiliaries require that the verb following them be in the bare form. Perfective *have* and passive *be* require the participial form, and the progressive *be* takes the gerund. Based on the following data, is *to* more like a modal, a perfective auxiliary or a progressive auxiliary?

(4) (a) George wants to leave.

(b) *George wants to left.

(c) *George wants to leaving.

Discussion The *to* found in non-finite clauses selects a bare form of verbs, just like modals. Modals are of category T, so perhaps we can presume that *to* is of category T too. This makes sense, in a twisted way, because *to* marks the absence of tense morphology (i.e. the definition of non-finite clauses).

Now that we know what category *to* is, we need to set up a feature structure for it. Recall the feature structure we developed for *will*. We'll use this as a starting point.

(5) *will*

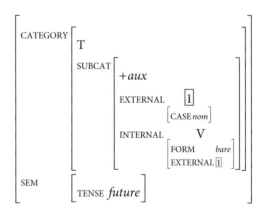

A couple of things must change here for *to*. The SEM feature must be different. We will propose that the value here would be *non-finite*. The other major difference is that in most circumstances the subject of the non-finite clauses must be absent. We used the [CASE *nom*] feature to require a subject in tensed clauses. Obviously, this must be different here. For the moment, let us leave the nature of the EXTERNAL feature of *to* as unspecified. We'll return to this feature later in the unit once we examine the difference between raising and control features. (But to give you a hint, think PRO!)

(6)   *to*$_T$

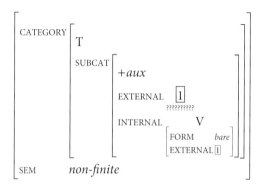

With this feature structure, we get a tree like (7) for non-finite clauses (again leaving aside the EXTERNAL argument, and assuming that *want* has a TP as its INTERNAL argument).

(7)

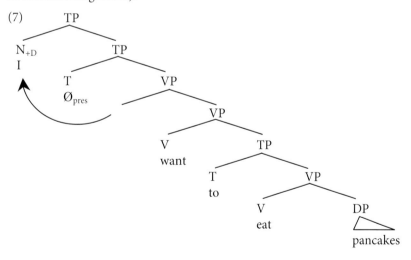

Exercise **Q5** 📖 One of the pet peeves of prescriptive grammarians is the so-called "split infinitive" like the famous *To boldly go where no man has gone before.* In split infinitives, one finds an adverb between the *to* and the verb (such as *boldly* in the famous sentence). The origins of this prescription are dubious at best – see, for example, the extensive discussion in Pinker (1995). In addition, one finds frequent examples of "split infinitives" in the works of Shakespeare and other famous authors. Nevertheless, it is taught religiously in grammar classes around the world. Think about where adverbs adjoin in tree structures for sentences like *I boldly ate a pepper*. Now, look at the tree in (7): where would these same adverbs adjoin to a verb like *eat*. Does our theory predict that a sentence like (8) below is grammatical or not? What does this tell us about prescriptive grammar?

(8) I want to boldly eat a pepper.

Exercise **Q6** 📖 Draw the tree for sentence (8).

20.3 *Is ready*

Comment One of the most common constructions where one finds non-finite clauses is as the complement to predicates such as *is ready*, *is eager* and *is able*. In order to study these we need to briefly look at how such predicates are formed.

Definition The *is* verb here is not an auxiliary that we've already seen. Instead, this one is known as the **copula**. The copula is a special form of *be* used to link a non-verbal predicate (a property being attributed to the subject) to the subject. For example, in the following sentences the copula (underlined) links the predicate (italics) to the subject.

(9) (a) Pangur is *happy*.

(b) Jean is *the teacher*.

(c) Fiona is *in bed*.

In each of these sentences, we have a predicate that isn't a verb. In (9a), the predicate is an adjective; in (9b), it's a DP; and in (9c), it's a PP.

Exercise **Q7** 🖝 Using the tests you learned about in Unit 4, determine the parts of speech for the following words (some of these may be tricky, but do your best). These words are often found with non-finite complements.

(a)	likely	N V A P
(b)	eager	N V A P
(c)	easy	N V A P
(d)	able	N V A P
(e)	reluctant	N V A P
(f)	anxious	N V A P
(g)	apt	N V A P
(h)	certain	N V A P
(i)	bound	N V A P
(j)	ready	N V A P

Comment   Copular *be* (*be$_{cop}$*) can appear with any non-verb complement, but we'll focus here on the cases where it takes an adjective complement.

Exercise   **Q8** 📖 Think about the meaning of the sentence *George is ready*. What element is *George* the EXTERNAL argument of? Is it *ready*, *is* or both? In many languages, sentences like *George is ready* are expressed without any copular verb (e.g. the Turkish sentence *Deniz mavi* "The sea is blue," literally "The sea blue"). Does this affect your answer?

Definition   Adjectives (and other categories) that take arguments are said to be **predicative**. The presence of EXTERNAL features alone suffices to make an adjective a predicate. All the adjectives in Q7 are predicative. This contrasts with **attributive** uses of adjectives which are blessed with a MOD feature, and attach into the sentence using the rule of ADJOIN. So in the DP *the big man*, *big* is attributive and attaches into the tree using MOD and ADJOIN. By contrast, in the sentence *the man is big*, *big* is predicative and takes *the man* as an EXTERNAL argument. *The man* is merged into the tree using S-MERGE because of *big*'s EXTERNAL feature.

Exercise   **Q9** 🖚 Determine if the adjectives in the following forms are attributive or predicative.

(a) The smelly shoes walked off on their own.   A   P

(b) Roderick is ready.   A   P

(c) Fred was scared of the dangerous road. (*Note: two adjectives in this sentence*)

                                                                         i.   A   P

                                                                        ii.   A   P

(d) The shoes are smelly.   A   P

(e) The evil cat was happy. (*Note: two adjectives in this sentence*)

                                                                        i.   A   P

                                                                        ii.   A   P

Discussion   Next we have to determine the feature structure for *be$_{cop}$*. In previous units, we resolved situations where a single DP is the external argument of more than one item by tagging the two positions together and then forcing movement. We can do the same here. We also have to make sure it selects for the correct category. This *be* is found with any predicate that is not a verb, but that has an external argument. The highlighted portion of this feature structure expresses this:

247

(10) *be*_{cop}

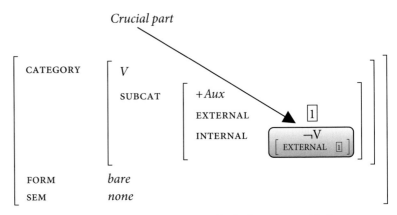

Crucial part

The ¬V here means "any category except V." The [EXTERNAL ①] feature entails that the category be predicative (having an EXTERNAL feature), and that the EXTERNAL argument is moved to the specifier position of *be*_{cop} (indicated with tagging). The semantic feature here is valued as *none*, because this verb is completely missing in other languages, which can express the same notions without a verb.[2]

Exercise **Q10** 📖 Give the feature structure for *is*_{cop}.

Discussion Let's now work on the structure of a sentence with a simple attributive adjective (one that does not take an infinitival complement; we'll return to these below):

(11) George is big.

Let's assume that (part of) the feature structure for *big* is something like (12):

(12) *big*

$$\begin{bmatrix} \text{CATEGORY} & \begin{bmatrix} A \\ \text{SUBCAT} \begin{bmatrix} \text{EXTERNAL } D \end{bmatrix} \end{bmatrix} \\ \text{SEM} & big \end{bmatrix}$$

---

2   It might alternately be given a semantics like "has the property of X" and languages apparently without *be*_{cop} simply have a null copular verb. There isn't much evidence to distinguish the two options, so we'll leave this possibility aside here.

This predicative adjective takes an EXTERNAL argument (the DP *George*) with which it S-MERGES:

(13)

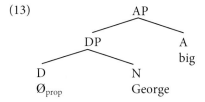

This C-MERGES with *is*$_{cop}$, to satisfy *is*$_{cop}$'s INTERNAL feature:

(14)

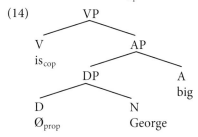

In order to satisfy the tagged EXTERNAL feature of *is*$_{cop}$, we move the DP to the specifier of the VP:

(15)

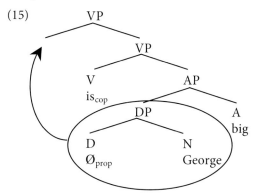

Finally, merge Ø$_{pres}$ T node and do the requisite movement to its specifier.

(16)

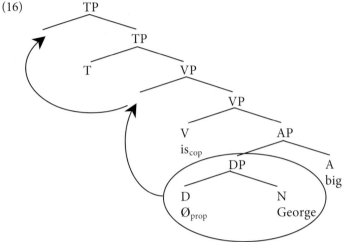

Discussion Next let's start on the derivation for *George is ready to leave*. A first pass at the feature structure for *ready* is given in (17). We'll need to revise this slightly later on in this unit.

(17) *ready* (preliminary)

$$
\begin{bmatrix}
\text{CATEGORY} & \begin{bmatrix} A \end{bmatrix} \\
& \text{SUBCAT} \begin{bmatrix} \text{EXTERNAL} & D \\ \text{INTERNAL} & T \\ & \begin{bmatrix} \text{FORM } non\text{-}finite \end{bmatrix} \end{bmatrix} \\
\text{SEM} & ready
\end{bmatrix}
$$

Exercise **Q11** 📖 Using the information in (17), and modeling the tree on a combination of (7) and (16), draw the tree for *George is ready to leave*.

Exercise **Q12** 📖 Not all predicates that take non-finite complements are adjectives. Some are verbs. For example, *want* takes a non-finite TP complement as in *I want to leave*. Can you think of at least five other verbs that take non-finite TP complements?

20.4 The missing subject

Comment Now we turn to the problem of the missing subject in infinitivals. In many non-finite constructions the subject of the embedded verb is absent or implied. Consider the sentences in (18):

(18) (a)   Phillip ate a waffle.

    (b)   Phillip wants a cookie.

    (c)   Phillip wants to eat a waffle.

In (18a) we see that the verb *eat* requires someone to do the eating (the eater, *Phillip*) and takes an object to be eaten (*a waffle*). In (18b) we see that *want* requires both a wanter (*Phillip*) and something wanted (*a cookie*). When we combine the two together in (18c), we still have a wanter (*Phillip*), and something wanted (the eating of the waffle) and something eaten (*a waffle*), but the eater is implied as being the same individual as the wanter (i.e. *Phillip*). There is no overt realization of the eater.

In the last unit, we saw a similar situation with passives, where there was an implied "doer" of the action. Here too we have an implied "doer" of the action in the non-finite clause. In unit 19, we solved this with PRO. We can do the same here for many of the sentences lacking overt subjects with infinitives. We'll make this part of the lexical entry for *to$_T$*, which we left unfinished above:

(19) *to$_T$*

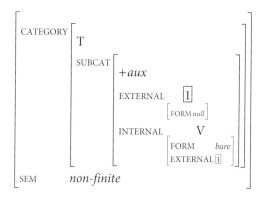

The external argument of to_T must be null (i.e. PRO). Therefore, the tree for a sentence like *I want to eat pancakes* would be:

(20)

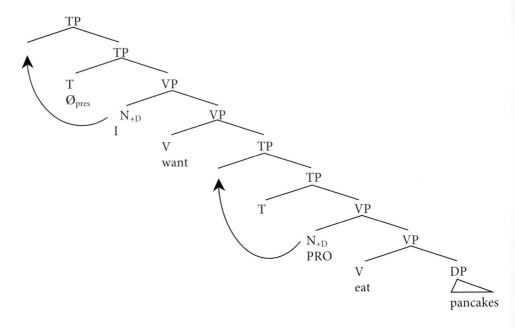

Exercise **Q13** 📖 Redraw the tree for *George is ready to leave*. This time make sure you include PRO.

Challenge Not all non-finite clauses contain PRO specifiers.[3] For example, with many verbs you can have an overt subject marked with the word *for*:

(a) I asked <u>for Susan</u> to buy me some potatoes.

What are we to make of these structures? What adjustments to the lexical entry for *to* are needed in order to allow a subject in these cases? What is *for*? Is it a complementizer like *that* or is it a preposition? How would you figure out the difference?

Exercise **Q14** 📖 In unit 19, we saw that *by*-phrases could attach to certain structures containing PRO. This option is not available here. The PRO in control constructions cannot be coindexed with a *by*-phrase:

(a) *I want to leave by me.

Study the lexical entry for *by* given in the previous unit and explain why that feature structure predicts the unacceptability of (a) and sentences like it.

---

[3] We'll see other examples of non-finite clauses without PRO in the next unit.

What is it about the restrictions on *by* that prevents it from attaching in cases like (a)? (*Bonus*: note that *by*-phrases are OK in sentences like *I want to be left alone by the police.* Why is the *by*-phrase OK in this sentence and not in (a)?)

Comment   One thing remains to be established with respect to these sentences. With the verb *want*, and the copula + adjective combo *is ready*, the PRO argument must refer to the same individual as the wanter or the person who is ready. Just as we did for *by* phrases in the last unit, we stipulate this coreference by using an index. As we will see below, not all coreference relations are between the two external arguments. The coindexation depends upon which main predicate is used. We will stipulate in the lexical entry for *want* that the external argument of *want* has to be the same as the external argument of the embedded predicate.

(21) *wants* (taking a non-finite clause complement)

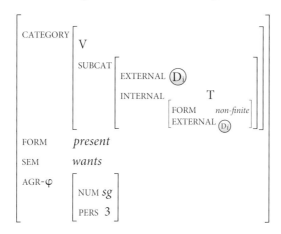

Discussion   In this feature structure, the obligatory coreference between the EXTERNAL argument of *want* and PRO is accomplished by indexing the two together here. Note that indexing and tagging are not the same thing. Tagging indicates an identity in features (which typically triggers movement); indexing, by contrast, doesn't trigger movement. Indexing just indicates that two items refer to the same individual.

Challenge   In unit 16, we claimed that subject/verb agreement and determiner/noun agreement was done with tagging. However, there is no movement in those relationships. Evaluate whether agreement relationships should be done with tagging or with coindexing. What kind of evidence would distinguish these hypotheses? Is there a technical reason to prefer one over the other?

Definition A **control predicate** is a verb like *want* or a predicative adjective like *ready*, which take non-finite embedded clauses as complements and where the external argument of the embedded predicate is realized as a PRO.

Exercise **Q15** 📖 Draw the feature structure for predicative *ready* (using (17) and (21) as starting points). Be sure to indicate any coindexing relations.

20.5 Object control

Exercise **Q16** ✏ In the following sentences who is the buyer of the cereal, Michael or Josh?

(a)	Michael promised Josh to buy a box of cereal.	M	J
(b)	Michael persuaded Josh to buy a box of cereal.	M	J
(c)	Michael ordered Josh to buy a box of cereal.	M	J
(d)	Michael forced Josh to buy a box of cereal.	M	J

Exercise **Q17** 📖 In sentences (b, c and d) above, does *Josh* appear to be the internal argument of the main verb (*persuade, order, force*), the external argument of the embedded verb (*buy*) or both?

Discussion With *ready, promise,* and the intransitive usage of *want,* the PRO in the embedded clause is coindexed with the EXTERNAL argument of the main verb. However, with *persuade, order* and *force* (and many other verbs) the coindexation seems to be with an INTERNAL argument of the main verb (*Josh* in the sentences above).

Definition: Control constructions where the external argument of the embedded clause is the same as the internal argument of the main verb are called **object control** constructions. Other control constructions (like that for *is ready*) are called **subject control** constructions.

Exercise **Q18** ✏ Consider the following verbs and predicates. Are they subject control (SC) or object control (OC)? A few of these can be either!

(a)	want	SC	OC	either
(b)	ask	SC	OC	either
(c)	persuade	SC	OC	either
(d)	is eager	SC	OC	either
(e)	is ready	SC	OC	either
(f)	promise	SC	OC	either
(g)	expect	SC	OC	either
(h)	urge	SC	OC	either
(i)	force	SC	OC	either

(j)	intend	SC	OC	either
(k)	requested	SC	OC	either
(l)	tell	SC	OC	either
(m)	consent	SC	OC	either
(n)	hope	SC	OC	either

Notation The sentences in exercise Q16 all have two complements (i.e. they are ditransitive). The first complement is the object *Josh*, the second complement is the non-finite clause. Recall from unit 8 that the way we notated having two internal arguments was to use the pair-bracket notation. For example, we said that the INTERNAL feature of one version of the verb *put* is [INTERNAL <D, P>] because *put* requires both a DP and a PP complement: *John put the book on the table*. One version of the verb *give* allows two DPs: *Trixie gave Marsha the wand*. Therefore, the feature is [INTERNAL <D, D>]. The trees for such structures involve three branches (**ternary branching**):

(22)
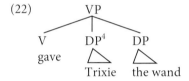

Exercise Q19 📖 Draw the feature structure for *persuaded*. Be sure to have two complements (a D and a non-finite T) and pay careful attention to what elements are coindexed in the structure.

Exercise Q20 📖 Draw the tree for *I persuaded him to leave*. Be careful that you have a PRO as the external argument of *leave*.

Challenge What do you think the lexical entries for verbs like *want, beg, expect*, etc. should look like? These verbs allow either subject control or object control. Would it be easiest to have two different lexical entries for each of these verbs?

Summary In this unit, we looked at the structure of non-finite clauses – clauses that don't express tense. We practiced identifying these structures and we looked at the nature of the modal to_T. We also took a brief tangent and looked at the structure of predicative adjectives with copular *be*. This let us provide a description for constructions like *is ready*. The modal to_T requires a null EXTERNAL argument (PRO). The fact that the reference of PRO must be identical to the subject of verbs like *want* and to the object of verbs like *persuade* is accomplished through coindexation in the feature structure for these verbs.

---

[4] I am, as in previous units, using triangles to obscure irrelevant details of trees, but you should avoid using this notational service.

In this unit, we've looked exclusively at control constructions. These are sentences where the external argument of the non-finite verb is PRO. In the next unit, we're going to look at a kind of sentence which, on the surface, looks very similar to control constructions, but on a deeper analysis we find that there is no PRO involved, and we have a movement relation a little bit like what we find with the passive; these are called raising sentences.

Suggested further reading

- Adger (2003), chapter 8
- Bresnan (2001), chapter 13
- Carnie (2006), chapter 14
- Davies and Dubinsky (2004)
- Falk (2001), chapter 5
- Haegeman (1994), chapter 5
- Huddleston and Pullum (2005), chapter 13
- Kim and Sells (2008), chapter 7
- Landau (1999)
- Larson (2010), unit 21
- Manzini (1992)
- Sag, Wasow and Bender (2003), chapter 12
- Soames and Perlmutter (1979), parts 2 and 3
- van Gelderen (2010), chapter 8

Answers to questions

Q1 (a) finite, (b) finite, (c) non-finite, (d) finite, (e) non-finite, (f) finite, (g) non-finite.

Q2 (a) non-finite, (b) finite, (c) non-finite, (d) non-finite (tricky because there is no *to* here), (e) non-finite, (f) finite.

Q3 The two words are pronounced alike, but that's where the similarities end. The preposition to must be followed by a DP (*I gave the book to the man*, **I gave the book to red*, **I gave the book to leave.*). Non-finite *to* is always followed by a VP (*I want to leave, *I want to them*). They mean different things too. The preposition *to* marks DPs as being the goals or end points of actions; the *to* in non-finite sentences marks the lack of tense.

Q4 Like modals, non-finite *to* requires the bare form of a verb.

Q5 Adverbs such as *boldly* adjoin to the VP. This will place them right between the *to* and the verb. This is the normal place for adverbs in English, so the prescriptive grammarian's ban on "splitting infinitives" is very likely unnatural, and inconsistent with other grammatical rules we know to be operating in the syntax of English.

Q6

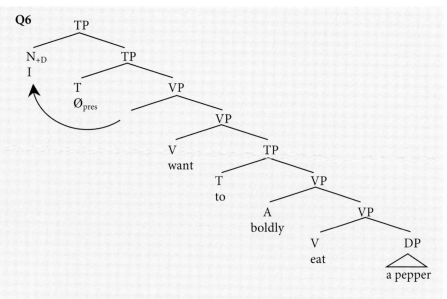

(Note this tree is missing the EXTERNAL argument of *eat* – we'll fix this problem later in this unit.)

Q7 All the words here are adjectives. They can follow a determiner and precede a noun (e.g. *the eager beaver, the reluctant president,* etc.). Some are a little tricky, but with the right context, you can get them (e.g. *the likely winner, the able workman, the ready forces, the certain victory*). *Bound* is perhaps the most difficult word to determine, at least with the intended reading, as in *he is bound to leave.* When *bound* appears in a DP it tends to mean "tied up" (*the bound man*) rather than "is likely."

Q8 Just as in cases where we have an auxiliary (such as *George is leaving.*), it appears as if *George* is the EXTERNAL argument of both *is* and *ready.* Semantically, the individual who is ready is George, suggesting that *George* is an EXTERNAL argument of the adjective *ready.* The fact that some languages lack *is* in these constructions supports this. On the other hand, *George* clearly comes before *is,* suggesting that it is also the EXTERNAL argument of *is.* In previous units, we resolved situations where a single DP is the external argument of more than one item by tagging the two positions together and then forcing movement.

Q9 (a) attributive, (b) predicative, (c) i. *scared*: predicative, ii. *dangerous*: attributive, (d) predicative, (e) i. *evil*: attributive, ii. *happy*: predicative

Q10 *is_cop*

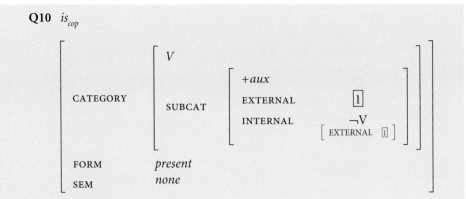

Q11

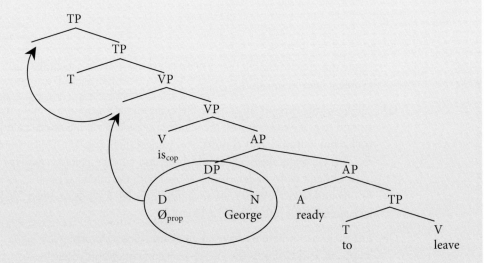

(Note that this tree is missing the EXTERNAL argument of *leave*; we return to this shortly.)

Q12 Among the many verbs that take non-finite TP complements: *want, ask, persuade, promise, expect, urge, force, intend, seems, requested, tell, consent, hope,* as well as the passives *is believed, is assured, is encouraged, is advised, is imagined.* There are probably many more.

Q13

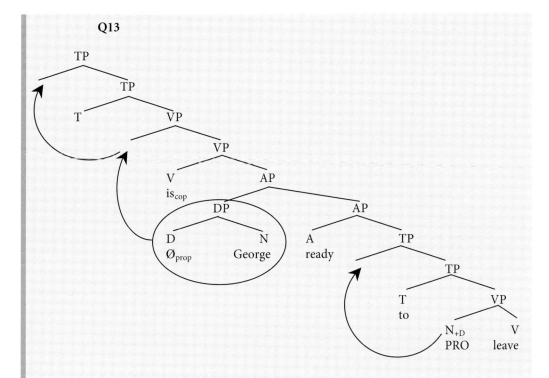

Q14 The lexical entry for *by* restricts it so that it only attaches to participles with a PRO in their specifier (i.e. only in passives). Sentence (a) is ungrammatical because *leave* is a bare verb form, not a participle. (Bonus: This sentence is OK because it has a passive in its non-finite clause. There are actually two PROs. One is the external argument of *left alone*, which can be coindexed with *by the police*, and the other is the PRO that is the specifier of the TP, which is the underlying INTERNAL argument of *left alone*.)

Q15 *ready* (final)

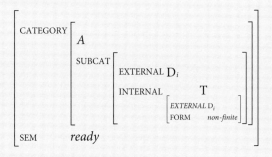

Q16 (a) M, (b) J, (c) J, (d) J

Q17 *Josh* appears to be both the EXTERNAL argument of *buy* (he's the buyer in b, c, d) *and* the INTERNAL argument of the main verb. He's who is being persuaded, ordered and forced. This is like the subject in sentences like *George wants to leave.* Josh is the object of the main verb, but is acting as the implied subject of the embedded verb too. This is the hallmark of a control construction with PRO.

Q18 (a) want   either

I want to leave (SC)

I want Bill to leave (OC)

(b) ask   either

I asked to leave (SC)

I asked Bill to leave (OC)

(c) persuade   OC

(d) is eager   SC

(e) is ready   SC

(f) promise   SC

(g) expect   either

I expected to leave (SC)

I expected Bill to leave (OC)

(h) urge   OC

(i) force   OC

(j) intend   either

I intended to leave (SC)

I intended Bill to be the winner (OC)

(k) requested   either

I requested to leave (SC)

I requested Bill to leave (OC)

(l) tell   OC

(m) consent   SC

(n) hope   SC

Q19   *persuaded*

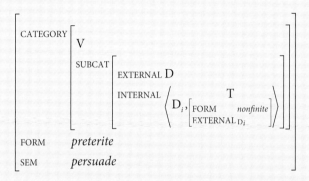

Q20

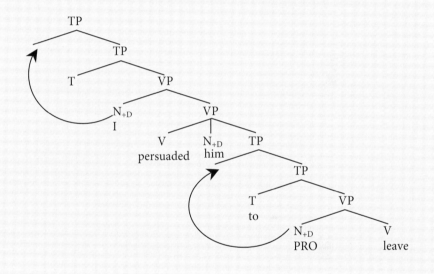

UNIT 21 NON-FINITE CLAUSES 2: RAISING SENTENCES

> **Objectives:**
> - Learn to distinguish raising sentences from control sentences.
> - Formulate the feature structures for raising predicates.
> - Draw trees for raising constructions.

21.1 Subject control vs. raising to subject

Comment In the last unit, you learned all about control constructions. In control constructions there seems to be a "missing" argument, realized by the silent PRO, which is coindexed with either the EXTERNAL or INTERNAL feature of the main clause predicate, depending upon which predicate is used. In this unit, we look at sentences that appear to be very similar, but actually have very different structures. We are going to contrast control predicates like *is ready* or *is eager* with another kind of construction called a raising construction, found with predicates like *is likely*. Look at the sentences in (1):

(1) (a) Gilbert is eager to leave. *control*

    (b) Gilbert is likely to leave. *raising*

These sentences look very much alike don't they? However, don't judge a book by its cover – surface appearances can be quite deceiving! These two sentences have very different structures and the feature structures for *eager* and *likely* are very different.

Discussion Let's start with who's doing what in (1a). Note that in (1a), the "leaver" is *Gilbert*. *Gilbert* also appears to be the person who is eager. In the last unit, we got around the fact that *George* seemed to be the argument of both *eager* and *leave* by using PRO and coindexing PRO with the EXTERNAL argument of the control predicate *is eager* (we used *is ready* in unit 20, but it is the same case):

(2) [Gilbert$_i$ is eager [PRO$_i$ to leave]]

But who is doing what in (1b) is very different. As in (1a), *Gilbert* is the "leaver." However, note that *Gilbert* is *not likely*! What is likely? Gilbert leaving is the likely thing, *not* Gilbert alone. This is true even though Gilbert is the subject of the whole sentence.

Exercise **Q1** 📖 Consider the following sentences:

(a) Gilbert is bound to leave.

(b) Gilbert is able to leave.

(c) Gilbert is certain to leave.

(d) Gilbert is anxious to leave.

(e) Gilbert seems to have gone.

(f) Gilbert is believed to have gone.

For each sentence, determine if *Gilbert* is the person who *is anxious, is believed, is certain* etc., or if instead the thing that is certain, is anxious, etc. is the action described by the non-finite clause (e.g. Gilbert's leaving is likely). If Gilbert alone has the property, then it's a control sentence. If the embedded non-finite clause has the property, then it's a raising sentence.

Discussion You may have found this exercise a little hard, but I hope the idea behind it is clear. In control sentences, there are two predicates and two subjects (which happen to be coindexed and corefer). In raising constructions, the higher predicate doesn't have its "own" EXTERNAL argument; instead, the EXTERNAL argument of the lower non-finite predicate appears to function also as the EXTERNAL argument of the higher predicate. This is very similar to what happens with auxiliaries, which share (via tagging and movement) the EXTERNAL argument of their main verb.

(3)   [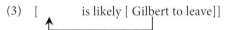 is likely [Gilbert to leave]]

Definition **Raising predicates** are predicates (like *seem, is likely, is certain,* etc.) which take a non-finite TP complement, and move the embedded EXTERNAL argument into their own subject position. They do not use PRO.

Comment Before we look at the mechanics of raising constructions let's briefly look at a couple of other tests we can use to distinguish between raising and control constructions.

21.2 The idiom test

Definition An **idiom** is a phrase or clause that has an arbitrary non-literal meaning that cannot be deduced from the component words in the phrase. The example we're going to use here is *The shit hit the fan.*[1]

---

[1] For non-native speakers this idiom means "bad things have happened" or "things got very wild in a bad way." This idiom contains the vulgarity *shit*, and may offend some readers, but I've chosen it for a reason. I'm not attempting to be shocking or disrespectful to the reader. This particular idiom has the property that it gets very silly interpretations under control constructions and gives very clear judgments. Other idioms work for this test, but the judgments aren't as clear-cut as with this one.

Discussion Idioms must be constituents. For example, one never finds an idiom that is just the subject and the object of a sentence, but excludes the verb. However, one can find plenty of VP idioms (*He let the cat out of the bag*), or sentential idioms like *The shit hit the fan.*

Idioms are usually ambiguous between a literal meaning and an idiomatic meaning. The sentence *He let the cat out of the bag* can mean either that he actually let a feline escape from a sack (literal meaning), or that he revealed a secret (non-literal meaning).

Interestingly, non-literal/idiomatic readings are often maintained even when parts of the idiom are moved around. For example, if we passivize *He let the cat out of the bag*, we get *The cat was let out of the bag*. Both the literal and non-literal meanings are maintained when we do movement for the passive. So idiomatic meanings are preserved under movement. We can use this to probe the structure of control and raising constructions.

We'll start with a pair of predicates that we've already identified as either control or raising: *is likely* (raising) and *is eager* (control). Let's put the idiom *The shit hit the fan* into these:

(4) (a) The shit is likely to hit the fan. *raising*

(b) #The shit is eager to hit the fan. *control*

In (4a), the raising construction, both the literal and non-literal meanings are available. Recall that idioms must be constituents; this means that the DP *the shit* must have started out as the subject of *hit*, even though it is the surface subject of *is likely*. The fact that the idiomatic meaning is retained is diagnostic of a movement relation. By contrast (4b) is just out-and-out strange (as marked with the # symbol). It cannot, except in really bad poetry, have the idiomatic/non-literal meaning. Instead, we get a very strange literal meaning where the shit is eager to do something (again only possible in bad poetry).

Definition **The idiom test**: if an idiomatic/non-literal meaning is available to a structure with a non-finite embedded clause, then the sentence is a raising construction. If it only allows a literal meaning (often with a very strange interpretation), then it is a control construction.

Exercise **Q2** 📖 Using the idiom test, determine if the following are raising or control constructions:

(a) is bound

(b) is able

(c) is certain

(d) is anxious

(e)   seems (put the embedded clause in the perfective: . . . *to have hit* . . .)

(f)   is believed (put the embedded clause in the perfective: . . . *to have hit*
       . . .)

(g)   wants

Challenge   In the previous unit, we identified *is ready* as a control predicate, like *want*.
How does it fare with the idiom test? Does it behave like a raising predicate
or a control predicate? Is it more like *is likely* or like *is eager*? Can you think
of an explanation for this. (In later tests we do below, *is ready* behaves like a
control predicate.)

21.3 The clausal subject test

Comment   As we saw in unit 8, it is possible to have a clause as the external argument of
a sentence:

(5)   [$_{CP}$ That Bill likes beef waffles] bothers me.

Predicates that are raising predicates typically allow a similar thing, whereas
control predicates do not:

(6)   (a)   [That Bill likes beef waffles] is likely.

       (b)   *[That Bill likes beef waffles] is eager.

Definition   **The clausal subject test:** If a tensed version of the embedded clause can be
used as the subject of a predicate, then it is a raising predicate.

Exercise   **Q3** 📖 Using the clausal subject test, determine if the following are raising or
control constructions:

(a)   is bound (add "to be the case" to the end to make this one work)

(b)   is able

(c)   is certain

(d)   is anxious

(e)   is ready

(f)   is believed (add "widely" to the end to make this one work)

(g)   wants

Challenge   In the previous section, where we used the idiom test, we identified *seems*
as a raising predicate, like *is likely*. How does it fare with the clausal subject
test? Does it behave like a raising predicate or a control predicate? Is it more
like *is likely* or like *is eager*? Can you think of an explanation for this. (In
later tests we do below, *seems* still behaves like a raising predicate.)

21.4 The pleonastic test

Exercise **Q4** 📖 Consider the word *it* in the following sentences. What does the *it* refer to in each sentence?

(a) It bothers me that Frank likes beef waffles.

(b) It rained.

(c) It is likely that Frank likes beef waffles.

Exercise **Q5** 📖 Now consider the pair of sentences below. Do these sentences mean the same thing? What does this tell us about the meaning of the word *it* in sentences like the (b) case below?

(a) That Bill left is likely.

(b) It is likely that Bill left.

Definition **Pleonastics** (also sometimes called **expletives**[2]) are pronouns that appear to have no meaning associated with them. In English, pleonastic pronouns are used when there is no other subject available in the sentence. For example, they are used as the subjects of weather verbs (which have no arguments), such as *rain* or *snow* (*it is raining, it is snowing*), or in contexts that we will identify as raising constructions.

Exercise In Spanish, most pronouns are optional, including the one meaning "it." In normal speech, you don't say the pronouns because the ending on the verb tells you what person you are referring to. If you want to emphasize the person you are referring to, you say the pronoun. Therefore, in (7a) we have the simple form that means "it arrived," and in (7b) we have the form that means "IT arrived."

(7) (a) Llegó.

arrived.3s

"It arrived."

(b) El llegó.

it arrived.3s

"IT arrived."

---

[2] This word is ambiguous: it can be used to refer to pleonastic pronouns or it can mean swear words. The latter usage is more common outside of linguistics, and the former usage is found extensively within the discipline. To avoid confusion, we'll use the term pleonastic instead.

Interestingly, with weather verbs (rain, snow etc.), the pronoun may not be present. The verb must stand on its own.

(8) (a) Llovió.

        rained.3s

        "It rained."

   (b) *El llovió.

Q6 📖 Discuss how the facts in (8) point to an analysis where the *it* in weather verbs in English is a pleonastic.

Discussion It appears as if English has two pronouns of the form *it*. One is the third-person singular neuter pronoun that is used to refer to things instead of people (*The lamp is over there but it isn't working*). The other is a pleonastic pronoun, which seems to be used when there is no other subject in the sentence. Not all *it* pronouns are pleonastic!

Exercise **Q7** ✏ Determine if the following *it*s are real pronouns or pleonastics. Circle the correct answer. Think about whether the *it* refers to a real entity in the world or is present just for grammatical reasons.

(a)	It's snowing.	pronoun	pleonastic
(b)	It ran away.	pronoun	pleonastic
(c)	I love it!	pronoun	pleonastic
(d)	It was really boring.	pronoun	pleonastic
(e)	It seems that Frank likes baseball.	pronoun	pleonastic
(f)	It appears that Pangur lost his toy.	pronoun	pleonastic

Comment Raising predicates and control predicates differ from one another in whether or not they allow pleonastic *it* subjects. Raising predicates (usually) allow three different structures:

(9) (a) Bill is likely to hate beef waffles.   *raising*

   (b) That Bill hates beef waffles is likely.   *sentential subject*

   (c) It is likely that Bill hates beef waffles.   *pleonastic subject*

Control predicates do not allow the second two types:

(10) (a) Bill is ready to hate beef waffles.   *raising*

   (b) *That Bill hates beef waffles is ready.   *sentential subject*

   (c) *It is ready that Bill hates beef waffles.   *pleonastic subject*

The fact that raising predicates take pleonastics is unsurprising if we remember that the subject in sentences like (9a) doesn't really belong to the main verb, instead it's really the argument of the embedded predicate. The fact that control predicates don't allow them is equally unsurprising. The subjects of control predicates are "real" arguments, so pleonastics are not allowed in this position.

Definition   The **pleonastic subject test**: If a pleonastic pronoun can be used in subject position of the main clause then the main clause predicate is a raising predicate. (Note: be very careful not to assume that all *it* pronouns are pleonastics. You can find *it* with control predicates, as in *It is eager to catch the ball*, where *it* refers to something – in this case, probably a dog. Don't let these cases throw you off!)

Exercise   **Q8** 📖 Using the pleonastic subject test, determine if the following are raising or control constructions:

(a)   is bound (add *to be the case* after the verb to make this one work)

(b)   is able

(c)   is certain

(d)   is anxious

(e)   is ready

(f)   is believed

(g)   wants

(h)   seems

Summary   We have seen that not all is as it might appear when you are dealing with sentences that have non-finite embedded clauses. There are really two types of such sentences. One type, the focus of the last unit, are control predicates where we have two different arguments as the EXTERNAL arguments of the two different clauses. The lower clause EXTERNAL argument is PRO. With raising predicates, by contrast, the EXTERNAL argument of the main clause actually starts out as the EXTERNAL argument of the embedded clauses and moves to that position. We distinguished between these two cases with three tests, which work in most cases (although there are some exceptions): the idiom test, the clausal subject test and the pleonastic subject test.

Next, we have to work out the feature structure for raising predicates and look at how the trees for these sentences are drawn.

21.5   The structure of raising predicates

Comment   Let's start by reminding ourselves of the structure of a control predicate such as *wants*:

(11) *wants* (taking a non-finite clause complement)

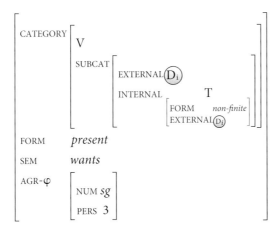

In (11) we see two Ds, which represent the two distinct arguments of the two predicates in a control sentence. The higher one is the subject of the main clause predicates, the lower one is the EXTERNAL argument of the embedded non-finite T. These two Ds happen to be coindexed, which ensures their coreference, but they are distinct DPs.

Let's contrast this with a raising predicate. In a raising predicate, there aren't two distinct DPs. Instead, there is a single DP that has occupied both positions. As before, this can be accomplished by making use of tags:

(12) *seems* (taking a non-finite clause complement)

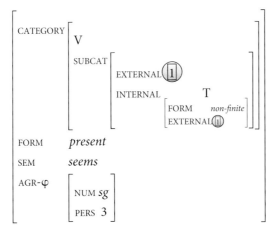

This says that the EXTERNAL argument of the main predicate is filled by the actual external argument of the non-finite T.

Exercise **Q9** 📖 Draw the feature structure for *likely* (as in *is likely*).

Challenge The feature structure for *seems* and *is likely* above requires a non-finite TP as an internal argument. Can you use this same feature structure for clausal subject constructions or pleonastic subjects? Draw two feature structures for *likely* that would work for *It is likely that Bill left* and *That Bill left is likely*. Draw the trees for these.

Comment Recall now the tree for a sentence with a control predicate:

(13)

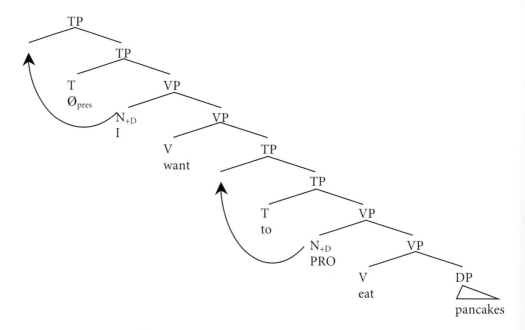

Here we have two DPs (well, actually $N_{[+D]}$s), one for each of the Ds mentioned in the feature structure for *wants*. In a raising construction, by contrast, we only have one DP, which moves through all the specifier positions because of all the tagging:

(14)

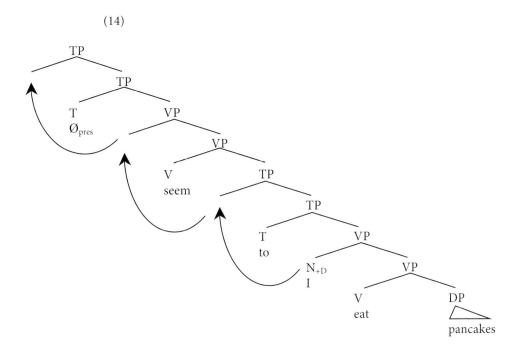

Exercise **Q10** 📖 Draw the tree for *He is likely to leave.*

Challenge Look at the tree in (14). You'll notice that the DP that shows up at the
EXTERNAL argument of *to*$_T$ is the pronoun *I*. Recall from the last unit that
the EXTERNAL argument of *to*$_T$ should be null, but *I* isn't null! Two solutions
to this have been proposed in the linguistics literature. The first one holds
that once the overt N has moved on to the higher clause, then there is no
longer any phonological content in the specifier of *to*$_T$, so this counts as null.
The problem with this hypothesis is that our feature structure stipulates a
null external argument, but doesn't say when the null quality is achieved.
An alternative view is that there are really two non-finite *to*s: one requiring
a null DP, the other allowing an overt subject. What would the feature
structure of these two *to*s look like if we went that route? Is there a way to
distinguish the two *to*s approach from the view that once the noun moves
out of that position it is considered null? What kind of data would you need
to look for to distinguish these two hypotheses?

21.6 Raising to object vs. object control

Comment In unit 20, we argued that there was a second kind of control construction found with predicates like *persuade* or *urged*. With object control, the DP that PRO was coindexed with was the first INTERNAL argument (the object). These are sentences like (15a). However, just as we found nearly surface-identical raising sentences that looked like subject control, we find another kind of raising, this time raising to the internal argument position of the main verb. This is the kind of sentence seen in (15b), which we'll call a raising to object construction.

(15) (a)   Susan persuaded Bill to eat the beef waffles.

(b)   Susan wanted Bill to eat the beef waffles.

Again, these two sentences look very similar. However, they have profoundly different structures.

Discussion Two of our tests for raising and control won't work here, because they test for the nature of the subject position (the pleonastic subject test and clausal subject test) and what we're looking at here are object positions. However, we can still use our basic judgments and the idiom test.

Exercise **Q11** ✏ In the sentence *Susan persuaded Bill to eat the beef waffles*, did Susan persuade Bill?

Q12 ✏ In the sentence *Susan wanted Bill to eat the beef waffles*, did Susan want Bill?

Definition When one sentence logically requires that another sentence be true, we say the first sentence **entails** the second. The symbol we use for entails is ⊨. The symbol that we use to say that one sentence does not entail another is ⊭.

Discussion When we have an object control sentence, the sentence as a whole entails that the object participates in the main verb action:

(16) Susan persuaded Bill to eat the beef waffles. ⊨ Susan persuaded Bill.

With raising to object constructions this is not true: the whole sentence does not entail that the object participates in the main verb action:

(17) Susan wanted Bill to eat the beef waffles. ⊭ Susan wanted Bill.

Exercise **Q13** 📖 Using the same kinds of judgments (the entailment task just given above) as you did in Q11 and Q12, try to determine if the following predicates are raising to object or object control predicates. Sometimes you'll need to be creative with which predicates you put under these verbs. For example, the predicates *consider, report* require that their embedded non-finite clauses have a stative predicate. So with these verbs you should use a non-finite clause like *to be foolish*. With other verbs a more active predicate is required, so for these use *to eat the beef waffles.*

(a) expect

(b) urge

(c) consider

(d) force

(e) intend

(f) report

(g) ask

(h) believe

(i) tell

(j) has known

(k) encouraged

(l) understood

Comment   The other test we can use to see if we have raising to object or object control is the idiom test. With raising to object predicates, idioms retain their non-literal meaning. With object control predicates, idioms only allow a literal meaning (which is silly in this case):

(18) (a)   John wants the shit to hit the fan.

(b)   *John persuaded the shit to hit the fan.

So, we can use this test to distinguish object control from subject control.

Exercise   **Q14** ☐ Using the idiom test, try to determine if the following predicates are raising to object or object control predicates.

(a) expect

(b) urge

(c) consider (use the perfective *to have hit the fan*)

(d) force

(e) intend

(f) report (use the perfective *to have hit the fan*)

(g) ask

(h) believe (use the perfective *to have hit the fan*)

(i) tell

(j) has known

(k) encouraged

(l) understood (use the perfective *to have hit the fan*)

273

Exercise   The apparent object in (15b) is not an underlying object of the verb *want*. Susan does not want Bill. So we know we have a raising sentence. Above, we used coindexation to indicate control and tagging to indicate raising.

Q15 📖 Draw the feature structure for the raising verb *expected*. (Hint: use the answer to Q19 in unit 20 as a starting point.)

Q16 📖 Draw the tree for *I expected him to leave*.

Summary   In this unit, we've looked at structures that appear to be very similar to control constructions on the surface. A deeper examination, however, shows that raising constructions behave very differently from control constructions. Control constructions involve a null embedded subject (PRO), which is coindexed with an actual argument in the main clause. Raising constructions, by contrast, take an argument from inside the embedded clause and move it into the main clause. Formally, control constructions utilize coindexation to ensure that PRO agrees with the higher subject. (This isn't necessary in raising constructions because the higher subject *is* the same element as the lower subject.) To motivate movement we use tags instead of coindexation.

Suggested further reading

- Adger (2003), chapter 8
- Carnie (2006), chapter 14
- Cowper (1992), chapter 5
- Culicover (2009), chapter 7
- Davies and Dubinsky (2004)
- Déprez (1992)
- Falk (2001), chapter 5
- Huddleston and Pullum (2005), chapter 13
- Kim and Sells (2008), chapter 7
- Kroeger (2004), chapter 5
- Postal (1974)
- Radford (1988), chapter 8; (2004), chapter 8
- Sag, Wasow and Bender (2003), chapters 11 and 12

Answers to questions

Q1 (a) raising: Gilbert's leaving is what is bound.

(b) control: Gilbert is able.

(c) raising: Gilbert's leaving is certain (note Gilbert is not certain!)

(d) control: Gilbert is anxious.

(e) raising: It seems that Gilbert is gone.

(f) raising: It is believed that Gilbert is gone. (Gilbert isn't believed.)

Don't worry if you found this exercise hard, we'll do some slightly less subjective tests for the raising/control distinction below.

Q2 (a) raising: The shit is bound to hit the fan.

(b) control: #The shit is able to hit the fan.

(c) raising: The shit is certain to hit the fan.

(d) control: #The shit is anxious to hit the fan.

(e) raising: The shit seems to have hit the fan.

(f) raising: The shit is believed to have hit the fan.

(g) control: #The shit wants to hit the fan.

Q3 (a) raising: [That Bill likes beef waffles] is bound to be the case.

(b) control: *[That Bill likes beef waffles] is able.

(c) raising: [That Bill likes beef waffles] is certain.

(d) control: *[That Bill likes beef waffles] is anxious.

(e) control: *[That Bill likes beef waffles] is ready.

(f) raising: [That Bill likes beef waffles] is believed widely.

(g) control: *[That Bill likes beef waffles] wants.

Q4 There are two typical answers to this question. The first is that in (a) and (c) the pronoun refers to the thing that is likely or that is bothering me and in (b) it refers to the weather. The other answer is that they refer to nothing at all. They are meaningless placeholders. We're going to go with the latter interpretation because of the behavior this *it* pronoun has in the next two exercises.

Q5 The two sentences appear to mean exactly the same thing. Since one of them lacks the pronoun *it* entirely, this suggests that *it* makes no contribution to the meaning of the sentence, i.e., it is meaningless.

Q6 The Spanish examples suggest that with weather verbs there is no pronoun at all. This suggests that with the equivalent English verbs the *it* is nothing more than a grammatical conceit. It does not contribute to the meaning of the sentences in these forms. One possible explanation for this is that English has a rule that every sentence must have a subject. The pleonastic pronoun serves this purpose in sentences with no other subject.

275

Q7 (a) pleonastic, (b) pronoun, (c) pronoun, (d) pronoun, (e) pleonastic, (f) pleonastic

Q8 (a) raising: It is bound to be the case that Bill likes beef waffles.

(b) control: *It is able that Bill likes beef waffles.

(c) raising: It is certain that Bill likes beef waffles.

(d) control: *It is anxious that Bill likes beef waffles. (This sentence is acceptable, but not with a pleonastic reading on the pronoun, only with a reading where there actually is something that is anxious.)

(e) control: *It is ready that Bill likes beef waffles.

(f) raising: It is believed that Bill likes beef waffles.

(g) control: *It wants that Bill likes beef waffles. (This sentence is marginally acceptable, but not with a pleonastic reading on the pronoun, only with a reading where there actually is something that wants.)

(h) raising: It seems that Bill likes beef waffles.

Q9 *likely*

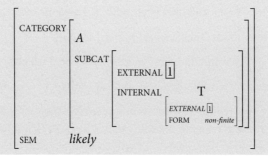

Q10

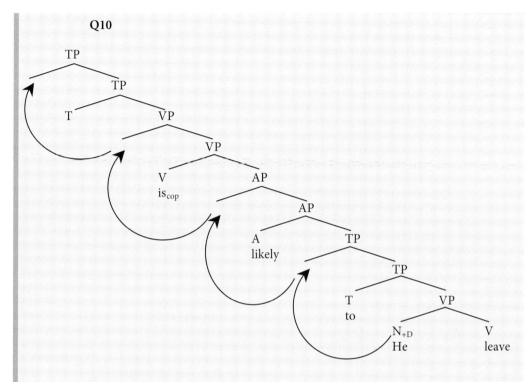

Q11 Yes, she persuaded him.

Q12 No, she didn't want him. Instead, she wants that he eat the waffles.

Q13 Using either the frame: *Sally* PREDICATE *Bill to eat beef waffles* or *Sally* PREDICATE *Bill to be foolish.*

(a) raising: Sally expects Bill to eat beef waffles ⊭ Sally expects Bill.

(b) control: Sally urged Bill to eat beef waffles ⊨ Sally urged Bill.

(c) raising: Sally considers Bill to be foolish ⊭ Sally considers Bill.

(d) control: Sally forced Bill to eat beef waffles ⊨ Sally forced Bill.

(e) raising: Sally intended Bill to eat the beef waffles ⊭ Sally intended Bill.

(f) raising: Sally reported Bill to be foolish ⊭ Sally reported Bill.

(g) control: Sally asked Bill to eat beef waffles ⊨ Sally asked Bill.

(h) raising: Sally believed Bill to be foolish ⊭ Sally believed Bill.

(i) control: Sally told Bill to eat beef waffles ⊨ Sally told Bill.

(j) raising: Sally has known Bill to eat beef waffles ⊭ Sally has known Bill.

(k) control: Sally encouraged Bill to eat beef waffles ⊨ Sally encouraged Bill.

(l) raising: Sally understood Bill to be a fool ⊭ Sally understood Bill.

277

Q14 (a) raising: I expected the shit to hit the fan.

(b) control: #I urged the shit to hit the fan.

(c) raising: I consider the shit to have hit the fan.

(d) control: #I forced the shit to hit the fan.

(e) raising: I intended the shit to hit the fan.

(f) report: I reported the shit to have hit the fan.

(g) control: #I asked the shit to hit the fan.

(h) raising: I believe the shit to have hit the fan.

(i) control: #I told the shit to hit the fan.

(j) raising: I have known the shit to hit the fan.

(k) control: #I encouraged the shit to hit the fan.

(l) raising: I understood the shit to have hit the fan.

Q15 *expected*

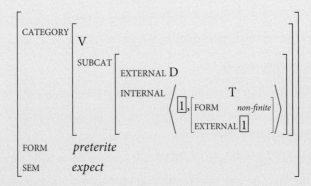

Q16

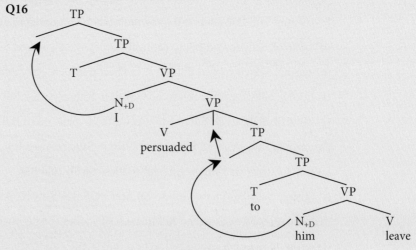

UNIT 22 HEAD-TO-HEAD MOVEMENT 1: AUXILIARIES

Objectives:

- Review the phenomenon of Subject/Auxiliary Inversion (SAI).
- Develop an analysis of SAI with modals, involving tagging the FORM feature.
- Reinvestigate the position of tensed auxiliaries.
- Write up new feature structures for different kinds of Tense.
- Draw trees for tensed auxiliaries and for SAI with tensed auxiliaries.

22.1 Subject/Auxiliary Inversion and complementizers

Comment   Recall the phenomenon of Subject/Auxiliary Inversion (SAI) from units
1 and 10. When the sentence is a yes/no question, modals and tensed
auxiliaries invert order with their subjects:

(1) (a) You will eat beef waffles.   *statement*

    (b) Will you eat beef waffles?   *question*

In this section, we'll try to figure out what is going on in these sentences.

Comment   In many languages, such as Mandarin, Japanese, Irish and many others,
yes/no questions are indicated not by SAI, but by a special question
particle. These question particles usually appear in the same position as
complementizers do. Take the following sentence from the African Khoisan
language !Xóõ (data from Traill 1994: 18) as an example:

(2) lú tûu   →   sîi

     Q people PAST come

     "Did the people come?"

A common analysis of these particles is that they are in fact complementizers,
because they are in complementary distribution[1] with other complementizers.
For example, in Irish, main clauses can start with a complementizer *go*, which
indicates that the speaker wishes something[2] (optative mood):

---

[1]   Recall from unit 15 that complementary distribution means that you have two items that
    never appear in the same place at the same time.
[2]   This usage is archaic, but one can easily find examples of it in literary works. It can also be
    found in the idiom meaning "thank you": *Go raibh maith agat.*

(3)   Go   raibh   tú   go   maith.

OPT be.DEP you ADV good

"May you be well."

This complementizer can be replaced with a question marker:

(4)   An raibh   tú   go   maith?

Q   be.DEP you ADV good

Were you well?

However, you cannot have both:

(5)   (a)   *Go an raibh tú go maith

(b)   *An go raibh tú go maith

Since you can't have both a complementizer and a question particle, this suggests that question particle and complementizers are part of the same category, i.e. complementizers.

Exercise   **Q1** ☐ Extrapolating from languages with question complementizers, can you make a guess about where the word *will* is in English questions? Think about where complementizers come in English relative to the rest of the clause. Is this where inverted auxiliaries are too?

Challenge   In Chinese and Japanese, the question particles go at the end of the sentence. Where do you think complementizers go in these languages?

Exercise   **Q2** ☐ Think about the words *whether* and *if* in English (in particular in their usage in the following sentences). What syntactic category are these words? What is their meaning/function?

(6)   (a)   I asked if Bill likes beef waffles.

(b)   I wonder whether Bill likes beef waffles.

Discussion   Let's consider the possibility then that inverted auxiliaries in English occupy the complementizer position in English, just like question particles do in other languages.

Exercise   If inverted auxiliaries appear in the position of complementizers, this predicts that you shouldn't have both an inverted auxiliary and a complementizer at the same time. They should be in complementary distribution.

Q3 📖 Explain how the following data supports the hypothesis that inverted auxiliaries are in the complementizer position in English. Assume the judgments given. Don't worry about whether or not there should be quotation marks around the embedded clause; that is irrelevant to the answer.

(7) (a) I asked will you be in class this afternoon.

     (b) I asked if you will be in class this afternoon.

     (c) *I asked if will you be in class this afternoon.

Comment There is clearly something to the idea that complementizers are somehow involved in SAI. This makes a certain amount of sense when you think about what complementizers do in a sentence. Complementizers seem to be tied in a deep way to what the speaker's intent for the use of the expression is. For example, we use a complementizer *that* to indicate we are making a statement (e.g. *He said that Jean left*), but we use the complementizer *if* to indicate a question[3] (e.g. *He asked if Jean left*). SAI serves the same function in *yes/no* question contexts.

However, we have a problem! Auxiliaries and modals like *will, should, can,* etc. are of category T and tensed auxiliaries like *has* or *is* are of category V! How could items like these appear in the position of complementizers? We will try to answer this in the next section.

22.2 Question complementizers

Comment In previous units, movement was posited when we have a single item that appears to have two or more functions. For example, the EXTERNAL argument of the passive *be* is the INTERNAL argument of the main verb. To solve this dichotomy of function, we moved elements from one position to another. This was notated by tagging two positions in the INTERNAL and EXTERNAL features of the verb or auxiliary.

With SAI, we seem to have another case of movement. In SAI the future marker *will* seems to be both of category T (indicating future tense) and of category C (indicating that we have a question). We accomplish this in a very similar way to the other kinds of movement we've seen, except that the feature that will be tagged is the FORM feature of the C rather than one of its EXTERNAL/INTERNAL features. This is because the C in SAI sentences doesn't have a FORM of its own, but takes on the form of the auxiliary that is underneath it:

---

[3] *If* is also used in conditionals (again marking the speaker's intent). *Whether* is a complementizer used exclusively in questions.

(8) Question complementizer ($C_{[+Q]}$)

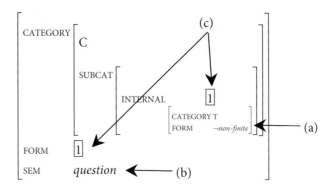

Let's look at the various bits of this feature structure. It is, obviously, of category C. This complementizer takes a finite T (a) as a complement. Non-finite clauses are not allowed, because *to* never inverts (*To John leave?*). It expresses the semantics of a question (b). The newest thing here is the tagging of the internal argument with the FORM feature of the complementizer (c). This says that the complementizer takes the FORM of the head of its complement (the T – or auxiliary). In other words, the T head moves into the head of the CP.

We can represent this in tree notation with an arrow moving the T into the C.

(9) *Will you leave?*

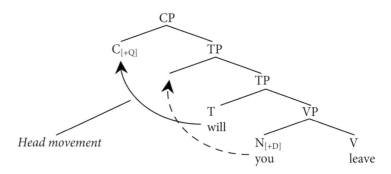

Definition **Head-to-head movement** (or **head movement**) is the movement of the contents of the head of one phrase into the head of another. For example, the movement of the contents of the T head into the C. This is triggered by the tagging of a word's FORM feature with its INTERNAL feature.

Exercise **Q4** 📖 Draw the tree structure for the sentence: *Should I go?*

Exercise **Q5** 📖 SAI in English isn't limited to *yes/no* questions. It also shows up in conditionals, especially in very formal registers of the language. For example, in many dialects of English we get sentences like the following: *Should he get the new job, there will be a vacancy in shipping.* (In less formal registers, we would find *If he should get . . .*) Draw the feature structure for the complementizer found in these conditional forms.

Challenge What would the feature structure for the !Xóõ question particle *lú* look like? Would it also involve tagging? Why or why not?

22.3 Tensed auxiliaries

Comment Recall our treatment of tensed auxiliaries. These are of category V, with the special feature *+aux*. Here, for example, is the feature structure for passive *was*.

(10) *was*_{pass}

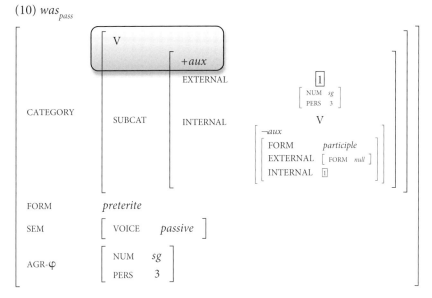

In unit 18, we proposed that the Tense node used with these is null:

(11) Ø_{past}

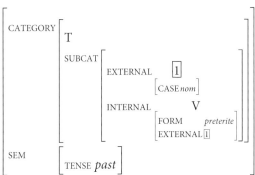

283

So, the tree structure for such sentences looks like (12) (obscuring some irrelevant details with a triangle):

(12)

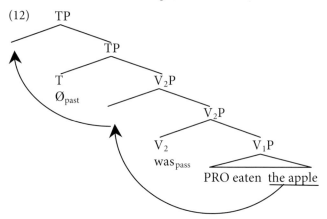

Exercise **Q6** 📖 Given the tree in (12), what head should undergo SAI (movement to C) when a tree like this is inverted? What is the predicted word order of a question of a simple passive like this?

Discussion The question order with tensed auxiliaries like the passive auxiliary *was*$_{pass}$ has the tensed auxiliary appearing first, as if it has undergone SAI.

(13) Was the apple eaten?

However, the question complementizer looks for T heads, not V heads!

Exercise Consider the position of modals, tensed auxiliaries, non-tensed auxiliaries and main verbs relative to negation (*not*) in English:

(14) (a) People should not eat apples.   *modal*

    (b) *People not should eat apples.   *modal*

    (c) People are not eating apples.   *tensed auxiliary*

    (d) *People not are eating apples.   *tensed auxiliary*

    (e) People will not have eaten apples.   *untensed auxiliary*

    (f) *People will have not eaten apples.   *untensed auxiliary*

    (g) People do not eat apples.   *main verb*

    (h) *People eat not apples.   *main verb*

Q7 ➥ Do modals come before or after negation?   before   after

Q8 ➥ Do tensed auxiliaries come before or after negation?   before   after

Q9 ➥ Do untensed auxiliaries come before or after negation?   before   after

Q10 ➥ Do main verbs come before or after negation?   before   after

Discussion   Tensed auxiliaries (like *has, is, was*, etc.), which are all of category V,
appear in exactly the same position as modals (like *should, will, can* etc),
which are all of category T, relative to negation. This suggests that tensed
auxiliaries are actually in the T position in the clause. However, we don't
want to say that they aren't also verbs. So we have a dichotomy like the one
we saw above, where we had an item that appeared to have properties of both
T and C, except here it is an element that has properties of both T and V. The
fact that tensed auxiliaries appear in T makes sense, since they are tensed.

In unit 13, we proposed that all tensed verbs (including tensed auxiliaries)
were the complements to null tense nodes like Ø$_{past}$ or Ø$_{pres}$. However,
clearly this can't be correct for sentences with tensed auxiliaries, since they
are appearing **in** the T node. To accomplish this we'll propose the following
structure for the T node that expresses past and takes a tensed auxiliary as a
complement.

(15) T$_{past}$

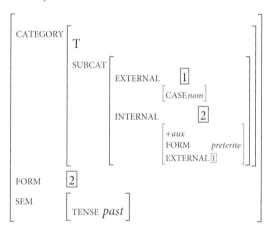

This feature structure holds only of cases when we have an auxiliary (as
specified by the +*aux* feature). Main verbs will have to have a separate
treatment, which we'll turn to in the next unit. The ② tag forces movement
of the head of the auxiliary into T. Therefore, the tree structure for a tensed
auxiliary will look like (16):

(16)

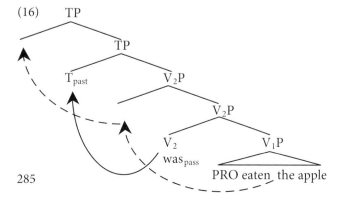

285

Exercise **Q11** 📖 Draw the feature structure for T~~present~~ (present tense T).

Q12 📖 Draw the tree for *He is leaving.* Do not use triangles.

Challenge You may have noticed that I haven't given you a tree with a negation in it. You might think that it would be trivial to simply put a NegP between the T and the V. However, there is a problem. Recall our feature structure for *not* from unit 18.

(17) *not*

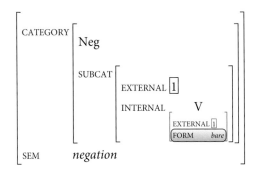

This feature structure requires that the complement to *not* be a bare verb. However, in cases with tensed *is, has,* etc. the complement is not bare; it is, in fact, the present or preterite form. How might we go about solving this problem?

Exercise **Q13** 📖 How do feature structures like (15) above explain why tensed auxiliaries can undergo SAI?

Exercise **Q14** 📖 Draw the tree for the sentence *Is he leaving?*

Summary The interaction between heads has been the focus of this unit. Subject/ Auxiliary Inversion appears to be a phenomenon linking two head positions: the question-marking complementizer and some element in the T head. The question complementizer of English has a FORM feature that is tagged to the element that is in its INTERNAL feature. This tagging motivates head-to-head movement of the T into the C. We also saw that when we have a tensed auxiliary in English, it behaves just like a T head with respect to Subject/ Auxiliary Inversion. We also saw this confirmed by their position relative to *not*. So we proposed that, at least in the case of tensed auxiliaries, the T nodes are not actually null, but instead have a FORM feature that is tagged so that the embedded tensed auxiliary raises into the T head. This T+V combo can then move on to the question complementizer in questions.

There are a couple of other flies in the ointment, however. And we'll take a swat at killing them in the next unit. First, we have the problem of tensed main verbs in English. These do *not* appear to have the properties of T (i.e. they don't precede negation and they don't undergo SAI). So we need to explain how those are structured. Coupled with that problem are some cross-linguistic facts. In many languages, main verbs *do* behave like English tensed auxiliaries. In French, for example, main verbs precede negation and undergo SAI. We'll extend our analysis of English tensed auxiliaries to these elements too. This in turn, in combination with a slight difference in DP movement, will allow us to explain how Verb Subject Object (VSO) order is derived in languages like Irish Gaelic.

Suggested further reading

- Adger (2005), chapter 5
- Carnie (2006), chapter 9
- Huddleston and Pullum (2005), chapter 9
- Kroeger (1993)
- Radford (1988), chapter 8; (2004), chapters 4 and 5

Answers to questions

Q1 The data from other languages is suggestive that inverted auxiliaries occupy the complementizer position. If question particles appear in this position in one language, it is likely that they also appear there in English. Note that in English complementizers appear immediately to the left of subjects. This is also where the inverted auxiliary appears.

Q2 It appears as if the words *if* and *whether* are complementizers. They appear in the same position in the sentence as complementizers like *that*. They express a meaning akin to that of *yes/no* questions but in an embedded context. It appears as if English also has question particles, and they are indeed complementizers.

Q3 To the extent that sentence (7a) is grammatical without quotation marks, it appears as if you can have either an inverted auxiliary or a question particle like *if*, but not both of them as in (7c). This is good evidence that complementizers and inverted auxiliaries are in complementary distribution, and thus part of the same category.

Q4

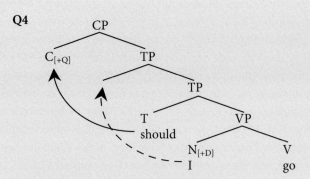

Q5 Conditional complementizer (C_{cond})

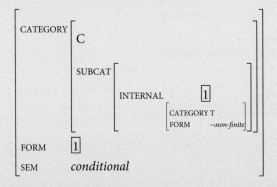

Q6 SAI targets T heads and moves them into the C head. Since the T head here is null ($\emptyset_{past}$) we predict the order $\emptyset_{past}$ *the apple was eaten.* In terms of the words that are actually pronounced, the order is the same as the statement!

Q7–10 Tensed auxiliaries and modals both must appear before *not.*
Untensed auxiliaries (i.e. those in bare form, gerund form or participle form) and main verbs must follow *not.*

Q11

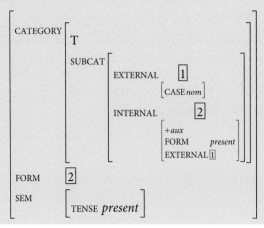

Q12

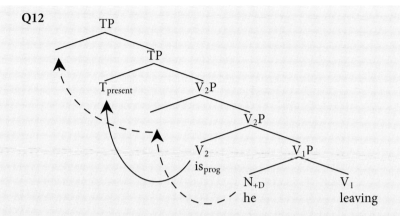

Q13 If the $C_{[+Q]}$ moves the T head it selects for, and the T it selects for in turn triggers the movement of the embedded tensed auxiliary, then we have movement of V to T and from T to C.

Q14

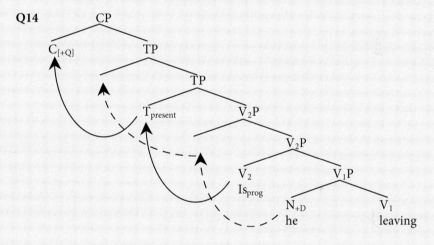

Notice in this tree that the elements are in the correct order already before you do all the movement. However, we understand that the movement happens anyway, so that the T and C requirements are met.

UNIT 23 HEAD-TO-HEAD MOVEMENT 2: MAIN VERBS

> **Objectives:**
> - Compare French and English main verbs, and develop an analysis of French T.
> - Look at other languages with respect to head movement.
> - Develop an analysis of VSO order in languages like Irish Gaelic.

23.1 English main verbs and tense

Comment In the last unit, we saw that modal verbs and tensed auxiliary verbs behave alike, in that they appear before negation (1a) and (1b), but that main verbs must follow negation (and take a *do* auxiliary) (1c):

(1) (a) He will not eat beef waffles.

 (b) He is not eating beef waffles.

 (c) *He eats not beef waffles.[1] (Cf. He does not eat beef waffles.)

We attributed the position of the auxiliary in (1a and b) to a process whereby the tensed auxiliary verb underwent head-to-head movement into the T head (motivated by a tagged FORM feature in the T head). Abstractly this looks like the tree in (2):

(2)

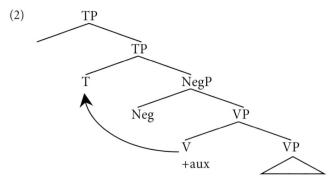

---

[1] This form was grammatical in older forms of the language. Leave that fact aside here, as we are looking at contemporary English.

We need to explain why main verbs (as in (1c)) don't undergo this movement. First, note that the feature structure for the English T that triggers head-to-head movement explicitly mentions that the complement verb must be +*aux* (3). Main verbs don't have this feature, so they won't appear with this particular T head.

(3) T

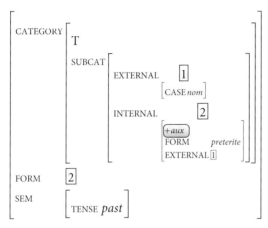

We have to have a different T node when we have a main verb. Here's the solution to our problem: with main verbs, tense is expressed with a null T node (just like the ones we proposed in unit 13), which does *not* have a tagged FORM feature. Instead, the FORM feature is specified as *null*.[2]

(4) Ø

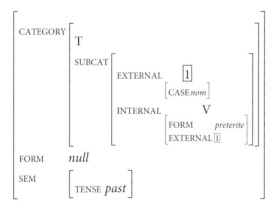

----

[2] In sentences with negation, the polarity *do/did/does* is used.

291

This means that with main verbs in English, there is no raising to T:

(5)

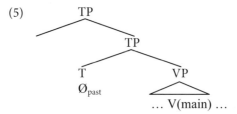

Exercise Q1 📖 Draw the feature structure for the T node used with present tense main verbs.

Exercise Q2 📖 Use the data in (6) about Subject/Auxiliary Inversion (SAI) to construct an argument that tensed main verbs in English do not raise to the T node, unlike tensed auxiliaries.

(6) (a) Should he leave?   *Modal*

      (b) Is he leaving?   *Tensed Auxiliary*

      (c) *Left he?   *Tensed Main Verb*

23.2 French main verbs and tense

Exercise Q3 📖 *Pas* is the French equivalent of the English word *not*. Explain the difference between English and French with respect to the position of the negatives *pas* and *not*. (The position of *ne* here is not relevant. It is typically omitted in spoken French.)

(7) (a) Il ne-doit pas manger des   gaufres au   boeuf.

            he must   not eat   of.the waffles with beef

            "He must not eat beef waffles."

      (b) Il n'a pas mangé des   gaufres au   boeuf.

            he has not eaten   of.the waffles with beef

            "He has not eaten beef waffles."

      (c) Il ne-mange pas des   gaufres au   boeuf.

            he eat   not of.the waffles with beef

            "He does not eat beef waffles."

Comment *Souvent* is the French equivalent of the English word *often*. These words are adjuncts that modify the main verb. In English, the word *often* typically follows tensed auxiliaries and modals, but it must precede tensed main verbs (and their objects).[3]

---

[3] We can, of course, always put *often* at the end of the sentence (*I eat beef waffles often*). This is beside the point because adverbs can adjoin either to the left or the right. We are only interested in the case where the adverb adjoins to the left of the verb and its object because it's only in this position that the adverb flags the position of the verb.

(8)   (a)   I will often eat beef waffles.

      (b)   I have often eaten beef waffles.

      (c)   I often eat beef waffles.

      (d)   *I eat often beef waffles.

This behavior parallels that of negation. The tree for (8c) is something like (9):

(9)

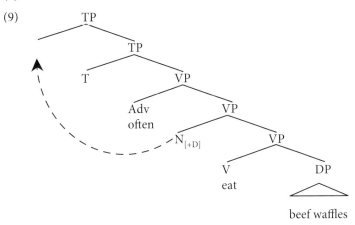

The main verb doesn't move, as we argued above.

Exercise   **Q4** 📖 Now consider the facts in (10). Explain the difference between English and French with respect to the position of the adverbs *souvent* and *often*, and how this bears on the position of tensed main verbs in the French tree.

Q5 📖 Draw the tree for sentence (10c) :

(10) (a)   Il doit souvent manger des   gaufres au   boeuf.

            he must often   eat   of.the waffles with beef

            "He must often eat beef waffles."

      (b)   Il a   souvent mangé des   gaufres au   boeuf.

            he has often   eaten of.the waffles with beef

            "He has often eaten beef waffles."

      (c)   Il mange souvent des   gaufres au   boeuf.

            he eat   often   of.the waffles with beef

            "He often eats beef waffles."

      (d)   *Il souvent mange des gaufres au boeuf.

Comment   Notice the alternation in position exhibited in French. When we have an auxiliary or modal, the untensed main verb follows the adverb or negation.

(11) French:

    (a)   Tensed Aux   negation/adverb   untensed V

    (b)   Modal   negation/adverb   untensed V

    (c)   Tensed V   negation/adverb

As such, main verbs seem to flip from one side of the negation or adverb to the other. This would be consistent with main verbs raising into T in French.

Exercise Look at the following data from French *yes/no* questions.

Q6 📖 How is French different from English with respect to the formation of *yes/no* questions? How does your answer bear on the question of where main verbs are in French?

(12) (a)   Devez-vous manger des   gaufres au   boeuf?

         must you eat   of.the waffles with beef

         "Must you eat beef waffles?"

    (b)   Avez-vous mangé des   gaufres au   boeuf?

         have you eaten of.the waffles with beef

         "Have you eaten beef waffles?"

    (c)   Mangez-vous des   gaufres au   boeuf?

         eat   you of.the waffles with beef

         "Do you eat beef waffles?"

Discussion All tensed verbs in French (including both main verbs and auxiliaries) undergo V to T movement. The evidence for this comes from the position of main verbs with respect to negation and adverbs like *often*, and whether or not the main verb undergoes SAI.

Exercise **Q7** 📖 What would the feature structure for present tense T be in French? Hint: start with the feature structure given for the present tense in the previous unit and make appropriate adjustments so that it targets all verbs, not just auxiliaries.

Exercise **Q8** 📖 Draw the tree for sentence (12c). Assume that SAI in French works like the equivalent phenomenon in English, except that main verbs are also in T.

23.3 Verb raising in other languages

Comment Main verbs move to T in many languages. For example, the linguist Hilda Koopman first noticed the phenomenon in a language called Vata, spoken in Africa and belonging to the Kru family of languages. In Vata, when you have an auxiliary in the sentence (13a), the auxiliary appears right after the subject and before the object (in Vata objects appear to the left of the main verb). The main verb is at the end. When there is no auxiliary (13b), the main verb appears before the object – in the same position that the auxiliary would normally appear in:

(13) (a)   A la   saki li.

we have rice eaten

"We have eaten rice."

(b)   A li   saki.

we eat rice

"We eat rice."

Exercise **Q9** 📖 Draw the tree for sentence (13b); you may use a triangle for the DP *saki*.

Discussion In all of the cases we've seen thus far, we have identified verb raising by virtue of comparing sentences with tensed auxiliaries with sentences that have tensed main verbs. In each case, we've seen that main verbs alternate in position relative to some particular word (an adverb or a negation in the case of French, the direct object in the case of Vata). In each case, the main verb appears in the same position as the tensed auxiliaries and modals, when it itself is tensed. The logical landing spot for tensed verbs is of course the Tense node. This can only be deduced when we have some element that allows us to distinguish two positions in the sentence, such as negation, adverbs or objects.

Definition The **landmark test** allows us to determine if a language has V to T movement (like French or Vata) or leaves its tensed verbs in place[4] (like English). If we find an alternation in position of tensed verbs and untensed verbs relative to some other syntactic constituent, where the tensed verb appears exactly in the same position as tensed auxiliaries or modals, we know that the verb has raised into T.

Exercise **Q10** 📖 Using the landmark test, determine if Finnish is like French and raises its verbs to T or if it is like English and does not move the verb into T.

(14) (a)   Markko usein puhuu Englanti.

Markko often speaks English

"Markko often speaks English."

(b)   Markko on usein puhunut Englanti.

Markko be often spoken   English

"Markko has often spoken English."

---

[4] The technical term for leaving an element in the position where it might start its syntactic journey is to say that the item is "in situ."

Exercise **Q11** 📖 Using the landmark test, determine if Portuguese is like French and raises its verbs to T or if it is like English and does not move the verb into T.

(15) (a) Maria é frequentemente falam   Inglês.

Maria is often   speaking English

"Maria is often speaking English."

(b) Maria fala   frequentemente Inglês.

Maria speaks often   English

"Maria often speaks English."

Comment The other piece of evidence we use to determine if a language has raising of tensed main verbs to T comes from the behavior of *yes/no* question formation in the language.

Definition The **subject/verb inversion test**: If the language creates questions using SAI (rather than, for example, using a particle) and tensed main verbs undergo inversion with their subject just like auxiliaries, then it has verb to T movement.

Exercise **Q12** 📖 Using the subject/verb inversion test, determine if German is like French and raises its verbs to T or if it is like English and does not move the verb into T.

(16) (a) Ich spreche Deutsch.

I   speak   German

"I speak German."

(b) Sprechen Sie Deutsch?

speak   you German

"Do you speak German?"

Exercise **Q13** 📖 Using the landmark test, determine if German is like French and raises its verbs to T or if it is like English and does not move the verb into T.

(17) (a) Er sitzt nicht auf diesem Tisch.

he sits not   on this   table

"He does not sit on this table."

(b) Sie soll   nicht auf diesem Tisch sitzen.

she must not   on this   table sit

"She must not sit on this table."

23.4 Verb subject object (VSO) languages

Comment   About 9 percent[5] of the world's languages regularly express simple sentences
with a word order where the verb comes first, followed by the subject
(EXTERNAL argument), followed by an object (INTERNAL argument). This
order is called VSO reflecting the order of the basic elements. An example
from Irish is given in (18):

(18) D'ith mé vaiféal na   mairteola.

     Ate   I   waffle of.thc beef

     "I ate the beef waffle."

VSO order is problematic for the theory of tree building we developed
earlier in this book. In our system, complements (i.e. INTERNAL arguments)
are C-MERGED before we S-MERGE specifiers (i.e. EXTERNAL arguments).
With this in mind, it is hard to see how we'd get subjects between the verb
and its internal argument. In (18), we'd merge the verb *d'ith* and its internal
argument *vaiféal na mairteola* first:

(19)

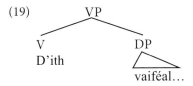

S-MERGE of *mé* "I" should put the subject either to the left or to the right
of this VP constituent, but of course in a VSO language it appears to be
plonked right into the middle.

The linguist Richard Sproat[6] noticed that fog surrounding the structure of
VSO order was lifted if you looked at the interaction of Tense and verbs.

Exercise   **Q14** 📖 Consider the following data from Welsh below. Using the landmark
test,[7] construct an argument that Welsh has V to T movement. Do not worry
about the alternation in the form of the word for "dragon"; it is irrelevant to
the answer to the question. (Data from Kroeger 1993.)

(20) (a)   Gwelodd   Siôn   ddraig.

           saw.PAST   John   dragon

           "John saw a dragon."

---

[5] Tomlin (1984).
[6] Sproat (1985).
[7] We can't use the subject/verb inversion test, because Welsh uses particles to mark questions
(and obviously, the subject and the verb are already inverted in statements!).

(b) Gwnaeth   Siôn   weld   draig.

do.PAST   John   seen   dragon

"John did see a dragon."

Discussion The landmark test tells us that Welsh VSO order shows some similarities with French verb raising, because we find a difference in position with tensed and untensed verbs.

However, note that there is still a problem here. If the verb in (20a) and the auxiliary in (20b) are in the T head, where is the subject? Think about this in terms of trees, and you'll see that the subject is precisely where we'd predict it to be if the subject has not moved to the specifier of DP, i.e. it remains in its base position within the VP:

(21)

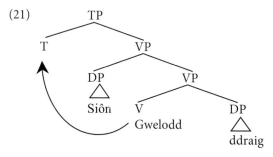

What we need for a VSO language, then, is a feature structure for T that does not have an EXTERNAL argument feature (so that *Siôn* is not moved up into the specifier of TP).

Exercise **Q15** 📖 Draw the feature structure for Welsh T_{past}. It should trigger V to T movement (like the French T_{past}), but it should not trigger the DP movement of *Siôn* into the specifier of TP.

Summary In this unit, we looked at two different kinds of languages. There are languages like English, which do not raise tensed main verbs into T. Instead, they take a null T head. By contrast, we identified a class of languages where tensed main verbs and tensed auxiliaries alike moved into T. We can identify these languages by making use of the subject/verb inversion test and the landmark test. Finally, we looked at the tricky VSO languages, which have verb head movement to T, but lack movement of their subject into the specifier of the TP.

Suggested further reading

- Carnie (1995); (2006), chapter 9
- Carnie and Guilfoyle (2000)
- Emonds (1980)
- Koopman (1984)
- Koopman and Sportiche (1991)
- Lightfoot and Hornstein (1994)
- McCloskey (1983); (1991)
- Poole (2002), chapter 10
- Radford (2004), chapter 5
- Ritter (1988)
- Sproat (1984)

Answers to questions

Q1 $\varnothing_{pres}$

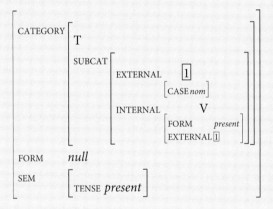

Q2 We know that SAI targets whatever element is in the T node. This can be either a modal that starts in that position or a tensed auxiliary that raises to that position. The fact that main verbs in English do not undergo SAI is evidence that they haven't moved to the T position. They are never targeted by this rule, which entails that they cannot be in T.

Q3 Like English, modals and tensed auxiliaries in French precede negation. However, French tensed main verbs behave differently from English main verbs. French main verbs appear before *pas*, just like tensed auxiliaries.

Q4 The pattern is very similar to that of negation above. French tensed verbs appear before the adverb that modifies them, in exactly the same position as tensed auxiliaries and modals. This suggests that they have undergone head movement to T, unlike main verbs in English.

Q5

```
                        TP
               ┌─────────┴──────────┐
               N                    TP
               ↑           ┌────────┴────────┐
               ┆           T                 VP
               ┆              ┌───────────────┴───────┐
               ┆             Adv                      VP
               ┆            souvent         ┌──────────┴──────┐
               ┆                            N                 VP
               ┆                            Il        ┌───────┴──────┐
                                                      V              DP
                                                    mange            ...
```

Q6 In English, main verbs never undergo SAI, but in French, they do. This entails that verbs raise into the T node in French, since the rule only targets those things in T.

Q7 T_{pres}

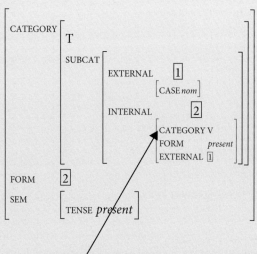

$$
\begin{bmatrix}
\text{CATEGORY} & T \\
\text{SUBCAT} & \begin{bmatrix}
\text{EXTERNAL} & \boxed{1} \\
& \begin{bmatrix}\text{CASE } nom\end{bmatrix} \\
\text{INTERNAL} & \boxed{2} \\
& \begin{bmatrix}\text{CATEGORY} & V \\ \text{FORM} & present \\ \text{EXTERNAL} & \boxed{1}\end{bmatrix}
\end{bmatrix} \\
\text{FORM} & \boxed{2} \\
\text{SEM} & \begin{bmatrix}\text{TENSE } present\end{bmatrix}
\end{bmatrix}
$$

The crucial difference between this feature structure and the English one is that it targets all verbs, not just auxiliaries.

Q8

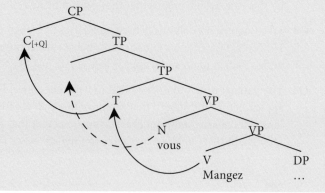

```
                              CP
                    ┌──────────┴──────────┐
                 C[+Q]                    TP
                    ↑           ┌──────────┴─────────┐
                    ┆                                TP
                    ┆                      ┌──────────┴────────┐
                    ┆          ↑           T                   VP
                    ┆          ┆                     ┌──────────┴──────┐
                    ┆          ┆                     N                 VP
                    ┆          ┆                   vous        ┌───────┴──────┐
                                                               V              DP
                                                             Mangez           ...
```

Q9

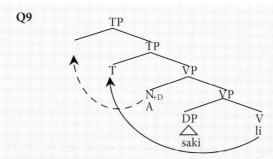

Q10 Finnish is like English: both tensed and untensed main verbs come after the landmark adverb.

Q11 Portuguese is like French: tensed main verbs appear to the left of adverbs and untensed verbs (found when there is a tensed auxiliary) appear to the right of adverbs.

Q12 German does verb/subject inversion with tensed main verbs. This tells us that the main verb has raised into T.

Q13 German tensed verbs appear before *nicht* when tensed, and after it when untensed. This is another clue that German moves its Vs into T.

Q14 The relevant landmark here is the subject. Participial (untensed) main verbs follow the subject. Tensed verbs precede the subject. The position right before the subject is also where auxiliaries like *gwnaeth* are found. This suggests that we have V to T raising.

Q15 T$_{past}$

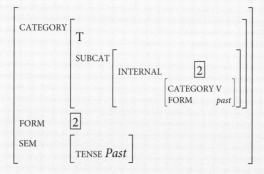

The crucial difference between this feature structure and the French one is the absence of an external feature for the T. This ensures that the subject stays in its base position: lower than T.

UNIT 24 *WH*-QUESTIONS

> **Objectives:**
> - Identify *wh*-questions.
> - Compare *wh*-questions to echo questions.
> - Motivate *wh*-movement.
> - Draw trees for *wh*-movement.
> - Develop constraints limiting the scope of *wh*-movement.

24.1 Finding *wh*-questions

Exercise **Q1** 📖 Consider the following sentences. What kind of answers might you give for such questions? Can you answer these questions with *yes, no* or *maybe*?

(1) (a) How have you been?

(b) What did you find in the bucket?

(c) Who was eating in the bathroom?

(d) Where did you put the cat food?

(e) When is Brad going to get a new computer?

(f) Why are you grating parmesan cheese on your ice cream?

(g) Which book are you going to read tonight?

Definition Questions that are answered with a constituent are called either **wh-questions** or **constituent questions**. They are called wh-questions because the words that begin such questions in English typically begin with the letters *wh* (*what, who, where, when, why, which*). The word *how* is also considered a *wh*-element even though it doesn't begin with *wh*.

Exercise **Q2** 📖 Change the sentences in Q1 above into statements. In order to do this, you may have to change the *you* in these sentences into *I*. For example, we would change the question *What did you eat?* into something like *I ate a peanut*. You can be inventive about what replaces the *wh*-element. Don't try to answer the question; try to turn the question into a statement instead.

Q3 📖 Can the *wh*-elements be replaced by just single words or can they also be replaced by more complex constituents?

Q4 📖 What does your answer to Q3 tell you about whether the *wh*-elements in (1) are phrases or not?

Comment   Compare the position of the *wh*-element in (1) with the related phrase in your sentences in response to Q2. It appears as if there is a movement relationship between the two positions. In (2), we see that the question form of a sentence has a gap in the position where there is a DP in the statement. Similarly, in (3) we see a gap where there is a PP in the statement.

(2) (a)   I   bought a flatbed.
     (b)   What did you buy   _____?

(3) (a)   I   got this suit at a flea market.
     (b)   Where did you get that suit _____?

24.2 Formalizing the process

Exercise   **Q5** ➥ In the sentences in (1), has Subject/Auxiliary Inversion applied?   Y   N

Q6 ➥ Where does the *wh*-phrase appear relative to the auxiliary?
                                                                before   after

Q7 📖 What conclusion might you draw about the landing site of the *wh*-movement given the position of the auxiliary. Could you make a hypothesis about where the *wh*-element lands?

Exercise   **Q8** 📖 Once more, look back at the sentences in (1). What kind of elements (in terms of category) seem to be able to undergo *wh*-movement?

Q9 📖 What subcategory do each of the *wh*-moved elements serve in their position before movement?

Comment   Bringing together your answers to Q5–9, we can now make some suppositions about what's going on in *wh*-movement. It appears as if *wh*-movement applies so that the *wh*-phrase appears in the specifier of the CP, so the landing site will be triggered by tagging the EXTERNAL feature of the C involved in *wh*-questions. If complementizers are involved in typing sentences as questions or statements, we might hypothesize a special C for *wh*-questions. Let's call it $C_{[+wh]}$.

Notation   The thing that moves has to be a phrase headed by a *wh*-word. We can code this with the FORM feature: [FORM *wh*]. It doesn't matter what function this phrase plays within the clause so long as it bears this feature.

Notice that in a sentence like (2b) above, the element that moves isn't necessarily in the immediate complement of the C head. It can be quite far down the tree. It can satisfy the INTERNAL feature of a VP, or be an adjunct on some element under T. As such, we're going to have to introduce a kind of uncertainty into the structure, such that the process can search down the tree more than into just its complement.[1] We indicate this with a triangle in the feature structure (indicating "containing"):

(4) $C_{[+wh]}$

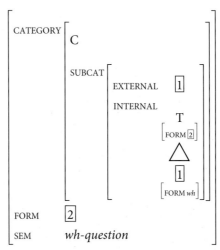

Discussion   Wow, that's a complicated feature structure! However, it contains all the relevant information we need. The semantics indicate that we have a constituent question. The FORM feature is tagged to the T node using the number 2. This indicates that we have head movement (SAI) of the T into the C head. The SUBCAT features are where all the action is, however. The EXTERNAL feature is tagged with ①. This links it to the element under the triangle. The triangle under the T node is meant to indicate that somewhere uncertain under the TP we need to find an element that has a *wh* FORM. That element then moves into the specifier of the CP to satisfy the C's EXTERNAL feature. An example of this is given in (5):

---

[1]   This idea is borrowed from the theory called Lexical–Functional Grammar and is called "Functional Uncertainty" there.

304

(5)

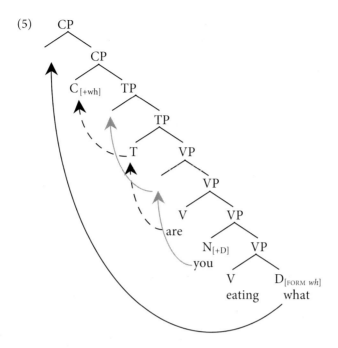

There is a lot going on in this tree. We have head-to-head movement (indicated with the dotted line) of the auxiliary verb *are*, from V to T and then from T to C (SAI). Those movements are motivated by the FORM feature of each of the higher heads. Next, we have the movement of the subject from the specifier of the lowest VP, to the higher VP and then to the specifier of the TP indicated by the gray arrows. These movements are triggered by the tags in the EXTERNAL features of each of these elements. Finally, we have the long movement of the object, triggered by the tag in the EXTERNAL feature of the C$_{[+wh]}$. The triangle in the feature structure means that there is an indeterminacy as to which element is targeted, except that in this sentence there is a single *wh*-element – the object – which meets the [FORM *wh*] requirement and this element moves into the specifier of the CP as indicated by the large black arrow.

Exercise **Q10** 📖 Draw the tree for the sentence *When are you leaving?* Assume that *when* is an Adv and is adjoined to the V *leaving*.

Challenge Consider the sentence *Who is eating the apple?* Which element (the subject? the object? etc.?) is in the first position in the sentence? Can you tell if SAI has applied here? If so how? If not can you tell if the subject question word has raised into the specifier of CP or not? What do you think? Has the subject *wh*-word raised into the specifier of CP or is it in the normal subject position in the specifier of TP?

24.3 Embedded *wh*-movement

Comment   *Wh*-movement is also found in embedded clauses. In these forms, the embedded clause isn't exactly a question, but is the complement to a verb of questioning like *ask, question, wonder, ponder*, etc. The examples in (6) are typical:

(6)   (a)   I asked what he ate for supper.

     (b)   I wondered when he'd leave.

     (c)   I pondered who my secret admirer is.

Exercise   Apart from the subtle semantic difference between a real question and an embedded one, there is a major syntactic difference between embedded clauses in (6) and main clause *wh*-questions.

    Q11 📖 Is there SAI in the embedded clause in the sentences in (6)?

Exercise   **Q12** 📖 Keeping in mind your answer to Q11, draw the feature structure for embedded $C_{[+wh]}$. Start with the feature structure in (4) and make the relevant modifications.

    Q13 📖 Draw the tree for the sentence *He asked what you are eating.*

24.4 Constraints on *wh*-movement

Exercise   **Q14** 📖 The sentence in (7) is an acceptable sentence of English. (It isn't beautiful, but it's acceptable to most English speakers.) Look back at the lexical entry in (4). Is the acceptability of this sentence predicted by the lexical entry in (4)?

(7)   What did Bill say that Mary claimed that Fred ate?

Comment   *Wh*-movement differs from DP movement and head-to-head movement in that it appears to allow **long-distance** properties. That is, the starting point of the movement can be indeterminately far away from the specifier of the CP. With DP movement and head-to-head movement, the relationship is always **local**, usually holding between a specifier of a head and some element in the complement of that head. The long-distance nature of *wh*-movement falls out from the fact that that the C has a triangle in it, introducing uncertainty into what element undergoes the movement. However, as we will see below, this uncertainty has some restrictions on it.

Exercise   **Q15** 📖 Consider now the sentence in (8). Is its unacceptability predicted by the feature structure in (4)?

(8)   * What did Bill say that Mary made the claim that Fred ate?

    (Cf. Bill said that Mary made the claim that Fred ate apples.)

Comment   The long-distance nature of *wh*-movement isn't without limitations. While the uncertainty introduced by the triangle allows us to do movement from a wide variety of positions within a clause and from embedded clauses, there are some circumstances we must exclude. The main difference between (7) and (8) is that in (8), the *wh*-word is moving from a clause that is part of a DP (*the claim that Fred ate what*), whereas in (7) the *wh*-word is moving from a clause that is immediately part of a VP. The difference is abstractly represented in (9) and (10).

(9)   *Wh*-movement is OK:

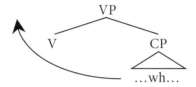

(10) *Wh*-movement is bad:

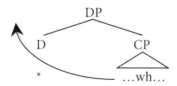

Notation   We can impose a restriction on our understanding of uncertainty in feature structures like (4) to exclude examples like (8) by writing a constraint.

(11) *The Complex DP Constraint (CDPC) on Uncertainty*

The triangle denoting uncertainty (a):

(a)   XP

         Y

may not contain any structures where a DP is dominated by XP and dominates Y:

(b)   *XP

           DP

           Y

Definition   The constraint in (11) uses the term "dominates." The definition of domination should be intuitive. When some element higher in the tree is connected to some element lower in the tree by tree branches, we say the first element **dominates** the second.

Comment   Consider the sentence in (12). This sentence is an example of what Ross (1969) called a **Wh-island Violation**. This sentence is unacceptable to most English speakers.

(12) *What did Bill ask who ate?

 (Cf. Bill asked who ate the apple.)

Ross observed that long-distance *wh*-movement cannot cross over another *wh*-word that's in a specifier position. Abstractly:

(13)   ....   wh   ...   wh

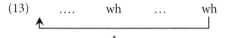

Exercise   **Q16** 📖 Construct a constraint similar to (11) to explain *wh*-islands. You will need to refer to a specifier here, so the structure in the second part of the constraint will have to be a little more complicated.

Challenge   *Wh*-movement is also restricted from applying to elements that are conjoined (a) or are within structures that are conjoined (b).

(a)   *What did Bill drink milk and? (Cf. Bill drank milk and whisky.)

(b)   *What did Bill drink milk and eat? (Cf. Bill drank milk and ate cookies.)

Formulate a constraint (or multiple constraints) to restrict the application of uncertainty to conjoined structures.

Summary   *Wh*-questions are formed in a very different way from *yes/no* questions and statements. They involve an operation that uses long-distance movement from an uncertain position. This movement is allowed whenever there is an element that has a [FORM *wh*] feature that can be found within the domain of "uncertainty" (the triangle) and the constraints discussed in section 24.4 aren't violated.

The discussion of *wh*-questions in this unit is only the tip of the iceberg when it comes to long-distance relationships. For example, similar relationships hold in topicalization structures and certain kinds of cleft constructions (e.g. *Beans are what I like to eat*) as well as in relative clauses. There are also many other constraints like those discussed in section 24.4. It would also be nice if we could explain why constraints like those in section 24.4 might exist in the first place. For reasons of space, we simply can't get into all these issues here, but try some of the readings in the further reading section below.

Suggested further reading

- Adger (2003), chapters 9 and 10
- Bayer (1984)
- Carnie (2006), chapters 11 and 12
- Cheng (1997)
- Chomsky (1973), (1977) and (1991)
- Cinque (1981)
- Cowper (1992), chapters 7 and 12
- Falk (2001), chapter 6
- Haegeman (1994), chapters 7 and 12
- Hornstein, Nunes and Grohman (2005), chapter 5
- Huang (1982)
- Huddleston and Pullum (2005), chapters 9, 10, 11, 14 and 15
- Kim and Sells (2008), chapter 10
- Kroeger (2004), chapter 7
- Larson (2010), units 24, 25, 26 and 27
- Manzini (1992)
- McCloskey (1979)
- Poole (2002), chapter 6
- Radford (1988), chapter 9; (2004), chapters 5, 6 and 10
- Richards (1997)
- Rizzi (1990)
- Roberts (1997), chapter 4
- Ross (1967)
- Sag, Wasow and Bender (2003), chapter 14
- Soames and Perlmutter (1979), chapter 7
- Tallerman (2005), chapter 8
- van Gelderen (2010), chapter 11

Answers to questions

Q1 None of these questions can be answered with *yes, no* or *maybe*. They are not *yes/no* questions. Instead, these questions must be answered with a constituent. For example, (b) might be answered "crabs and oysters."

Q2 Some possible answers (these are not the only possible sentences, but give an idea of how we might answer this question):

(a)   I have been very well.

(b)   I found pearls in the bucket.

(c) Elvis was eating in the bathroom.

(d) I put the cat food in the cabinet.

(e) Brad is going to get a new computer on Friday.

(f) I'm grating parmesan cheese on my ice cream because the ice cream is spaghetti flavored.

(g) I'm going to read *Syntactic Structures* tonight.

Q3 The *wh*-elements in (1) can be replaced by complex constituents, such as *very well* or even clauses like *because the ice cream is spaghetti flavored.*

Q4 This suggests that the *wh*-elements in (1) are in fact phrases and not just words (but can be words!). Further evidence for this is the *wh*-element in (1g) which itself is a phrase (*which book*). This suggests it isn't head-to-head movement.

Q5 Yes, at least in the ones where the element that has moved is not the subject.

Q6 Before

Q7 *Wh*-element moves to the beginning of the sentence, before the inverted auxiliary. If the inverted auxiliary is in the C of the clause, this means that the moved *wh*-element is before the C. The most likely position for this is the specifier of the CP:

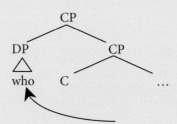

Q8 (a) Adverb, (b) DP, (c) DP, (d) probably a PP, (e) either a PP (on Tuesday) or an Adverb (yesterday), (f) probably a CP, but other categories are possible, (g) a DP.

Q9 (a) a MOD feature, (b) an EXTERNAL feature, (c) an EXTERNAL feature, (d) an INTERNAL feature, (e) a MOD feature, (f) a MOD feature, (g) an INTERNAL feature.

Q10

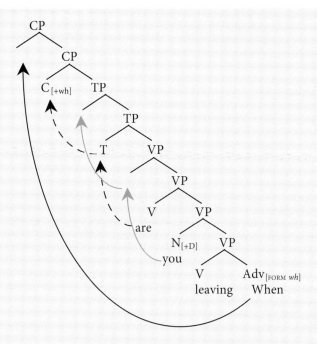

Q11 There is no SAI in embedded clauses in English.

Q12 $C_{[+wh]}$

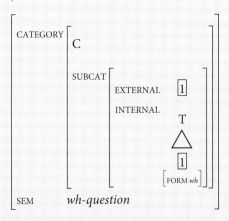

The difference between (4) and this feature structure is the lack of the ② tag, which triggers SAI in main clauses but is absent here.

Q13

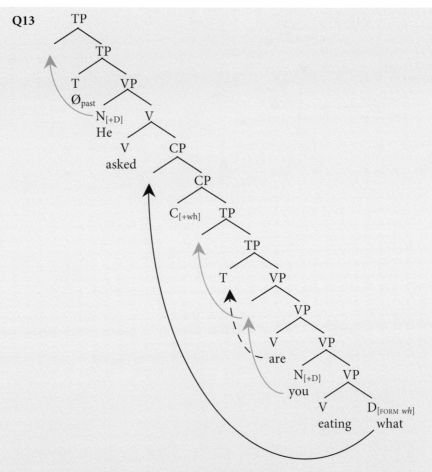

Q14 Yes, this sentence is predicted to be acceptable. There are no restrictions on the triangle in the lexical entry that prevent the *wh*-element starting out in an embedded clause or even in an embedded clause inside another embedded clause, as in this case. The "uncertainty" of the triangle allows the lexical entry to go infinitely deep to find the *wh*-word to satisfy the EXTERNAL feature of the C.

Q15 No, the ungrammaticality of this form is not predicted by the feature structure in (4). The *wh*-element should be able to move in such a case, just as it does in (6).

Q16 *The* Wh-*island Constraint on Uncertainty*

The triangle denoting uncertainty (a):

(a)   XP

312

may not contain any structures where there is a ZP that is dominated by XP and dominates Y and that ZP has a *wh*-element in its specifier:

(b)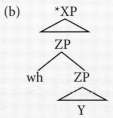

Other formalizations of this constraint may be possible.

GROUP 4 REVIEW

The following were the major ideas introduced in group 4:

- The INTERNAL argument of a passive verb appears as the EXTERNAL argument of the passive *be* auxiliary, using tags in the feature structure for $be_{pass.}$
- The EXTERNAL argument of a passive is apparently null (it shows up as PRO), but can be optionally expressed overtly by a *by*-phrase adjunct.
- Non-finite clauses are clauses marked by the absence of past, present or future tense, and are marked with the marker to_T in English.
- The EXTERNAL arguments of the complements to control predicates like *is ready* lack phonological expression and are generated as PRO. This is determined by the feature structure for the control predicate itself.
- We distinguished object control from subject control, using tests like the clausal subject test, the pleonastic test, the idiom test and the entailment test.
- Control predicates have an underlying EXTERNAL argument. Raising predicates inherit their EXTERNAL argument from the non-finite clause they embed, via tagging and movement.
- We distinguish raising to subject position from raising to object position, again encoded in the SUBCAT features of the raising predicate.
- Subject/Auxiliary Inversion (SAI) is encoded as movement of a T head into a question complementizer head. This is triggered by a tagging between the C's INTERNAL feature and FORM feature.
- In English, main verbs don't raise into T, but in French they do. Again this is encoded by taking an INTERNAL feature with a FORM feature.
- English auxiliary verbs behave like French main verbs.
- We can distinguish between languages that raise main verbs to T using the landmark test, and subject/verb inversion test.
- VSO languages involve V to T movement around a VP internal subject (i.e. one that has not raised to the specifier of TP).
- *Wh*-questions involve movement of some constituent into the specifier of CP, triggered – like all movement – by tagging.

- *Wh*-movement differs from other kinds of movement in that the movement isn't immediately local; instead, it is long-distance. This is encoded using a triangle in the feature structure that marks uncertainty in the depth of embedding of the $[+wh]$ feature.
- Despite the fact that *wh*-movement is long-distance there are restrictions on *wh*-movement, called island constraints. Two island constraints are discussed here: the *wh*-island constraint and the complex DP island constraint.
- The complex DP constraint (CDPC) does not allow a dominating DP to intervene in the middle of the uncertainty triangle.
- The *Wh*-Island Constraint disallows a CP with a *wh*-phrase in its specifier to intervene in the uncertainty triangle.

5 Conclusions

UNIT 25 EVALUATING OUR PROGRESS

Objectives:

- Review the major ideas in this book by drawing the tree of a complex sentence.
- Evaluate the system presented by looking to see if it is scientific and meets the criteria of observational, descriptive, explanatory and formal adequacy.

25.1 A tree for review

Comment   In this text, we've covered a fair amount of ground hitting on many (but by no means all) of the main questions in syntactic theory. One way to see if you've mastered this material is to try drawing the tree for a fairly complex sentence. You'll do this in the exercise below. In the following sections, you'll then have an opportunity to think about what we have accomplished, and what work we still have to do to come up with a good theory of syntax.

Exercise   **Q1** 📖 Draw the tree for the following sentence. Since this sentence is quite complex, you may want to break it down into bits, as I have done in the answer key.

(1)   What is he likely to want to have been read by his students on Tuesday?

A couple of hints:

   (a)   There is an instance of V to T to C movement in the highest clause.

   (b)   *want* is an object-raising predicate (this is tricky!)

   (c)   *be read* is a passive verb.

   (d)   *is likely* is a subject-raising predicate.

   (e)   don't forget about how possessive pronouns like *his* are formed.

   (f)   Assume that *on Tuesday* modifies *read* (although other interpretations are possible).

   (g)   *Wh*-movement applies from the second clause down to the main clause.

25.2 Evaluating our grammar

Comment   Let's now take a pause to think about how well our grammar has done with the standards we set out for it in the first few units of this book.

Exercise   **Q2** 📖 Think carefully about the definition of science given at the beginning of this book. Have we done a good job in sticking to the scientific method? Think carefully about when we've made formal proposals because of the data and when we've stipulated something just to make the whole picture hold together.

Exercise   **Q3** 📖 We claimed that our grammar should meet four levels of adequacy (observational, descriptive, explanatory and formal). How well did we do on these? Are there facts that we haven't accounted for? Does the grammar correspond to your judgments about form? Does the grammar explain how a child acquires the language? Is the grammar sufficiently formalized?

Answers to questions

Q1   Let's start with the embedded clause.

(a) First let's put together PP *on Tuesday*. This one is easy, but don't forget the empty D head. This structure is created through two instances of C-MERGE, due to the INTERNAL features of the P and the D.

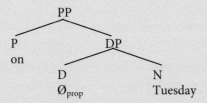

In the rest of the derivation we'll represent this structure with a triangle, just to save on space:

The P *on* still has a MOD feature that must be checked; we'll fix this below.

(b) Next let's do the DP *his students*, and the PP *by his students*. Remember that *his* is really *he+'s*. First we have the N *students*, which has an EXTERNAL argument attached via S-MERGE:

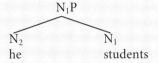

This is C-MERGED with *'s* to satisfy the determiner's INTERNAL feature. Then N₂ moves to the specifier of the DP to satisfy the D's EXTERNAL feature. The fact that movement occurs is due to the tag in the D's feature structure. The morphological readjustment rule applies rendering *his* out of *he+'s*:

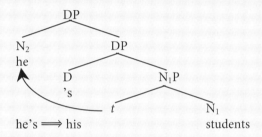

This structure is then attached as a complement via C-MERGE to satisfy the INTERNAL feature of the P *by*:

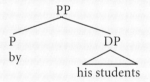

The preposition *by* still has a MOD feature that must be checked to meet the Principle of Full Interpretation, but first we need to start assembling other parts of the VP.

(c) Next, we C-MERGE together the V with the object *what* to satisfy the V's INTERNAL feature:

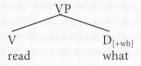

(d) Now we can ADJOIN the two PPs, satisfying each preposition's MOD feature:

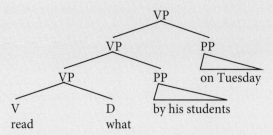

(e) The last thing we have to do to this VP is to attach the external argument via S-MERGE. Here we're using PRO because this is a passive and the feature structure for passive *be* (the next thing we're going to attach) is going to require that the external argument of the embedded verb have the feature [form *null*]. PRO serves this function. The PRO is coindexed with the *by*-phrase due to the coindexing requirement imposed by *by*.

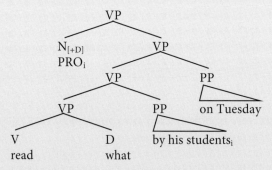

(f) The VP in (e) becomes the complement of the passive auxiliary verb *been*, through C-MERGE. The passive auxiliary stipulates that the INTERNAL argument of its complement (*what*) becomes the specifier through MERGE:

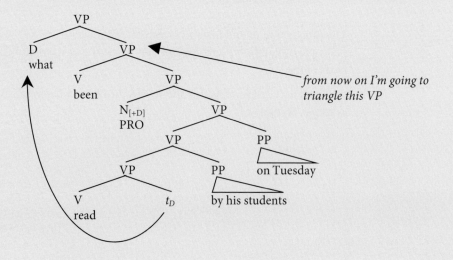

from now on I'm going to triangle this VP

(g) This VP in turn is C-MERGED with the perfective auxiliary *have* and the non-finite T node *to$_T$*. Due to the tags in each of these elements' EXTERNAL features, we have further raising of *what* to each specifier position.

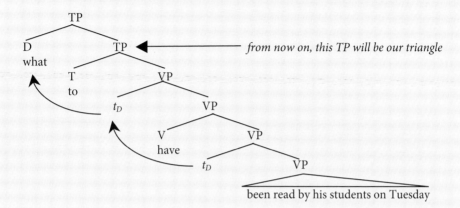

from now on, this TP will be our triangle

been read by his students on Tuesday

(h) This non-finite TP will be a complement to the object-raising verb *want*. *Want* also requires an EXTERNAL argument to be S-MERGED. In this case it's the pronoun *he*.

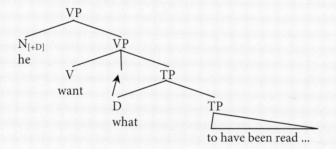

to have been read ...

(i) This structure is also a non-finite clause, and the external argument of the VP is tagged to move to the specifier of the non-finite T.

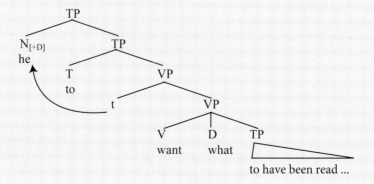

to have been read ...

(j) The pronoun he cannot stay in this place, however, since the external argument of the non-finite clause must be null. Fortunately, we can move it, leaving a null trace in this position. To move it, we'll merge this TP with the raising predicate *is likely. He* raises through each specifier on its way up to the specifier of TP. Because *is* is a tensed auxiliary, it raises into the T head due to the tagged FORM feature.

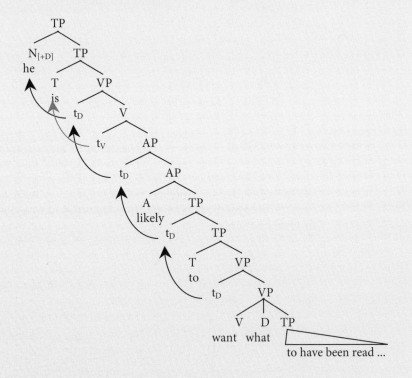

This is the final stop for the pronoun *he.*

(k) Finally, we MERGE the *wh*-question complementizer. This complementizer's FORM feature is tagged to that of the T head. So *is* undergoes Subject/Auxiliary Inversion by moving to C. The complementizer also requires a *wh*-specifier. There is a *wh*-phrase in the object position of *want*. Due to uncertainty, the C can reach down and grab this and move it to satisfy the [+wh] requirement of its EXTERNAL feature.

This results in the final string.

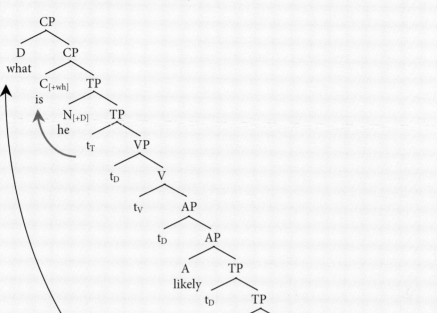

Q2 The answer to this question is largely a matter of opinion, but I'll give you my thoughts. I think overall I've tried to give you a theoretical proposal that corresponds to the facts that I've presented to you. To a certain degree, any scientific theory is going to have to work with some stipulations. This is true here too. For example, I had to stipulate that C-MERGE applied before ADJOIN and ADJOIN applied before S-MERGE. The island constraints mentioned in unit 24 also feel a bit stipulative, even if supported by the data. We'd really like a better treatment of those facts. The sheer number of phonologically empty categories that we've had to propose is consistent with the facts, but also seems to have a bit of stipulative quality to it.

Q3 Again the answers to these questions are matters of opinion! So there are no right or wrong answers here. You could be happy with what we've done or highly suspicious. As a textbook author I hope you're happy, but as a teacher I'm hoping you'll be very suspicious and will investigate the material further, given the readings in the next unit.

My own opinion is that our system fares not too badly on each of the levels of adequacy, although there is room for improvement in each. With respect to observational adequacy, we've covered a fairly hefty chunk of sentences that you might find in a corpus – at least basic statements and questions. But I can think of a lot of sentence types we can't deal with. We can't (yet) deal with relative clauses (*the book that he read*), imperatives (*Go now*), clefts (*It wasn't beef waffles that he wanted*), topicalizations (*Beef waffles, now those I like*), sentences with heavy objects shifted to the right (*He ate with gusto the pizza that I bought him*) and existential sentences (*There was a fight*) among many others. The story gets worse when we start looking at other languages. Some languages have fairly robust case systems and a freer word order. Obviously, none of these fall into the scope of what we've done here, and you may be able to think of more cases. Nevertheless, I think we've done not bad with the data we've covered.

From a descriptive perspective, I think we have a strong case for success. The constituency facts, as well as the distinctions among complements, adjuncts and specifiers, correspond closely with my own syntactic judgments (yours, of course, may differ).

With respect to explanatory adequacy, there is a puzzle. Look at appendix 3, and you'll see that with relatively simple formal rules (only four of them), and a couple of constraints and principles, we can do a lot of work. On the other hand, the feature structures we've proposed are quite complex, so what the child has to learn is much more complex when it comes to learning feature structures.

Finally, formal adequacy seems to be a strong point of the system. Our grammar is precise, and hopefully the predictions it makes are clear and straightforward.

You may well disagree with my evaluation of these measures of adequacy. Indeed, many syntacticians do! But I hope the approach given here is at least a step in the right direction.

UNIT 26 THE NEXT STEPS

26.1 "Modern" syntax

Discussion   As stated at the outset of this book, the "modern" part of the title is meant to imply a broad, non-theory-specific approach to the study of syntax. It is, of course, impossible to be completely atheoretic about any scientific study. It is part of the definition of science that the researcher pursue hypotheses and theories. Nevertheless, I wanted the reader of this book to get exposure to ideas in syntax that weren't too closely tied to one particular framework or theory of syntax. My solution to this problem was to take three of the most common frameworks of analysis (MP, HPSG and LFG) and lift the things I thought they did best and create a blend.

The reaction to this has been mixed among professional syntacticians. Most of them tend to see the blended theory presented here only in terms of the things they disagree with. For example, among my colleagues who work in MP who have looked at the manuscript version of the book, this has come to be known as "Carnie's HPSG book." The irony to this statement is that HPSG colleagues have complained to me that the book here has all the hallmarks of being written by someone who primarily works in MP (as I do) and doesn't understand the "truth" behind HPSG. Practitioners of LFG seem equally disturbed by all the movement and tagging. Fortunately for me, the audience of this book is none of these professional syntacticians, but you: the open-minded interested beginning syntactician.

I've really tried here, as much as possible, to give you a foundation that will serve you well, no matter what theoretical approach you end up working in. Nevertheless, you will probably end up choosing to work in one particular framework of syntax (one of MP, HPSG or LFG, or even one of the many other approaches you can find out there). So, the point of this unit is to provide you with some guidance for where to take it from here. I'll try to give you both the similarities and differences between the analysis presented here and the major frameworks. For each theory, I'll also point you to both textbooks and primary sources that will help you further your studies in syntax.

327

26.2 The paradigm of generative grammar

Discussion In 1957, Noam Chomsky published his famous work *Syntactic Structures*. In this work, he set out the beginnings of a general approach to syntax that all three of the main theories found in this book belong to. This paradigm is called Generative Grammar. The term "generative" here is meant to refer to a mathematical notion where a formal system is said to "generate" the sentences of a language. There is a great deal of confusion about this term, at least partly because Chomsky has argued that a significant portion of Generative Grammar is an innate property of humans, and often speaks of a mental "organ" for language. However, the original intent of the term was not that the formal system actually is the mechanism for producing sentences as we speak and understand them. Instead, "generate" was intended to be used in its mathematical sense (perhaps closer to "enumerate" or "identify"). Despite this confusion, Generative Grammar as a whole is perhaps the most influential view of syntax. It concentrates on the form of a sentence and identifying formal mechanisms for describing those forms.

The earliest form of Generative Grammar is often called Transformational Grammar (TG), and is closely associated with Chomsky's (1957) and (1965) works. Transformations are rules that turn one tree structure into another. In the loosest sense of the word, our MOVE operation has the effect of a transformation (although, technically, it isn't a transformation because it doesn't map between trees, only changes a single tree). In the 1970s, Generative Grammar fractured into several different factions, including LFG (see section 26.4), Generalized Phrase Structure Grammar (GPSG), which later became HPSG (see section 26.5), and the Extended Standard Theory (EST). The EST itself underwent two major revisions, first becoming Government and Binding Theory (GB) and then the Minimalist Program (MP) (and even MP has gone through several different iterations). The latter two theories are often grouped together into a framework of theories known as Principles and Parameters (P&P).

Further reading

As an introduction to the framework as a whole, I'm unsurprisingly very partial to one book in particular:

* Carnie (2006)

This book is an introduction to the general approach current in Chomskyan circles. The book you are holding in your hands right now is a more experimental work and more of a hybrid. Carnie (2006), by contrast, is a much more conservative introduction to the main ideas in Generative Grammar. It is couched in the Principles and Parameters framework. Among the topics covered there and not discussed in this book are X-bar theory, theta theory, binding theory, split VPs and minimalist accounts of island effects.

Other introductions to the Principles and Parameters model include the following books, all of which are excellent. Although, as should be self-evident, not as excellent as my own!

* Cook and Newson (1996)
* Cowper (1992)
* Culicover (1997)
* Friedin (1991)
* Haegeman (1994)
* Larson (2010)
* Ouhalla (1999)
* Poole (2002)
* Radford (1997b)
* Roberts (1997)
* van Gelderen (2010)

26.3 The Minimalist Program (MP)

Discussion The Minimalist Program (Chomsky 1993, 1995) represented a methodological turn in the way Principles and Parameters analysis was done. The reasons for this change need not concern us here (see Uriagereka 1998 for discussion), but it amounts to a shift towards looking for simple formal rules.

In this book, the various MERGE, ADJOIN and MOVE rules come directly from this tradition (Chomsky 1995, chapter 4), albeit in a slightly different form. Also borrowed from this tradition are the Principle of Full Interpretation, and the notion of feature checking. Some of the things that are not part of MP are the complex feature structures (especially SUBCAT features), tagging and structural uncertainty.

Further reading

MP is not a monolithic theory. There are several different versions of it, and it has evolved over time. The textbooks listed below offer various perspectives on minimalism.
- Adger (2003)
- Radford (1997a), (1997b), (2004)

26.4 Lexical–Functional Grammar (LFG)

Discussion   LFG is perhaps the least represented theory in this book. One reason for this is that, since it is an early offshoot of Generative Grammar, it has developed a large number of assumptions that are contrary to the view developed in this book. While LFG uses feature structures similar to those we use here (called F-structures or functional structures), these structures have both contentful and ontological differences with our feature structures. The bigger of these is the ontological difference: F-structures differ from our feature structures in that they represent entire sentences instead of the meaningful representations of individual words and phrases. These representations are separate from tree structures (we have combined the two) and are related to one another only by an abstract mapping. The trees in LFG are not constructed via operations that reference the featural/functional content of the words. This in turn relates to the contentful difference between LFG and this book. In this book, we've referred to SUBCAT features. In LFG, the equivalent functions aren't merely about the selectional requirements of words. Instead, they represent grammatical functions like subject and object. Another important difference between LFG and the view in this book lies in the importance of the lexicon. In this book, I've been fairly loose in my interpretation of what the lexicon does and does not do. For example, I've allowed inflectional information to be constructed in the syntax (e.g. *he+'s* becoming *his*). Under the assumptions of LFG – a perspective known as lexicalism – this is not allowed. Similarly, there are no syntactic transformational rules in LFG. Some of these ideas are discussed at length in Kaplan and Bresnan (1982) and Dalrymple *et al.* (1995).

On the other hand, I've borrowed some important ideas from LFG. The notion of uncertainty is borrowed directly from LFG, allowing long-distance dependencies like those found in *wh*-questions. While it still involves movement in the version presented here, the idea that head movement involves the form and category features of the target is inspired by the LFG treatment known as head-mobility.

26.5 Head-driven Phrase Structure Grammar (HPSG)

Discussion   On a purely visual level, the approach given here owes much to HPSG. The feature structures, although different in content from those found in HPSG, look very similar to HPSG representations. The notation of tagging is also taken straight from the conventions of HPSG – although since HPSG has no syntactic movement, it indicates only identity in features, not the trigger for movement. The treatment of auxiliaries and their complements is also lifted from the HPSG literature.

However, there are many deep differences between this book and HPSG. Like LFG, HPSG is a lexicalist theory; it does not allow syntactic movement transformations. Similarly, phrase level structures also have feature structures (this latter stance could apply to the theory described in this book, although I was never explicit about it). The HPSG treatment of *wh*-movement is completely different.

A classical version of HPSG is described in Pollard and Sag (1994), although newer conceptions without rules (using instead complex feature inheritance hierarchies) have also been recently proposed.

26.6 Other approaches to syntax

Discussion   The generative approach to grammar is by no means the only one. There is an alphabet soup of grammars and their acronyms. We find Word Grammar (WG), Relational Grammar (RG), Arc Pair Grammar (APG), Functional Grammar (FG), Cognitive Grammar (CG), Construction Grammar (also CG), Categorial Grammar (yet another CG), Tree-Adjoining Grammar (TAG), Dependency Grammar (DP), Simpler Syntax (SS) and Role and Reference Grammar (RRG).

Further reading

All of these approaches have their adherents, and I can't possibly do justice to them all. Therefore, I'll limit my recommended readings to three of them.

The oldest approach mentioned here is Categorial Grammar. Categorial Grammar is not a Generative Grammar, but instead comes from the European proof-based mathematical approaches to syntax. The Categorial Grammar conceptions of specifier and complement to a head are borrowed by all three of MP, HPSG and LFG, and are reflected in the INTERNAL and EXTERNAL features described here (amounting to the symbols / and \ in Categorial Grammar). A good textbook treatment of Categorial Grammar:

- Carpenter (1997)

Perhaps one of the most popular non-generative approaches to syntax is Role and Reference Grammar. It differs from all of the approaches discussed above in previous sections in that it is a functionalist view of syntax. This means it focuses on the communicative function of a sentence rather than on a treatment of its form (although it also attempts to do that too). There is an extensive treatment of the major ideas in:

- Van Valin and LaPolla (1997)

The last theory I'll point you towards is perhaps the newest. It's Jackendoff and Culicover's Simpler Syntax model and it shares many of the same insights used here, but with a very different formalism. There is a textbook treatment in:

- Culicover (2009)

26.7 The last word

Conclusion I hope that this book has opened your eyes to the exciting world of syntactic theory. Although necessarily complex and detailed, the investigation of sentence structure gives us real insight into how we think and communicate. I sincerely hope you find investigations like these as exciting as I do.

APPENDIX 1: GLOSSARY, SYMBOLS AND ABBREVIATIONS

Glossary:

abstract Case	The formal CASE features associated with a particular DP, whether the features are realized morphologically or not.
acceptability	The degree to which a native speaker accepts a sentence.
accusative case	The form of nouns in direct object position.
active	The default voice, where the doer of the action is in subject position, and the entity that the action is done to is in the object position.
adjacency test for adjuncts	If there is a complement and an adjunct, the complement must appear adjacent to the head.
adjective (Adj)	A part of speech that is used to modify a noun. It appears between articles and nouns in English.
ADJOIN	A rule that combines two (or more) items together into a constituent, to satisfy a MOD feature. The combined category is given the label of the non-head.
adjunct	A modifier that is attached using ADJOIN to satisfy a MOD feature.
adposition	A preposition or postposition.
adverb (Adv)	A part of speech that is used to modify a verb or an adjective. It often (but not always) ends in *-ly*. Its position is relatively free in English.

anaphor	A special kind of pronoun which is obligatorily coreferent with another noun in the same clause. In English these are usually marked with the *-self* or *-selves* suffixes.
animate	Animate nouns refer to living things.
argument	Entities involved in the relation described by a predicate. Arguments are typically DPs, CPs or PPs.
aspect	Aspect is a kind of verbal inflection. It is defined by making reference to some point in time, other than the speech time, then looking at when the event happens relative to that reference point. Typical aspects include perfective and progressive.
attributive	Uses of adjectives which are blessed with a MOD feature, and attach into the sentence using the rule of ADJOIN are called attributive adjectives.
auxiliaries	A special class of verbs that have both the property of being a verb and expressing tense. These always appear first in the string of verbs.
case	The form a noun takes when it appears in particular positions in the sentence. When capitalized (Case) it can also refer to abstract Case (see above).
checked	When we do a MERGE operation that satisfies the requirements of a feature we say that feature is checked.
clausal subject test	If a tensed version of the embedded clause can be used as the subject of a predicate, then it is a raising predicate.
clause (TP)	A TP or tense phrase. This usually consists of a subject and a predicate.
closed class	A part of speech that does not allow new members.

334

coindexed	When two items in a feature structure or tree bear the same index (i, j, k, etc.) they are said to be ***coindexed***.
common nouns	Nouns that aren't proper names or pronouns.
complement	The word or phrase that is C-MERGED with the head as required by the head's INTERNAL feature.
COMPLEMENT-MERGE (C-MERGE)	A rule that combines two (or more) items together into a constituent as required by the INTERNAL features of one of the items. The constituent is given the label of the head.
complementary distribution	Two elements are in complementary distribution if they cannot appear at the same time.
Complementizer	A closed class part of speech that introduces a clause.
Complementizer Phrase (CP)	A phrase headed by a complementizer, normally takes TP as a complement.
Complex DP Constraint (CDPC) on uncertainty	A constraint that prevents *wh*-movement out of a DP structure. See appendix 3 for the exact formulation.
conjunction (Conj)	These words tie together two words or phrases (groups of words) on an equal level, e.g. *and, or, but*.
constituent	Either a single word or a group of words that functions as a unit.
constituent question	See ***wh*-question**.
constraint	Constraints are formal statements of structures that are impossible – structures that are claimed to be unacceptable to native speakers.
control predicate	A verb like *want* or a predicative adjective like *ready*, which takes non-finite embedded clauses as complements and where the external argument of the embedded predicate is realized as a PRO.

coordinator	See **conjunction**.
copula	A special verb that is used to introduce predicates that aren't verbs. In English this is usually one of the variants of the verb *is*.
corpus	(pl. corpora) A collection of written or spoken material representing real-world usage.
count nouns	Nouns that can be counted, require a determiner, can be made plural and take the quantifier *many*.
dative case	The form of nouns used with indirect objects.
declarative sentence	A sentence that asserts that an event or state of affairs has or has not occurred.
derivation	A formal description of how the grammatical structure is formed.
descriptive rules	Rules that represent actual corpus and judgment data.
descriptively adequate grammar	Such a grammar accounts not only for corpus data, but also for the judgments that a native speaker has about the acceptability of sentences.
determiner (D)	A closed class part of speech that comes before adjectives and nouns.
Determiner Phrase (DP)	A phrase introduced by a determiner such as *the, a, that, these*, etc.
displacement (or movement) test	If a string of words can be displaced (i.e. moved) as a unit, then it is a constituent.
distribution	Refers to the places the word appears, both with respect to other words and with respect to the prefixes and suffixes the word has on it.
ditransitive	A verb that takes three arguments (a subject, an object and an indirect object).
domination	When some element higher in the tree is connected to some element lower in the tree by tree branches, we say the first element *dominates* the second.

explanatorily adequate grammar	A grammar that offers an explanation for why the grammar is structured the way it is, usually by appealing to language acquisition.
EXTERNAL **argument**	An argument introduced by the EXTERNAL feature. This often corresponds to the subject of a phrase.
feature passing	The features of one head pass to the head of a functional category. This usually happens via tagging.
finite clause	A clause that morphologically expresses the tense relations of past, future or present.
formally adequate grammar	A grammar that is stated in a formal mathematical manner; one that is precise and simple, and makes its predictions obvious, yet does so in the most perspicuous way.
functional categories	Categories that express grammatical notion (P, D, C, T).
future tense	The event time (E) is going to happen after the utterance time (U): U < E.
gender	A property of nouns; in many languages dividing up into masculine, feminine and neuter.
genitive case	See **possessive case**.
gerund	The *-ing* form of a verb (e.g. *biting, walking*). Traditionally the term "gerund" is limited to nominal (noun) uses of the *-ing* form (e.g. *the biting*) and the term "present participle" is used to indicate the verbal usage. We'll use the term "gerund" for both.
grammar	A collection of descriptive rules and constraints.
head	The primary word in a phrase; typically subcategorizes for the other elements in a constituent.

337

head-to-head movement (or head movement)	The movement of the contents of the head of one phrase into the head of another. For example, the movement of the contents of the T head into the C. This is triggered by the tagging of a word's FORM feature with its INTERNAL feature.
idiom	A phrase or clause that has an arbitrary non-literal meaning that cannot be deduced from the component words in the phrase.
idiom test	If an idiomatic/non-literal meaning is available to a structure with a non-finite embedded clause, then the sentence is a raising construction. If it only allows a literal meaning (often with a very strange interpretation), then it is a control construction.
imperfect	An aspect which is the opposite of perfect. This is unmarked by affixes or auxiliaries in English.
infinitive	A special verb form that marks non-finite.
intensifier	A closed class part of speech that serves to modify adjectives and other adverbs, as in *very big* or *too rude* or *rather quickly*.
interjection	A closed class part of speech that a speaker uses to express an emotion (e.g. *Oh!, Ouch!*).
interlinear gloss	A word-by-word translation of a sentence.
INTERNAL	A subcategory feature that defines which complements must appear with a word.
intransitive	A verb that takes only one argument (e.g. *arrive, leave*).
lexical category	A category that expresses content (N, V, Adj, Adv).
local	A relationship between two items that are close to one another in the tree.
mass nouns	Nouns that describe a group or indivisible amount; these can be modified by *much*.
MOD	A SUBCAT feature that is used to indicate what elements an adjunct can modify.

modal auxiliary	An auxiliary that expresses mood.
mood	A verbal inflection that expresses the speaker's perspective on the event. In particular, whether the event described is a possibility, a probability, a necessity or an obligation.
Move/Remerge	A rule that takes an item already in the tree and moves it into another position in the tree.
native-speaker judgment task	A tool used by linguists to probe the structure of sentences.
negation (Neg)	Words like *no* and *not*.
neologism	A new word.
nominative case	Form of nouns in subject position.
non-finite clause	A clause that does not morphologically express the tense relations of past, future or present.
noun (N)	A part of speech used in argument positions. Nouns can be marked with determiners and adjectives.
number	Singular or plural.
observationally adequate grammar	A grammar that accounts for all the data that can be outwardly observed in corpora and other real-world usages.
open class	A class of words that permits new members.
paradigm	A list or table of forms that represents the combination of different grammatical dimensions.
participle	A form of the verb used in the perfect and passive. Usually ends in *-ed* or *-en* (e.g. *bitten*). In traditional grammars this is called the "past participle."
particles	Small words that often serve grammatical functions.
parts of speech	The groups of words that let us state rules and constraints about the form of sentences.

passive	A voice that highlights the element which is undergoing the action. This is marked in English with *be* + Participle.
past tense	The event being described (E) happened before the time of speech or writing (U): E < U.
perfect	The perfect happens when the time of the event (which we might represent abstractly as E) occurs before some reference point (R). So the perfect is E < R. In English, the perfect is marked by *have* + Participle.
person	1st person = speaker, 2nd person = listener, 3rd person = some other person.
phrase	Another name for constituent.
pleonastic subject test	If a pleonastic pronoun can be used in subject position of the main clause, then the main clause predicate is a raising predicate.
pleonastics	Pronouns that appear to have no meaning associated with them. In English, pleonastic pronouns are used when there is no other subject available in the sentence.
possessive case	The case form used on a noun that is acting as the possessor. Sometimes also called the **genitive case**.
postposition	Like a preposition but follows a noun instead preceding it.
predicate	A predicate that expresses a relation between individuals in the world.
predicative	Adjectives (and other categories) that take arguments are said to be **predicative**.
preposition	A closed class part of speech that is used to indicate case. It is always found before DPs, e.g. *to, from, of, along, with, on, under, off,* etc.
Prepositional Phrase (PP)	A phrase headed by a preposition.
prescriptive rules	Grammatical rules that prescribe how we should speak.

present tense	The event time (E) is at the same time as the speech time (U): E = U.
preterite	The form a verb takes when it shows up in past tense sentences. Typically this is the form ending in -*ed*, but it can also be an irregular form like *ate, rang, shook, stood, went*.
Principle of Full Interpretation (FI)	If two items are merged together their feature structures must be compatible.
Principle of Headedness	In any circumstance where a SUBCAT feature mentions a category, one may substitute in a phrase headed by that category and vice versa (e.g. you can freely substitute NP for N, and N for NP; DP for D and D for DP, VP for V, V for VP, etc.).
PRO	The phonologically empty pronoun that satisfies the external feature of passives and the complements of control predicates.
progressive	The progressive aspect indicates an on-going event relative to the reference time. In English, the progressive is marked by BE + GERUND.
pronouns	A special kind of noun, which can be used to refer to someone or something that has previously been mentioned or is obvious from the discourse, e.g. *I, me, you, he, him, his, she, her, it, its, we, us, they, them, their*.
proper nouns	Names; in English, these usually don't take determiners, e.g. *Andrew*.
raising predicates	Predicates (like *seem, is likely, is certain*, etc.) that take a non-finite TP complement, and move the embedded subject into their own subject position. They do not use PRO.
reflexive pronoun	A special kind of anaphor that ends in -*self* or -*selves*.
relative clause	A clause that is used to modify a noun.
reordering test for adjuncts	If two modifiers can be freely reordered, then both modifiers are adjuncts.

replacement test for constituency	If you can replace a string of words with a single word, without changing the meaning of the rest of the sentence, then that string is a constituent.
representation	The output of the derivation.
rule	Statement phrased in a positive form that describes *possible* structures – structures that are claimed to be acceptable to a native speaker.
semantic judgment	A judgment of acceptability that has to do with the meaning of a sentence.
semantic modification test for constituency	If one word modifies another, then they are part of the same constituent.
specifier	An argument that is required by the EXTERNAL feature.
SPECIFIER-MERGE (S-MERGE)	Combine two (or more) items together into a constituent as required by the EXTERNAL features of one of the items. The constituent is given the label of the head.
stand-alone test	If a string of words can stand alone in answer to a question, then it is a constituent.
Subject/Aux Inversion (SAI)	The mechanism for forming *yes/no* questions in English. The first auxiliary is inverted in order with the subject. So the statement *Gilbert is eating waffles* becomes *Is Gilbert eating waffles?* In this book, we analyze SAI as movement of the T head into an abstract initial question complementizer ($C_{[+Q]}$).
subject/verb inversion test	If the language creates questions using Subject/Auxiliary Inversion (SAI) (rather than, for example, using a particle) and tensed main verbs undergo inversion with their subject just like auxiliaries, then it has verb-to-T movement.
suppletion	The complete replacement of a word to indicate a morphological change. For example, the past tense of *go* is *went*.
syntactic categories	The groups of words that let us state rules and constraints about the form of sentences.

syntactic judgment	A judgment of acceptability that has to do with the form of a sentence.
syntax	The scientific study of sentence structure.
tags	Parts of feature structures that mark identity in values in feature structures. Tags are typically numbers written inside of a box. The identity of two numbers means that the values of the features are identical.
tense	The verbal inflection that refers to the time of an event relative to the time at which the sentence is either spoken or written.
transitive	A verb that takes two arguments (a subject and an object).
triangle notation	A notation used to obscure the depth and nature of syntactic embedding, used to indicate uncertainty in structure.
uncertainty	Indicated with the triangle notation in feature structure, uncertainty refers to the idea that a precise depth of embedding need not be stated for long-distance relations such as *wh*-movement.
verb	A part of speech that takes tense inflection, and governs the arguments in a sentence.
voice	A phenomenon that changes the number of participants that are described in an event.
***Wh*-island Constraint on Uncertainty**	A constraint that prevents *wh*-movement out of a CP that has a *wh*-phrase in the CP's specifier. See appendix 3 for the exact formulation.
***wh*-movement**	A kind of MOVE operation that takes some [+*wh*] element and moves it into the specifier of a CP.
***wh*-question**	A question that can be answered with a constituent. *Wh*-questions are usually marked with a question word like *who, what, where, when, why, how* and *which*.
***yes/no* question**	A question that can be answered by *yes, no* or *maybe*.

Symbols and Abbreviations

?	questionable acceptability or grammaticality
( )	optional
[ ]	can mark constituents; can also serve to mark a feature
{ }	choice of items
*	unacceptable/ungrammatical
/	(in a feature structure) "or"
#	semantically odd
→	(in morphological readjustment rules) changes to
+aux	Auxiliary
+intens	intensifier
+prop	proper (noun)
+R	reflexive
±*def*	definite
<	before
< >	ordered list of elements
¬	when used before a feature or a feature value, this symbol indicates that this value or feature cannot be used.
1	first person
$\boxed{1}$	tagged number
2	second person
3	third person
A	Adjective or Adverb
Acc	Accusative Case
Adj	Adjective
Adv	Adverb
AGR-φ	Agreement features
C-MERGE	Complement merge

CDPC   Complex DP constraint on *Wh*-movement

Conj   Conjunction

CP   Complementizer Phrase

DP   Determiner Phrase

E   event time

Fem   feminine

GEND   gender

Interj   interjection

Masc   masculine

N   Noun

Neg   negation

Neut   neuter

Nom   Nominative Case

NP   Noun Phrase

NUM   number

PERS   person

Poss   Possessive Case

S-MERGE   Specifier-merge

SEM   semantics

SUBCAT   subcategorization

t   trace

TP   Tense Phrase

U   utterance time

V   Verb

VP   Verb Phrase

APPENDIX 2: FEATURES AND THEIR VALUES

Feature	Possible values
CATEGORY	N (Noun) V (Verb) P (Preposition) Adj (Adjective) Adv (Adverb) D (Determiner) C (Complementizer) T (Tense) Conj (Conjunction) Interj (Interjection) SUBCAT

SUBCAT	For all categories:
	   EXTERNAL
	   INTERNAL
	   MOD
	For nouns:
	   +D (pronouns)
	   +*prop* (proper)
	   ±*animate* (animacy)
	   ±*count* (mass/count)
	For pronouns:
	   +R (reflexive)
	For verbs
	   +*aux*
	For adverbs
	   +*intens* (intensifier)

CASE	*Nom* (Nominative) *Acc* (Accusative) *Poss* (Possessive)

Feature	Possible values
AGR-φ	GEND (gender) NUM (number) PERS (person)
GEND	*masc* (masculine) *fem* (feminine) *neut* (neuter)
NUM	*sg* (singular) *pl* (plural)
PERS	1 (first person, speaker) 2 (second person, addressee) 3 (third person, non-participant)

SEM	For T or V categories
	  TENSE
	  ASPECT
	  VOICE
	  MOOD
	For D
	  ±*def*
	question
	statement
	emphatic
	±*animate*
	and many others

TENSE	*past* *present* *future*
ASPECT	*perfect* *progressive*
VOICE	*passive*
MOOD	*obligation* *permission* *necessity* (and other values)

Feature	Possible values
EXTERNAL	(There are many possible values, but typically these are DPs or CPs if the word is a verb)
INTERNAL	(There are many possible values, but typically these are a list of DPs and PPs if the word is a verb)
FORM	*preterite* *present* *bare* *gerund* *participle* *null* *+wh* (and other values)

APPENDIX 3: RULES, CONSTRAINTS AND PRINCIPLES

Syntactic rules

ADJOIN: combine two (or more) items together into a constituent, to satisfy a MOD feature. The combined category is given the label of the non-head.

***COMPLEMENT-MERGE* (C-MERGE)**: combine two (or more) items together into a constituent as required by the INTERNAL features of one of the items. The constituent is given the label of the head.

MOVE* or *REMERGE: take an item that is already present in the tree and remerge it to satisfy some feature higher up in the tree.

***SPECIFIER-MERGE* (S-MERGE)**: combine two (or more) items together into a constituent as required by the EXTERNAL features of one of the items. The constituent is given the label of the head.

Principles and constraints

Principle of Full Interpretation (FI): if two items are merged together their feature structures must be compatible.

Principle of Headedness: In any circumstance where a SUBCAT feature mentions a category, one may substitute in a phrase headed by that category and vice versa (e.g. you can freely substitute NP for N, and N for NP; DP for D and D for DP, VP for V, V for VP, etc.).

Mass/Pl Feature Co-occurrence Restriction:

$$\begin{bmatrix} -count \\ \pm pl \end{bmatrix}$$

The Complex DP Constraint (CDPC) on Uncertainty:

The triangle denoting uncertainty (a):

(a)   XP
$\overline{\triangle}$
Y

may not contain any structures where a DP is dominated by XP and dominates Y:

(b)   *XP

*The **Wh-island Constraint on Uncertainty**:*

The triangle denoting uncertainty (a):

(a)   XP

may not contain any structures where there is a ZP that is dominated by XP and dominates Y and that ZP has a *wh*-element in its specifier:

(b)   *XP

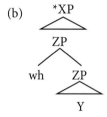

REFERENCES

Aarts, Bas (1997) *English Syntax and Argumentation.* New York: St. Martin's Press.

Abney, Steven (1987) The English Noun Phrase in its Sentential Aspect. Ph.D. dissertation, MIT.

Adger, David (2003) *Core Syntax: A Minimalist Approach.* Oxford University Press.

Bacheller, Irving (1903) *Darrell of the Blessed Isles.* Open source document at: www.gutenberg.org/files/12102/12102.txt

Baker, Mark (2003) *Lexical Categories.* Cambridge University Press.

Baker, Mark, Kyle Johnson and Ian Roberts (1989) Passive arguments raised. *Linguistic Inquiry* 20, 219–51.

Bard, Ellen G., Dan Robertson and Antonella Sorace (1996) Magnitude estimation of linguistic acceptability. *Language* 72, 32–68.

Bayer, J. (1984) COMP in Bavarian syntax. *The Linguistics Review* 3, 209–74.

Bobaljik, Jonathan (2008) Where's phi? Agreement as a post-syntactic operation. In S. Bejar, D. Harbour and D. Adger (eds.), *Phi Theory: Phi-Features across Modules and Interfaces.* Oxford University Press.

Borsley, Robert (1996) *Modern Phrase Structure Grammar.* Oxford: Blackwell.

Bresnan, Joan (1972) Theory of Complementation in English. Ph.D. dissertation, MIT.

(2001) *Lexical–Functional Syntax.* Oxford: Blackwell.

ed. (1982) *The Mental Representation of Grammatical Relations.* Cambridge, MA: MIT Press.

Carnie, Andrew (1995) Head Movement and Non-Verbal Predication. Ph.D. dissertation, MIT.

(2006) *Syntax: A Generative Introduction.* Oxford: Wiley-Blackwell.

Carnie, Andrew and Eithne Guilfoyle (2000) *The Syntax of Verb Initial Languages.* Oxford University Press.

Carpenter, Robert (1997) *Type-logical Semantics.* Cambridge, MA: MIT Press.

Carroll, Lewis (1872) *Through the Looking-Glass and What Alice Found There.* Public Domain Books.

Chametzky, Robert (1996) *A Theory of Phrase Markers and the Extended Base.* Albany: SUNY Press.

Cheng, Lisa (1997) *On the Typology of Wh-Questions.* New York: Garland Press.

Chomsky, Noam (1957) *Syntactic Structures.* Berlin: Mouton.

(1965) *Aspects of the Theory of Syntax.* Cambridge, MA: MIT Press.

(1970) Remarks on nominalization. In Roderick Jacobs and Peter
Rosenbaum (eds.), *Readings in English Transformational Grammar.*
Waltham, MA: Ginn, pp. 184–221.

(1973) Conditions on transformations. In Stephen Anderson and Paul
Kiparsky (eds.), *A Festschrift for Morris Halle.* New York: Holt, Rinehart
and Winston, pp. 232–86.

(1977) On *wh*-movement. In Peter Culicover, Thomas Wasow and Adrian
Akmajian (eds.), *Formal Syntax.* New York: Academic Press, pp. 71–132.

(1981) *Lectures on Government and Binding.* Dordrecht: Foris.

(1991) Some notes on economy of derivation and representation.
In Robert Friedin (ed.), *Principles and Parameters in Comparative
Grammar.* Cambridge, MA: MIT Press, pp. 417–54.

(1993) A Minimalist program for linguistic theory. In Kenneth L. Hale and
Samuel J. Keyser (eds.), *The View from Building 20: Essays in Honor of
Sylvain Bromberger.* Cambridge, MA: MIT Press, pp. 1–52.

(1995) *The Minimalist Program.* Cambridge, MA: MIT Press.

Cinque, Guglielmo (1981) *Types of A' Dependencies.* Cambridge, MA: MIT
Press.

Collins, Chris (2005) A smuggling approach to the passive. *Syntax* 8.2,
81–120.

Cook, V. J. and Mark Newson (1996) *Chomsky's Universal Grammar: An
Introduction,* 2nd edn. Oxford: Blackwell.

Cowper, Elizabeth (1992) *A Concise Introduction to Syntactic Theory: The
Government and Binding Approach.* Chicago: University of Chicago
Press.

Culicover, Peter (1997) *Principles and Parameters: An Introduction to
Syntactic Theory.* Oxford University Press.

(2009) *Natural Language Syntax.* Oxford University Press.

Dalrymple, Mary, Ronald Kaplan, John Maxwell and Annie Zaenen (eds.)
(1995) *Formal Issues in Lexical-Functional Grammar.* Stanford: CSLI
Publications.

Davies, William and Stan Dubinsky (2004) *The Grammar of Raising and
Control.* Oxford: Wiley-Blackwell.

Déprez, Vivienne (1992) Raising constructions in Haitian Creole. *Natural
Language and Linguistic Theory* 10, 191–231.

Edmondson, Jerold and Donald A. Burquest (1998) *A Survey of Linguistic
Theories,* 3rd edn. Dallas: Summer Institute of Linguistics.

Emonds, Joseph (1980) Word order in Generative Grammar. *Journal of
Linguistic Research* 1, 33–54.

Falk, Yehuda N. (2001) *Lexical–Functional Grammar: An Introduction to
Parallel Constraint-Based Syntax.* Stanford: CSLI Publications.

Feldstein, R. (2001) http://seelrc.org:8080/grammar/pdf/compgrammar_
   polish.pdf

Friedin, Robert (ed.) (1991) *Principles and Parameters in Comparative
   Grammar.* Cambridge, MA: MIT Press.

Goodall, Grant (1993) On case and the passive morpheme. *Natural Language
   and Linguistic Theory* 11, 31–44.

Grimshaw, Jane (1990) *Argument Structure.* Cambridge, MA: MIT Press.

Haegeman, Liliane (1994) *Introduction to Government and Binding Theory.*
   Oxford: Blackwell.

   (2006) *Thinking Syntactically.* Oxford: Wiley-Blackwell.

Harley, Heidi (2006) *English Words: A Linguistic Introduction.* Oxford:
   Blackwell.

Hornstein, Norbert (1999) Movement and control. *Linguistic Inquiry* 30,
   69–96.

   (2009) *A Theory of Syntax: Minimal Operations and Universal Grammar.*
   Cambridge University Press.

Hornstein, Norbert, Jairo Nunes and Kleanthes Grohmann (2005)
   Understanding Minimalism. Cambridge University Press.

Huang, C.-T. James (1982) Logical Relations in Chinese and the Theory of
   Grammar. Ph.D. dissertation, MIT.

Huddleston, Rodney and Geoffrey K. Pullum (2005) *A Student's Introduction
   to English Grammar.* Cambridge University Press.

Jackendoff, Ray and Peter Culicover (2005) *Simpler Syntax.* Oxford
   University Press.

Jaeggli, Osvaldo (1986) Passive. *Linguistic Inquiry* 17, 587–622.

Jelinek, Eloise and Richard Demers (1994) Predicates and pronominal arguments in Straits Salish. *Language* 70, 697–736.

Kane, Thomas (1994) *Oxford Guide to Writing.* Oxford University Press.

Kaplan, Ronald (1995) The formal architecture of Lexical–Functional
   Grammar. In Mary Dalrymple *et al.* (eds.), *Formal Issues in Lexical–
   Functional Grammar.* Stanford: CSLI Publications, pp. 7–27.

Kaplan, Ronald and Joan Bresnan (1982) Lexical–Functional Grammar: a
   formal system for grammatical representation. In Joan Bresnan (ed.),
   The Mental Representation of Grammatical Relations. Cambridge, MA:
   MIT Press, pp. 173–281.

Kim, Jong-Bok and Peter Sells (2008) *English Syntax: An Introduction.*
   Stanford: CSLI Publications.

Koopman, Hilda (1984) *The Syntax of Verbs: From Verb Movement Rules in
   the Kru Languages to Universal Grammar.* Dordrecht: Foris.

Koopman, Hilda and Dominique Sportiche (1991) The position of subjects.
   Lingua 85, 211–58.

Kroeger, Paul (1993) *Phrase Structure and Grammatical Relations in Tagalog.*
   Stanford: CSLI Publications.

(2004) *Analyzing Syntax: A Lexical–Functional Approach.* Cambridge University Press.

Landau, Idan (1999) Elements of Control. Ph.D. dissertation, MIT.

Larson, Richard (2010) *Grammar as Science.* Cambridge, MA: MIT Press.

Legate, Julie (2005) Two types of nominal splits. Paper presented at the North Eastern Linguistics Society Conference 36, October 29. Amherst, MA.

Levin, Beth (1993) *English Verb Classes and Alternations: A Preliminary Investigation.* University of Chicago Press.

Lightfoot, David and Norbert Hornstein (eds.) (1994) *Verb Movement.* Cambridge University Press.

Lobeck, Anne (2000) *Discovering Grammar: An Introduction to English Sentence Structure,* 3rd edn. Oxford University Press.

Manzini, Maria Rita (1983) On control and control theory. *Linguistic Inquiry* 14, 421–46.

(1992) *Locality: A Theory and Some of Its Empirical Consequences.* Cambridge, MA: MIT Press.

McCloskey, James (1979) *Transformational Syntax and Model Theoretic Semantics: A Case Study in Modern Irish.* Dordrecht: Reidel.

(1983) A VP in a VSO language. In Gerald Gazdar, Geoffrey Pullum and Ivan Sag (eds.), *Order Concord and Constituency.* Dordrecht: Foris, pp. 9–55.

(1991) Clause structure, ellipsis and proper government in Irish. *Lingua* 85, 259–302.

Ouhalla, Jamal (1999) *Introducing Transformational Grammar,* 2nd edn. London: Edward Arnold.

Pinker, Steven (1994) Grammar puss: the fallacies of the language mavens. *The New Republic* January 31, pp. 19–26.

(1995) *The Language Instinct.* New York: Harper Perennial.

Pollard, Carl and Ivan Sag (1994) *Head-Driven Phrase Structure Grammar.* Stanford: CSLI Publications and University of Chicago Press.

Pollock, Jean-Yves (1989) Verb-movement, Universal Grammar, and the structure of IP. *Linguistic Inquiry* 20, 365–424.

Poole, Geoffrey (2002) *Syntactic Theory.* New York: Palgrave.

Postal, Paul (1974) *On Raising.* Cambridge, MA: MIT Press.

Radford, Andrew (1988) *Transformational Grammar: A First Course.* Cambridge University Press.

(1997a) *Syntactic Theory and The Structure of English: A Minimalist Approach.* Cambridge University Press.

(1997b) *Syntax: A Minimalist Introduction.* Cambridge University Press.

(2004) *Minimalist Syntax: Exploring the Structure of English.* Cambridge University Press.

Richards, Norvin (1997) What Moves Where When in Which Language? Ph.D. dissertation, MIT.

Ritter, Elizabeth (1988) A head movement approach to construct state noun phrases. *Linguistics* 26, 909–29.

Rizzi, Luigi (1990) *Relativized Minimality*. Cambridge, MA: MIT Press.

Roberts, Ian (1997) *Comparative Syntax*. London: Edward Arnold.

Ross, J. R. (Haj) (1967) Constraints on Variables in Syntax. Ph.D. dissertation, MIT.

Rubin, Edward (2003). Determining Pair-Merge. *Linguistic Inquiry* 34, 660–8.

Sag, Ivan, Thomas Wasow and Emily Bender (2003) *Syntactic Theory: A Formal Introduction*, 2nd edn. Stanford: CSLI Publications.

Sapir, Edward (1929) The status of linguistics as a science. *Language* 5.4, 207–14.

Schütze, Carson (1992) *The Empirical Base of Linguistics*. University of Chicago Press.

Sells, Peter (1985) *Lectures on Contemporary Syntactic Theories*. Stanford: CSLI Publications.

Soames, Scott and David M. Perlmutter (1979) *Syntactic Argumentation and the Structure of English*. Berkeley: University of California Press.

Speas, Margaret (1990) *Phrase Structure in Natural Language*. Dordrecht: Kluwer Academic Publishers.

Sportiche, Dominique (1988) A theory of floating quantifiers and its corollaries for constituent structure. *Linguistic Inquiry* 19, 425–49.

Sproat, Richard (1985) Welsh syntax and VSO structure. *Natural Language and Linguistic Theory* 3, 173–216.

Standún, Pádraig (1992) *An tAinmhí*. Indreabhán: Cló Iar-chonnachta.

Stowell, Tim (1981) Origins of Phrase Structure. Ph.D. dissertation, MIT.

Szabolcsi, Anna (1994) The noun phrase. In *Syntax and Semantics 27: The Syntax of Hungarian*. New York: Academic Press, pp. 179–279.

Tallerman, Maggie (2005) *Understanding Syntax*, 2nd edn. London: Hodder Arnold.

Tomlin, Russell (1984) The frequency of basic constituent orders. *Research on Language and Social Interaction* 17, 163–96.

Traill, Anthony (1994) *A !Xóõ Dictionary*. Cologne: Rüdiger Köppe Verlag.

Uriagereka, Juan (1998) *Rhyme and Reason: An Introduction to Minimalist Syntax*. Cambridge, MA: MIT Press.

van Gelderen, Elly (2010) *An Introduction to the Grammar of English*. Amsterdam and Philadelphia: John Benjamins.

Van Valin, Robert D. Jr. and Randy J. LaPolla (1997) *Syntax: Structure, Meaning and Function*. Cambridge University Press.

Williams, Edwin (1983) Semantic vs. syntactic categories. *Linguistics and Philosophy* 6, 423–46.

INDEX